3.⁰⁰

ideals
Gourmet Treasury
COOKBOOK

by Naomi Arbit and June Turner

Here is a treasury of recipes compiled especially for today's cook who loves to serve dishes attractive to behold, and delicious to eat, while requiring a minimum of preparation time. Within this volume are recipes from four best-selling cookbooks of June Turner and Naomi Arbit— cookbooks created with the busy gourmet in mind. Each recipe has been tested and perfected by the authors in their cooking schools and demonstrations; and each of the three sections within this book focuses on a special area of menu preparation.

The first section features unique and tantalizing appetizers, a lovely and delicious beginning to any meal or an array of which can be served alone. Included are dips and spreads, hors d'oeuvres, sand-wiches and relishes, the majority of which can be prepared from the contents of any kitchen cupboard.

The second section features entreés, accompaniments, and desserts from the authors' best-selling cookbook, *Gourmet on the Go* and their highly successful *Gourmet Touch*. Here are hearty main meals, delicious and unusual vegetable dishes, rich and luscious desserts, and always popular sweet and quick breads. These recipes offer a complete menu which will elicit raves from guests and are guaranteed to be easily and quickly prepared.

The final section is a grand holiday assortment of the most festive food imaginable for Christmas—or, for that matter, any special occasion. From the traditional wassail bowl to the roast duck or chicken della robbia, the emphasis is on party recipes. Every dish is perfect for a gala event or impromptu gathering, and each will make the season special for both hostess and guests.

Modern conveniences and the year-round availability of fresh ingredients make it possible for even the busiest cook to prepare fine cuisine with a gourmet touch. Authors Arbit and Turner utilize today's conveniences and provide recipes which are delicious, attractive, and, best of all, fun and simple to prepare.

ISBN 0-89542-024-4 995

First Printing

Contents by Gourmet Section

Gourmet Appetizer

The recipes in this first section provide easy and time-saving methods for preparing delicious, taste-tempting appetizers which will add to any party or meal a feeling of richness and festivity. The authors have included chicken soufflés, Hawaiian kabobs, miniature crepes, and stuffed eggs elegantly garnished with caviar. These are just a few of the appetizer recipes with which you can treat your guests royally and pamper yourself as well.

Pictured opposite:
Sautéed Nuts, p. 41
Virginia Peanuts, p. 41

Cheeses

SAUCY CHEDDAR SPREAD

1 8-oz. pkg. sharp Cheddar cheese, grated
¼ c. margarine or butter
2 T. chili sauce
1 t. Worcestershire sauce
½ small onion, minced

Combine all ingredients, mixing well. Serve with crackers or rye slices. Makes about 1 cup.

POTTED CHEESE

1 lb. sharp Cheddar cheese, grated
¼ c. butter
1 T. brandy
1 T. mustard
Dash of Tabasco sauce

Combine all ingredients, mixing well. Chill and serve with crackers. Serves 6 to 8.

SWISS CHEESE AND OLIVE SPREAD

2 c. grated Swiss cheese
3 T. chopped pimiento-stuffed olives, drained
2 T. chopped green pepper
Mayonnaise to moisten

Thoroughly mix together all ingredients, making a thick paste; spread on toast rounds. Serves 12 to 16.

CUCUMBER-CHEESE SANDWICH

1 8-oz. pkg. cream cheese
1 8-oz. pkg. Roquefort or blue cheese
½ c. mayonnaise
1 t. Worcestershire sauce
Thin bread, white or wheat, crusts removed
1 medium-size cucumber, thinly sliced
1 c. snipped chives
Garlic salt (optional)

Mix together cheeses, mayonnaise, and Worcestershire sauce until smooth. Cut bread slices into quarters. Spread cheese mixture on bread, top each with a cucumber slice, a light dusting of garlic salt and a sprinkle of chives. Makes 2 to 3 dozen.

APPETIZER

Quick starter.

½ c. chopped ripe olives
¼ c. minced green onion
1 c. grated American cheese
¼ c. mayonnaise
1½ t. curry powder (optional)
¼ t. salt
Bread or English muffins, split and toasted

Combine all ingredients except muffins and mix thoroughly. Spread on bread or muffin halves and broil until hot and cheese is melted. Cut in squares or triangles to serve.

CHEESE FONDUE

1 8-oz. pkg. Muenster cheese, shredded
2 T. flour
1 c. beer
½ t. prepared mustard
  Cubes of bread *or*
  Frankfurters cut into 1-inch pieces

Toss cheese with flour. Heat beer in fondue pot or chafing dish until it bubbles (do not boil). Add small amounts of cheese mixture, stirring constantly; let cheese melt before adding more. Continue stirring until mixture bubbles lightly. Stir in mustard. Serve hot with bread or frankfurters for dipping. Makes 4 servings.

BLUE CHEESE MOLD

2 3-oz. pkgs. cream cheese, softened
1 4-oz. pkg. blue cheese
1 t. Worcestershire sauce
2 T. snipped parsley
½ t. salt
½ t. paprika
1 envelope unflavored gelatin
2 T. cold water
½ c. hot water
1 c. heavy cream, whipped

Mix cheeses together until well blended. Stir in Worcestershire sauce, parsley, salt, and paprika and set aside. Soften gelatin in cold water. Add hot water and stir until gelatin is dissolved. Blend in cheese mixture and chill until mixture is slightly thickened. Fold in whipped cream and pour into a lightly oiled 6-cup mold. Chill until firm. Makes 10 to 12 servings.

SWISS FONDUE

1 clove garlic, split
1 c. dry white wine
½ lb. Swiss cheese, shredded
½ lb. Gruyere cheese, shredded
  Dash of pepper, nutmeg and paprika
1 T. cornstarch
¼ c. Kirsch or cherry brandy
1 loaf French or Italian bread, cubed
  (leave crust on one side)

Rub the inside of saucepan, chafing dish, or fondue pot with garlic. Add wine and heat. Add shredded cheese in small amounts, stirring constantly with wooden spoon until smooth and melted. Add seasonings and remove from heat. Mix cornstarch and Kirsch into paste; add to fondue. Return to heat and cook another 2 minutes stirring constantly. Serve, keeping hot over burner, stirring occasionally. Spear bread cubes through soft side into crust and dip in fondue. Serves 24.

Note: It is best to make fondue in a heavy saucepan on the stove and then transfer to chafing dish or fondue pot before serving.

FONDUE OF BRIE

1½ to 2 lb. round of Brie cheese
1 c. toasted almond slices
  Melba toast or sliced hard rolls

One hour before serving, place Brie, bottom up, on a flameproof platter. After about 30 minutes, remove the thin layer of crust. Place under a preheated broiler until surface bubbles. Garnish with toasted almonds. Serve hot surrounded with toast or roll slices. Serves 18 to 24.

SHERRIED CHEESE

1 8-oz. pkg. cream cheese, softened
½ 10½-oz. can beef consommé
1 T. sherry
½ cucumber, drained and minced

Mix together all ingredients well. Chill and serve with rye chips. Serves 4 to 6.

WATERCRESS SPREAD

2 3-oz. pkgs. cream cheese with chives, softened
¼ c. butter, softened
1 T. minced onion
1 T. mayonnaise
1 bunch watercress, minced

Blend cheese with butter, onion, and mayonnaise until smooth. Blend in watercress. Spread on trimmed, thin white or whole wheat bread for sandwiches or serve with melba toast. Makes 1½ cups.

MOCK BOURSIN

1 8-oz. pkg. cream cheese
1 clove garlic, minced
1 t. caraway seed
1 t. basil
1 t. dill weed
½ t. Worcestershire sauce
Lemon pepper

Blend first 6 ingredients together. On waxed paper, pat into a flattened circle. Sprinkle another piece of waxed paper with lemon pepper; roll all sides of the cheese in the pepper. Shape again into a flattened circle. Wrap in plastic wrap and chill at least a day before serving. Serve with crackers. Serves 4 to 6.

CHEESE PUFFS

1 egg white
½ t. cream of tartar
¼ t. salt
1½ c. grated medium or sharp Cheddar cheese
18 buttered bread rounds

Beat egg white with cream of tartar and salt until light and frothy. Stir in cheese and mix well. Mound mixture on bread rounds and place on a baking sheet. Broil about 4 inches from burner for 3 to 5 minutes or until golden brown. Makes 18 puffs.

CHEESE SPREAD

8 oz. sharp Cheddar cheese, shredded
1 8-oz. pkg. cream cheese
¼ c. beer
½ t. dry mustard
Dash of cayenne pepper
1 T. snipped green onions or chives
1 t. chopped pimiento, optional

Combine cheeses, beer, mustard, and cayenne; mix until well-blended. Stir in green onion and pimiento, if desired. Chill several hours. Serve at room temperature with crackers. Makes 1¾ cups.

CHEESE AND NUT SPREAD

¼ lb. Cheddar cheese, grated
1 3-oz. pkg. cream cheese, softened
¼ c. sour cream
¼ t. garlic powder
½ t. Worcestershire sauce
½ c. finely chopped nuts, (walnuts or pecans)

Combine all ingredients and mix thoroughly. Serve with crackers. Makes 1½ cups.

CHEESE TARTS
CRUSTADES

24 slices of thin bread, crusts trimmed
Softened butter

Roll out bread slice to flatten slightly. Cut bread into 2½-inch rounds and butter both sides. Ease circle into miniature muffin tins so that edges ruffle. Place filling in center and bake in a 325° oven for 15 to 18 minutes until golden brown. Serve warm.

FILLINGS

24 cubes of Cheddar, Muenster, Swiss or blue cheese
24 t. of clam spread
24 t. of cream cheese, olive spread
24 t. of ham spread

Crustades may also be baked empty and filled with cold spread, such as chicken, ham, shrimp, or egg salad.

Pictured opposite:
Cheese Tarts

CHEESE BALLS

1 8-oz. pkg. Swiss cheese, grated or
   shredded
½ c. margarine or butter, softened
1 t. mustard
1 t. Worcestershire sauce
2 T. dry sherry
   Dash of Tabasco
½ to 1 c. finely chopped walnuts

Mix all ingredients together and shape into
1-inch balls. Spear with toothpicks. Makes
about 3 to 4 dozen.

QUICK CREAM CHEESE SPREAD

1 8-oz. pkg. cream cheese
   Pepper Jelly
   Crackers

Top cream cheese with Pepper Jelly, surround with crackers and serve. Makes about
1 cup.

PEPPER JELLY

¼ c. chopped sweet red pepper
¾ c. chopped green pepper
5½ c. sugar
1½ c. white vinegar
1 6-oz. bottle liquid pectin

In a saucepan, combine pepper, sugar, and
vinegar; boil 3 minutes. Remove from heat
and set aside for 5 minutes. Stir in pectin.
Pour into sterilized jars and seal. Makes 4 to
5 4-oz. jars.

READY RYE APPETIZERS

1 3 to 4-oz. pkg. sliced smoked beef,
   snipped
1 4-oz. pkg. shredded Cheddar cheese
1 can pitted ripe olives, sliced
1 c. mayonnaise
   Rye crackers

Combine first 4 ingredients, mixing well.
Spread about 1 tablespoon on each rye
cracker. Bake in a 375° oven for 5 to 7
minutes or until bubbly, or 45 seconds in a
microwave oven. Makes about 3 dozen.

CAMEMBERT CHEESE SPREAD

1 8-oz. pkg. camembert cheese, softened
½ c. margarine or butter, softened
2 T. brandy
1 T. sour cream
¼ c. toasted sesame seed

Combine all ingredients, mixing well. Chill
for 48 hours. Before serving, bring to room
temperature. Serve with assorted crackers.
Makes about 1 cup.

OLIVE-NUT SPREAD

1 8-oz. pkg. cream cheese, softened
1 T. mayonnaise
1 4½-oz. can ripe olives, chopped
½ t. garlic powder (optional)
¼ to ½ c. chopped nuts

Combine all ingredients, mixing thoroughly. Spread on bread rounds, chill, then
serve. Makes about 1 cup.

CHEESE BALLS

1 8-oz. pkg. cream cheese
1 4-oz. pkg. blue cheese
1 T. grated onion
   Finely snipped parsley *or* chopped nuts

Combine cheeses and onion. Form into small
balls and roll in parsley or nuts. Serve on
toothpicks. Makes about 1½ cups.

CRUNCHY SPREAD

1 8-oz. pkg. cream cheese, softened
¼ c. mayonnaise
1 medium onion, minced
1 large tomato, chopped
1 stalk celery, minced
5 to 6 slices chipped beef, torn in bits

Combine all ingredients, mixing well. Serve with crackers or toast. Makes about 1¼ cups.

CHEESE ROUNDS

½ c. mayonnaise
½ c. grated Parmesan cheese
1 T. minced onion

Combine all ingredients, mixing well. Spread on melba toast. Broil until bubbly. Makes 1½ to 2 dozen.

SAVORY CHEESE SPREAD

½ c. grated Cheddar cheese or
    cheese spread
2 T. mayonnaise
¼ t. dry mustard
1 T. chopped ripe olives
2 t. anchovy paste
1 t. lemon juice
    Salt and pepper to taste

Combine all ingredients, mixing well. Spread on whole wheat bread rounds. Serves 6 to 8.

SESAME CHEESE LOG

1 8-oz. pkg. cream cheese, softened
1 4-oz. pkg. blue cheese, softened
½ c. margarine, softened
½ c. chopped black olives
1 T. Worcestershire sauce
1 T. chopped chives
1 T. snipped parsley
½ c. toasted sesame seed

Combine all ingredients except sesame seed, mixing well. Form into a log or ball; roll in sesame seed. Serve with crackers or melba toast. Serves 8 to 10.

ALMOND OR PISTACHIO CHEESE LOG

1 c. shredded Cheddar cheese
1 16-oz. pkg. cream cheese, softened
2 t. prepared mustard
½ c. slivered almonds or chopped
    pistachio nuts

Cream cheeses with mustard. On waxed paper, shape into a roll 9 inches long. Roll in nuts, wrap in plastic and chill. Let stand at room temperature about 30 minutes before serving. Serves 12 to 16.

PARTY CHEESE SPREAD

1 c. Cheddar cheese spread
1 3-oz. pkg. cream cheese
1 c. small curd cottage cheese
¼ c. orange liqueur
½ c. chopped walnuts

Mix cheeses together until smooth. Add liqueur and nuts. Shape into ball or place in bowl; chill for several hours. Serve at room temperature with crackers. Makes 2 cups.

ANOTHER BOURSIN

1 8-oz. pkg. cream cheese, softened
¼ c. mayonnaise
1 clove garlic, minced
1 t. lemon juice
¼ t. salt
2 t. snipped chives
2 t. snipped parsley
1 t. freshly ground pepper

Mix together all ingredients except pepper. Form into a flattened circle. Sprinkle with pepper. Chill; serve with crackers. Serves 4 to 6.

Dips

GUACAMOLE

1 c. mashed avocado
1 T. lemon juice
1 t. salt
1½ t. grated onion

Note: For variety, add 1 or more of the following:

Dash of Tabasco
1 t. curry powder
1 t. Worcestershire sauce
½ t. chili powder

Combine all ingredients and mix well. Chill several hours. Serve with chips or crackers. Makes 1 cup Guacamole.

DIPPERS

Scallions
Green beans
Carrot or celery sticks
Fresh pineapple spears
Radishes
Green pepper slices
Cucumber or zucchini rounds
Cauliflowerets
Mushrooms
Kohlrabi slices
Turnip slices
Asparagus spears

Serve an assortment of these vegetables and fruits with the usual chips, pretzel sticks, and crackers.

CORN CHIPS

½ c. cornmeal (yellow or white)
1 t. salt
¾ c. boiling water
2 T. butter
Sesame, celery, or poppy seeds

Mix together cornmeal, salt, water, and butter. On foil-lined cookie sheets, place 1 to 2 teaspoonfuls of batter 2 inches apart. Sprinkle with choice of seeds; bake in a 425° oven about 8 minutes. Let harden slightly before removing to cool on rack. Makes 48 2-inch chips.

SHERRIED ONION DIP

½ c. sherry
½ pkg. onion soup mix
1 pt. sour cream or half and half

In a saucepan, warm sherry; add soup mix. Set aside for 30 minutes, then blend in sour cream. Serve with raw vegetables or crackers. Makes about 2½ cups dip.

CAVIAR DIP

1 c. yogurt or sour cream
1 4-oz. jar red caviar
1 t. minced parsley (optional)
1 T. grated onion

Combine all ingredients, mixing well. Serve with small rounds of melba toast for dipping. Makes about 1½ cups dip.

Pictured opposite:
Guacamole
Dippers

GREEN GODDESS DIP

1 c. cream-style cottage cheese
1 T. anchovy paste
4 sprigs of parsley
1 t. Worcestershire sauce
½ t. dry mustard
1 garlic clove
1 T. minced green onion or chives
4 T. mayonnaise

Place all ingredients in a blender or food processor and blend until smooth. Refrigerate several hours before serving with assorted bite-sized raw vegetables. Makes about 1¼ cups.

CLAM DIP

1 7½-oz. can minced clams, drained
1 T. clam juice
6 drops Tabasco sauce
½ t. Worcestershire sauce
½ t. salt
1 t. minced onion
1 8-oz. pkg. cream cheese *or* 1 c. cottage cheese

In a blender or food processor, combine all ingredients except clams. Process until smooth. Blend in clams and chill before serving. Makes 1½ cups.

LIPTAUER CHEESE DIP

2 8-oz. pkgs. cream cheese, softened
¼ c. butter, softened
2 to 3 T. anchovy paste *or* 4 to 5 anchovy fillets, mashed
½ t. minced onion
1 T. capers, drained
1 t. prepared mustard
⅓ c. milk

Combine all ingredients, mixing well. Chill and shape into a ball. Garnish with minced parsley and serve with crackers. Serves 10 to 12.

SHRIMP DIP

1 3-oz. pkg. cream cheese, softened
½ c. mayonnaise
½ c. snipped green onion (green part only)
1 T. lemon juice
1 dash of Tabasco sauce
1 4½-oz. can of shrimp

Rinse and drain shrimp. Combine all ingredients, mixing well. Chill for several hours before serving. Makes 1½ cups.

SOUR CREAM COTTAGE CHEESE

For calorie watchers.

1 c. creamed cottage cheese
1 T. lemon juice

Combine ingredients in a blender and process until smooth and creamy. May be used in place of yogurt or sour cream in any dip. Makes 1 cup.

JALAPEÑO DIP

2 10-oz. cans jalapeño bean dip
1 T. Worcestershire sauce
1 t. crushed dried chilies (remove seeds)
½ t. cumin
1 lb. grated Monterey Jack cheese

Heat bean dip and seasonings. When steaming hot, add cheese; stir until melted. Serve with corn chips. Makes about 2 cups.

CHILI DIP

½ c. mayonnaise
½ c. sour cream or yogurt
2 T. pickle relish
1 T. chopped stuffed olives
2 t. chili powder
1½ t. grated or minced onion

Combine all ingredients, mixing well. Chill for several hours. Serve with tortilla chips. Makes about 1 cup.

CHESTNUT DIP

16 oz. plain yogurt
1 8-oz. can water chestnuts, drained and chopped
2 T. snipped green onions
1 T. beef-flavored instant bouillon
2 T. snipped parsley
½ t. Worcestershire sauce
¼ t. garlic powder
Dash of Tabasco sauce

Combine all ingredients, mixing well. Chill; stir before serving with assorted fresh vegetables. Makes 2 cups.

BOMBAY DIP

1 c. mayonnaise or salad dressing
2 T. lemon juice
2 t. grated onion
2 t. sugar
1 t. curry powder or more to taste

Combine all ingredients, mixing well. Chill. Serve with raw vegetables. Makes 1 cup.

MOCK GUACAMOLE

Looks like guacamole, but has its own zip.

1 10-oz. pkg. frozen broccoli, cooked, drained
½ c. sour cream
2 T. grated Parmesan cheese
2 T. lemon juice
½ small onion

Place all ingredients in blender; blend until smooth. Serve with corn chips or raw vegetables. Makes about 1½ cups.

BOMBAY DIP (LOW CAL)

2 c. yogurt or sour half and half
4 T. minced fresh parsley or chives
2 T. lemon juice
Sugar substitute to equal 2 t. sugar
2 t. curry powder (or more to taste)

Combine all ingredients, mixing well. Chill. Serve with raw vegetables. Makes about 2 cups.

YOGURT DIP

1 large cucumber
1 c. plain yogurt
⅛ t. garlic powder
⅛ t. dill weed
Salt and white pepper to taste

Peel cucumber, remove seed, grate, and drain. Combine all ingredients and mix well. Chill for several hours before serving. Serve with chips or assorted raw vegetables. Makes 1½ cups.

AVOCADO DIP

1 ripe avocado, peeled and mashed
1 3-oz. pkg. cream cheese, softened
3 T. mayonnaise
Dash of lemon juice
¼ t. garlic powder
Dash of Tabasco

Combine all ingredients, mixing thoroughly. Chill. Serve with vegetables for dipping. Makes about 1 cup.

TUNA DIP

1 8-oz. pkg. cream cheese, softened
¼ c. mayonnaise
1 7-oz. can tuna fish
¼ t. salt
2 t. grated onion
4 to 6 drops Tabasco sauce
½ t. Worcestershire sauce

Rinse and drain tuna; flake. Combine all ingredients. Chill several hours before serving. Makes about 1½ cups.

Eggs

MINIATURE EGG FOO YONG

8 eggs, beaten
1 t. salt
¼ t. pepper
1 c. minced onions
1 c. diced celery
½ c. minced green pepper
1 T. soy sauce
2 c. flaked cooked crab meat, baby
   shrimp, or diced ham
4 T. vegetable oil

Combine all ingredients except oil; mix well. Heat oil in frying pan; by tablespoons fry small pancakes, browning on both sides. Keep hot in warm oven until ready to serve. Makes 25 pancakes.

FROSTED EGG PATÉ

6 to 8 hard-boiled eggs, minced
6 T. butter, softened
½ t. curry powder
   Dash of pepper
¼ c. mayonnaise
   Curry powder
   Snipped parsley

Combine eggs, butter, curry powder and pepper; mix well. Pat onto a serving plate to ½ to ¾-inch thickness. Chill until firm. Frost with mayonnaise, sprinkle with additional curry powder, and garnish with minced parsley. Serve with toast or crackers. Makes about 1 cup.

CHOPPED EGG APPETIZER

3 to 4 green onions
6 to 8 hard-boiled eggs
¼ c. rendered chicken fat
   Salt and freshly ground pepper to taste

Mince green onions, using all of the white and half the green. Finely chop eggs and mix with minced onion. Set aside. To render chicken fat, fry slowly in an ungreased pan. Pour off the fat, let cool. Mix fat with the egg and onion. Season to taste and chill for 2 hours. Serve on lettuce. Makes about 1 cup.

CREAMY EGG DIP

4 hard-boiled eggs, chopped
1 8-oz. pkg. creamed cottage cheese
¾ c. mayonnaise
4 green onions, snipped
   Salt and pepper to taste

Combine all ingredients, mixing well. Chill several hours. Serve with seasoned crackers. Makes 2½ cups.

Pictured opposite:
Frosted Egg Paté

15

EGG ROLLS

½ c. sifted flour
2 t. cornstarch
¼ t. salt
1 small egg, beaten
½ t. sugar
1 c. water
¼ c. peanut oil
1 T. flour
2 T. water

Sift together flour, cornstarch, and salt. Beat in egg and sugar. Slowly add 1 cup water, beating constantly, until batter is smooth. Lightly grease a hot 6-inch skillet with peanut oil. Pour 3 tablespoons batter into the skillet, tipping to spread batter evenly over bottom. Place over medium heat and fry until batter shrinks from sides of pan. Carefully slide onto a towel to cool. Place 1 tablespoon filling on each egg roll skin on lower section. Fold up and over the filling, away from you. Fold edges toward center. Roll firmly all the way up. Mix 1 tablespoon flour with 2 tablespoons water and brush edges to seal. Heat 1 inch of peanut oil in skillet and fry egg rolls, 2 at a time, until golden. Reheat on a cookie sheet in a 400° oven for 10 to 20 minutes until hot and crispy. Serve with Hot Mustard Sauce. Makes 8 Egg Rolls.

FILLING

¾ c. finely chopped celery
1 c. shredded cabbage
½ c. water
½ c. diced cooked shrimp
½ c. diced pork, ham, chicken, or veal
2 T. peanut oil
¾ c. finely chopped water chestnuts
4 scallions, chopped
1 clove garlic, minced
4 T. soy sauce

In saucepan, combine celery, cabbage, and water; bring to a boil. Drain thoroughly. Heat oil in skillet and sauté shrimp and meat for 2 or 3 minutes. Add remaining ingredients and cook, stirring constantly until lightly browned. Cool.

HOT MUSTARD SAUCE

3 T. dry mustard
Cold water

Stir enough water into mustard to make the consistency of mayonnaise.

STUFFED EGGS

6 hard-boiled eggs
1 7-oz. can tuna, shrimp, salmon or lobster, drained and flaked
½ c. mayonnaise
1 T. minced green onion
2 t. prepared mustard
Salt and pepper to taste

Cut eggs in half lengthwise. Remove yolks and mash. Add remaining ingredients to egg yolks and mix well. Mound mixture into egg white shells and garnish with parsley. Makes 12 Stuffed Eggs.

EGG SALAD MOLD

1½ envelopes gelatin
¼ c. cold water
12 hard-boiled eggs, chopped
½ c. chopped celery
½ c. chopped green pepper
2 t. grated onion
¼ t. white pepper
½ t. Worchestershire sauce
1 c. mayonnaise
2 t. salt
¾ c. hot water
1 1-oz. jar black caviar

Dissolve gelatin in cold water. Add remaining ingredients, except the caviar. Pour into a greased 6-cup mold. Chill until firm. Unmold and serve with bread rounds or crackers. Garnish with black caviar. Makes 12 to 24 servings.

DEVILED EGG BASKETS

1 cucumber, scored and sliced
6 hard-boiled eggs
1 t. prepared horseradish
¼ c. mayonnaise
½ t. prepared mustard

Slice cucumber, seed, and cut each slice in half. Score the slice and set aside to use as a "handle." Cut eggs in half lengthwise. Mash yolks with a fork, blender, or food processor. Add horseradish, mayonnaise, and mustard and beat until smooth. Heap into whites. Top each egg with cucumber slice to make a basket handle. Makes 12 "Baskets."
Note: For variety, add one of the following:
4 T. yogurt
¼ t. salt and dash of white pepper
¼ c. crumbled blue cheese

AVOCADO-FILLED EGGS

6 hard-boiled eggs
1 ripe avocado, mashed
1 t. lemon juice
1 T. olive oil
Salt to taste

Slice hard-boiled eggs in half lengthwise. Remove yolks and mash with an equal amount of mashed avocado. Moisten with lemon juice and olive oil; salt to taste. Heap mixture into each egg white. Sprinkle with paprika and serve chilled. Serves about 6.

HAM AND EGG BALLS

6 hard-boiled eggs, chopped
1 T. minced onion or chives
½ c. ground cooked ham
Dash of pepper
¼ c. mayonnaise
⅔ c. crushed cornflakes or chopped nuts

Combine all ingredients except cornflakes. Shape into small balls. Roll balls in cereal; chill. Makes about 40.

MORE EGG ROLLS

1 c. minced celery
½ c. minced bamboo shoots
½ c. chopped water chestnuts
½ c. shredded celery cabbage or bean sprouts
2 T. thinly sliced green onions
2 T. vegetable oil
1 c. minced cooked shrimp, chicken or turkey
1 T. soy sauce
Dash of pepper
2 c. flour
2¼ c. water
4 eggs

Stir fry vegetables in oil for 3 to 5 minutes. Add shrimp, soy sauce, and pepper; set aside. Combine flour, water, and eggs, mixing well. Heat a 6-inch skillet, brush lightly with oil. Pour about 2 tablespoons batter into skillet, tilting pan quickly to coat bottom. Cook until underside is lightly browned and dry on top. Turn out on tea towel, browned side up. Repeat until batter is used up. Place two tablespoons filling lengthwise on pancake. Fold pancake over filling; fold 1 inch of each side toward center. Roll pancake away from you and seal edge with a dab of beaten egg. Fry 3 or 4 egg rolls at a time in 375° fat until well browned and crisp. Drain on paper toweling. Serve with Mustard and Plum Sauces. Makes about 18.

MUSTARD SAUCE

1 t. dry mustard
1 T. prepared mustard
1 t. lemon juice
1 c. mayonnaise

Combine all ingredients, mixing well.

PLUM SAUCE

1 c. plum preserves
1 T. sugar
1 T. vinegar

Combine all ingredients, mixing well.

EGG AND ANCHOVY SPREAD

3 hard-boiled eggs, minced
2 T. mayonnaise
1 T. anchovy paste
1 t. lemon juice
1 t. snipped green onion

Combine all ingredients, mixing well. Makes about 1 cup.

ANCHOVY EGGS

12 hard-boiled eggs, halved
½ to ¾ c. mayonnaise
2 cans rolled anchovies with capers, drained

Mash egg yolks; blend in mayonnaise. Fill egg whites with yolk mixture and top each with an anchovy. Makes 24.

ANCHOVY STUFFED EGGS

6 hard-boiled eggs
⅓ c. yogurt or sour cream
2 T. anchovy paste
1 T. snipped scallions
Minced fresh parsley

Cut eggs in half lengthwise and remove the yolks. Mash with a fork, blending in the yogurt, anchovy paste, and onions. Fill whites with mixture. Sprinkle with minced fresh parsley and chill before serving. Makes 12 appetizers.
Note: For a variation, omit anchovy paste and garnish filled egg with caviar.

HAM AND EGG BOATS

12 hard-boiled eggs, peeled
1 c. minced ham
½ c. mayonnaise
½ small onion, minced
1 T. mustard
12 thin rounds sweet pickle, cut in half

Cut eggs in half lengthwise. Mash egg yolks; combine with ham, mayonnaise, onion, and mustard. Heap into egg white halves. Garnish with pickle slice. Makes 24.

CAVIAR A LA RUSSE

6 eggs, hard-boiled and chopped
4 T. butter, melted
1 t. minced onion or onion flakes
½ c. sour cream or sour cream substitute
1 4-oz. jar red or black caviar

Combine chopped eggs, butter, and onion. Spread on an 8-inch dessert or salad plate. Chill until firm. Frost with sour cream. Chill again. Just before serving, top with caviar. Cut into wedges and serve with toast or crackers. Serves 4 to 6.

CAVIAR EGGS

6 hard-boiled eggs
1 2-oz. jar small red caviar, drained
2 t. minced onion
¾ c. sour cream

Cut eggs lengthwise in half. Remove yolks. Mash only half of the yolks, adding onion and 1 tablespoon of the sour cream. Save the remaining half of the yolks for use elsewhere. Reserve 1 teaspoon of caviar for garnish; stir remaining caviar into the yolk mixture. Fill eggs. Frost top of eggs with sour cream and garnish each with 2 caviar eggs. Arrange with parsley on a serving dish. Makes 12 Caviar Eggs.

Pictured opposite: Caviar Eggs

18

Meat, Poultry, and Cold Cuts

BROILED GROUND BEEF TRIANGLES

4 to 5 slices of bread, toasted on 1 side
Softened butter
Prepared mustard
½ lb. ground round
¼ c. milk
½ t. salt
½ t. pepper
1 T. instant minced onion

Spread untoasted side of bread with butter and then lightly with mustard. Combine meat, milk, salt, pepper, and onion. Spread on top of mustard to the edges of bread. Broil, meat side up, 5 to 7 minutes until meat is done. Cut each sandwich into 4 triangles. Makes 16 to 20 triangles.

MINI HAMBURGERS

3 doz. miniature hamburger buns
1 lb. ground round steak
1 T. chili sauce
1 small onion, minced
1 clove garlic, minced
1 T. mustard
Sliced cheese, optional

Combine all ingredients, except hamburger buns. Spread round steak mixture on buns. Top with sliced cheese, if desired. Bake in a 400° oven for 30 minutes or until meat is no longer pink. Makes 3 dozen Mini Hamburgers.

BEEF TARTARE

1 lb. twice ground top round or sirloin steak, fat removed
1 egg yolk
1 t. salt
1 t. Worcestershire sauce or steak sauce
Dash of Tabasco sauce
1 T. minced onion
½ t. freshly ground pepper
1 t. capers, drained
4 anchovy fillets, for top of meat
Pimiento-stuffed olives
Cherry tomatoes
Onion rings

Gently combine all ingredients, except olives, tomatoes and onion rings. Shape into flattened circle; refrigerate. Just before serving, place on a platter. Top with anchovy strips and ring with olives, tomatoes, and onion rings. Serve with thin slices of pumpernickel or rye bread. Serves 6 to 8.

BEEF SANDWICHES

36 party rye slices, buttered
Very thin slices of roast beef
1 c. mayonnaise
2 T. horseradish
2 T. brown mustard

Top buttered bread with sliced beef. Combine remaining ingredients. Garnish sandwiches with a dollop of sauce. Makes 36 open-faced sandwiches.

DRIED BEEF PINWHEELS

1 3-oz. pkg. cream cheese, softened
2 T. snipped green onions
1 t. garlic powder *or* seasoning salt
1 to 2 T. mayonnaise
¼ lb. sliced dried beef

Mix cheese, onions, garlic powder, and mayonnaise together. Spread 2 slices of beef with mixture and place one on top of the other. Roll up tightly and chill several hours or overnight. Cut each roll into 1½ to 2-inch slices; insert a toothpick into edge of each slice. Makes about 36.

HOT CHIPPED BEEF ROLLS

1 8-oz. pkg. chipped beef
1 3-oz. pkg. cream cheese, softened with
    1 T. mayonnaise
1 T. minced onion
1 loaf thinly sliced bread, crusts removed
    Butter or margarine, softened

Mix beef with cheese and onion. Spread bread slices with butter or margarine. Turn over and spread with beef cheese mixture. Roll up and secure with toothpick. Place on baking sheet; bake in a 325° oven until golden brown. Serve warm. Makes 3 to 4 dozen.

BAR-B-Q BEEF BUNS

1 onion, chopped
1 T. butter
1 c. catsup
½ c. water
¼ c. vinegar
1 T. Worchestershire sauce
1 t. sugar
    Dash of salt
    Cocktail buns

In a saucepan sauté onion in butter until tender; add remaining ingredients and simmer for 10 to 15 minutes. Warm thinly sliced roast beef, brisket, or chicken in sauce. Place in cocktail buns. Makes enough for 3 to 4 dozen sandwiches.

TURKISH MEATBALLS WITH YOGURT

4 slices thin white bread, crusts trimmed, torn into 1-inch pieces
⅓ c. water
½ lb. ground lamb
¼ c. minced onion
½ t. salt
¼ t. ground cumin
¼ t. pepper
¼ c. flour
    Vegetable oil
1 c. yogurt

Soak bread in water until most of the water is absorbed. Squeeze out excess water. Combine all ingredients except flour, oil, and yogurt. Shape rounded teaspoons of mixture into balls. Roll each in flour. Fry in 1 inch of hot oil until golden. Drain on paper toweling. May be reheated in 350° oven until hot (about 20 minutes). Serve on toothpicks around a bowl of yogurt mixed with snipped parsley, mint, and salt. Makes 18 to 24 meatballs.

MEATBALLS MADRAS

2 eggs, beaten
1 c. chopped mixed dried fruits (apricots, prunes, raisins, apples)
½ c. finely chopped onion
½ c. crumbled fresh bread crumbs
1½ t. salt
1 dash of Tabasco sauce
1½ lbs. ground beef (may contain veal and pork)
2 T. vegetable oil or margarine
1 c. sweet vermouth

Combine all ingredients, except oil and vermouth, until evenly mixed. Shape into 1-inch balls. In a large skillet, sauté 1 layer of meatballs at a time in hot oil until evenly browned. Place in a heated chafing dish. Warm vermouth; pour over all, and serve. Makes about 50 meatballs.

SWEDISH MEATBALLS

1 lb. ground round
½ c. fine dry bread crumbs
½ c. milk
1 egg, slightly beaten
1 t. salt
½ t. nutmeg
Dash of pepper
2 T. Worcestershire sauce
3 T. flour
½ t. salt
2 c. light cream *plus* ½ c. milk
2 T. vegetable oil

Mix together first eight ingredients. Shape into 1-inch meatballs. Heat oil in a frying pan and sauté half of the meatballs until browned. Continue to cook until meatballs are done. Repeat with remaining meatballs. Blend flour and ½ teaspoon salt into drippings in frying pan. Gradually blend in cream and milk. Stir until thickened and comes to a boil. Mix in meatballs; heat through. Makes 60 to 80 meatballs.

MEATBALLS

1 lb. ground beef
¼ lb. pork sausage, cooked and drained
2 eggs, beaten
½ c. fine bread crumbs
1 can mincemeat pie filling
½ to 1 c. apple cider
1 T. wine vinegar

Combine meats, eggs, and crumbs. Mix well and form into 5 to 6 dozen tiny meatballs. Bake in a 375° oven for 15 to 20 minutes. Cool and drain. At serving time, combine pie filling, cider, and vinegar. Pour over meatballs and heat. Serve hot. Makes 5 to 6 dozen meatballs.

MEDITERRANEAN MEATBALLS

1 lb. ground beef
1 c. cooked rice
⅓ c. minced onion
¼ c. snipped fresh dill
¼ c. snipped fresh parsley
1 egg, beaten
1 t. salt
⅛ t. pepper
½ c. flour
1 egg, beaten
Vegetable oil

Combine first 8 ingredients; mix until smooth. Shape meat into balls and dip in flour, then egg. Heat 1 inch of oil in skillet; fry meatballs until golden. Makes 30 meatballs.

CHAFING DISH MEATBALLS

1½ lbs. ground round
½ c. diced bread crumbs
1 t. salt
¼ t. pepper
1 egg, slightly beaten
½ c. milk
2 T. vegetable oil
1 1-lb. 4-oz. can pineapple chunks, drained
1 17-oz. jar stuffed olives or 1 green pepper cut in chunks

Toss together ground round, bread crumbs, salt, pepper, egg, and milk until well blended. Shape into ¾-inch balls and chill for 2 hours. Bake meatballs in a shallow pan with oil in a 350° oven for 30 minutes. Drain all fat, cover with sauce and bake an additional 30 minutes. Spoon into chafing dish with pineapple chunks, green olives or green pepper chunks. Makes about 48 meatballs.

Sauce

1 bottle chili sauce
1 bottle water
1 small jar of grape jelly

Combine all ingredients and bring to a boil.

Pictured opposite:
Chafing Dish Meatballs

BARBECUED SPARERIBS

2 lbs. spareribs, cut in bite-size pieces
½ c. brown sugar
1 c. catsup
¼ c. soy sauce
¼ t. cumin
2 T. sherry
2 T. vinegar

Combine all ingredients except spareribs, mixing well. Marinate ribs 3 to 4 hours in sauce. Remove and bake, covered, in a 300° oven for 1½ hours. Remove cover, add sauce; bake and baste 1 hour longer. Makes 8 to 10 servings.

MOCK PATÉ DE FOIS GRAS

4 to 5 large mushrooms, sliced
2 T. butter
½ lb. liverwurst, mashed
1 3-oz. pkg. cream cheese, softened
1 T. Worcestershire sauce
½ t. thyme
¼ c. heavy cream

Sauté mushrooms in butter. Mix together all ingredients. Chill; serve with crackers or pumpernickel bread. Serves 4 to 6.

TURKEY ROLL-UPS

¼ c. mayonnaise
¼ t. curry powder
12 thin slices turkey
12 green pepper strips
12 Swiss cheese strips

Mix together mayonnaise and curry powder. Lightly spread each turkey slice with mayonnaise mixture. Place a green pepper strip and a Swiss cheese strip at one end of turkey slice. Roll up turkey jelly-roll fashion; secure with 2 toothpicks. Cut Turkey Roll-Up in half. Makes 24.

CHINESE RIBS

2 lbs. spareribs
½ c. soy sauce
3 T. catsup
1 T. dry sherry
1 T. brown sugar
½ t. ginger
¼ t. garlic powder
2 T. honey

Combine soy sauce, catsup, sherry, brown sugar, ginger, and garlic powder in pan large enough to hold ribs. In a separate cup combine honey with 1 tablespoon soy sauce marinade and set aside. Coat spareribs with soy sauce marinade; marinate for at least 1 hour, turning occasionally. Place ribs on a broiler pan; bake in a 350° oven for 1 to 1½ hours brushing frequently with marinade. During the last five minutes, brush ribs with the honey mixture. Serve hot. Makes 6 to 8 servings.

TURKEY SANDWICHES

¼ c. butter, softened
1 T. mustard
1 t. horseradish
36 fingers of thin white bread
Thin slices of turkey breast

Combine butter, mustard, and horseradish. Spread bread with seasoned butter; top with turkey. Makes 3 dozen fingers.

CURRIED CHICKEN OR TURKEY

2 c. minced cooked chicken or turkey
½ to ¾ c. mayonnaise
¼ c. minced celery
1 to 2 t. curry powder
4 to 6 dozen Crustades, p. 6

Mix all ingredients together. Serve in crustades with minced parsley or snipped chives on top. Makes 3 cups.

BAKED CHICKEN PATÉ

1 medium onion, chopped
1 clove garlic, minced
2 eggs
1 lb. chicken livers
¼ c. flour
½ t. allspice
1 t. salt
½ t. pepper
¼ c. butter
1 c. light cream

Place all ingredients in a blender; blend until smooth. Pour into a greased 1-quart baking dish; cover. Set in pan of hot water and bake in a 325° oven for 3 hours. Cool, then chill. Unmold and serve with unsalted crackers or melba toast.

CHICKEN SALAD SPREAD

2 c. cooked chicken, minced
¼ c. celery, minced
½ c. mayonnaise
2 T. sour cream
1 T. sherry
1 T. lemon juice
    Ripe olives, sliced, for garnish
    Paprika

Mix all together. Serve garnished with ripe olive slices and sprinkled with paprika. Makes about 2 cups.

CHICKEN LIVERS CANTON

1 to 2 lbs. chicken livers, fresh or frozen, thawed
1 c. soy sauce
¼ c. butter
¼ c. flour

Cover chicken livers with soy sauce and marinate overnight in the refrigerator. Drain well; dust with flour. Sauté in butter for about 5 minutes until no longer pink. Shake pan occasionally to brown livers on all sides. Serve with toothpicks. Makes 10 to 12 servings.

CHICKEN OR TURKEY SOUFFLÉS

2 c. minced chicken or turkey
1 3-oz. pkg. cream cheese, softened
½ c. mayonnaise
1 T. lemon juice
1 T. capers
    Dash of Tabasco
    Toast rounds

Mix all together. Mound onto toast rounds and broil until puffy. Makes 2 to 3 dozen.

CHICKEN SPREAD

2 c. finely chopped chicken or turkey (dark meat)
½ c. chopped ripe olives
    Salt and pepper to taste
    Mayonnaise to bind

Combine all ingredients, mixing well. Spread on choice of breads or toast. Serves 12 to 16.

SESAME SEED CHICKEN WINGS
BATTER

2 eggs
¾ c. flour
½ t. salt
¾ c. cold water

Beat eggs; gradually add flour and salt. Add water slowly and beat until smooth and thin. Refrigerate for 30 minutes. Remove from refrigerator 30 minutes before using.

12 to 16 chicken wings, discard tips
½ c. sesame seed
4 c. peanut or corn oil

Heat oil to 375° in skillet or deep fryer. Dip each chicken wing in batter; sprinkle with sesame seed. Deep fry four wings at a time for 10 to 12 minutes, turning several times. Remove from oil and drain on paper toweling. Repeat until all pieces are fried. Serve with bottled sweet sour sauce, if desired. Serves 6 to 12.

CHICKEN WINGS, MEXICANA

32 chicken wings
1 T. vegetable oil
1½ c. diced onion
1½ c. diced green and red pepper
1½ c. diced canned tomatoes
1½ T. tomato paste
2 cloves garlic, minced
1 t. salt
¼ t. pepper
¼ t. chili powder
½ envelope beef onion soup mix *or*
1 c. brown gravy mix

Sauté onion in oil until soft. Combine all ingredients and pour over chicken. Place in a baking dish. Bake in a 375° oven for 30 to 45 minutes until tender. Serve hot in sauce.

CHICKEN WINGS

32 chicken wings
⅔ c. melted butter
1 t. salt
½ t. garlic powder
1½ c. bread crumbs
½ c. grated Parmesan cheese

Discard wing tips; cut remaining wing into 2 pieces. Season melted butter with salt and garlic powder. Combine bread crumbs and grated cheese, stirring to mix well. Dip wings in butter, then in crumb-cheese mixture. Place on a 15 x 10-inch baking sheet; bake in a 400° oven for 30 minutes. Makes 32 appetizers.

HAWAIIAN KABOBS

1 lb. bologna, cut into 24 cubes
24 pineapple cubes
2 T. soy sauce
1 T. brown sugar
1 T. vinegar

Spear cubes of meat and pineapple on toothpick. Place on broil-and-serve platter. Brush with combined mixture of soy sauce, sugar, and vinegar. Broil, turning, until hot and golden. Makes 24.

FRANKLY HAWAIIAN

Cocktail wieners or frankfurters cut in
1-inch pieces
1 c. brown sugar
2 t. mustard
3 T. flour
1 c. pineapple juice
½ c. vinegar
1 T. soy sauce

Combine all ingredients, except wieners; heat, stirring until sauce comes to a boil. Add wieners and heat through. Serve in a chafing dish. Makes 4 to 5 dozen.

STIK & PIK

HOT KABOBS

With toothpicks, alternate pineapple chunks or pickled onions with one of the following and then broil:

Ham cubes
Cooked shrimp
Scallops
1-inch frankfurter pieces
Chicken livers

COLD KABOBS

Using toothpick, carrot or celery stick, alternate 2 or more of the following:

Melon balls
Pineapple chunks
Cold meat cubes
Chicken cubes
Cooked shrimp
Cheese cubes
Wiener chunks, cubed salami, cut in
1-inch pieces
Cubes of pickle
Cherry tomatoes
Cubes of cheese
Pickled onion
Stuffed green olive
Orange slices
Ham cubes
Canned mushroom
Radishes

Pictured opposite:
Chicken Wings
Hawaiian Kabobs

HAM AND SWISS SQUARES

12 slices boiled ham
2 8-oz. pkgs. Swiss cheese spread,
   softened
2 T. hot mustard
½ c. minced parsley

Mix together cheese, mustard and parsley. Spread half the mixture on 4 slices of ham, top with another slice of ham, then spread remaining cheese, and top with remaining ham. Chill for ½ hour. Cut into bite-sized cubes. Dip edges in minced parsley. Makes about 3 dozen.

HAM SPREAD

1 c. chopped ham
¼ c. finely grated Cheddar cheese
1 t. prepared mustard
2 t. pickle relish
3 T. mayonnaise

Combine all ingredients, mixing well. Serve on toast or crackers. Makes 1⅓ cups.

BACON STICKS

12 unsalted bread sticks
12 slices bacon

Wrap each bread stick, spiral fashion, with a bacon slice. Bake in a 400° oven for 10 to 12 minutes until bacon is crisp. Makes 12 sticks.

SALAMI TRIANGLES

1 8-oz. pkg. cream cheese, softened
2 T. prepared horseradish
¼ t. Tabasco sauce
36 slices salami

Blend cheese with horseradish and Tabasco sauce. Spread 12 slices of salami with the cheese mixture. Top with another slice of salami, more cheese and a third slice of salami. Cut each circle into quarters; spear each with a toothpick. Makes 48 triangles.

ZIPPY HAM SPREAD

2 c. ground ham
2 T. prepared mustard
2 T. horseradish
1 c. sour cream

Blend all ingredients together, mixing well. Serve with rye or pumpernickel bread. Makes about 3 cups.

DEVILED HAM SPREAD

2 cans deviled ham
2 hard-boiled eggs, minced
½ small onion, minced
1 T. minced sweet pickle
½ c. mayonnaise

Mix all ingredients together, blending well. Serve with party rye or crackers. Makes about 1 cup.

BACON BALLS

Stuffed green olives
Bacon slices

Wrap stuffed olive in ¼ to ½ of a bacon slice. Broil until bacon is done. Serve on toothpicks.

LIVER SAUSAGE SPREAD

1 8-oz. pkg. cream cheese, softened
1 8-oz. pkg. liver sausage or
   Braunschweiger
1 T. minced onion
2 t. lemon juice
1 t. Worcestershire sauce
Salt and pepper to taste

Blend all ingredients together, mixing well. Garnish with parsley; serve with crackers. Makes 2 cups.

TOASTED BRAUNSCHWEIGER

Braunschweiger or liver sausage
Bread rounds
Butter
Mustard
Grated onion
Stuffed olives, sliced

Butter bread rounds and spread with a little mustard. Mix braunschweiger and onion; spread thickly on top of butter. Broil for about 5 to 7 minutes until hot. Garnish with sliced olive. Serve hot.

BUFFET BAR-B-Q

1 large cabbage, red or green
1 small can sterno
  Cocktail sausages
  Shrimp
  Chunks of bologna and salami

Cut off slice from bottom of cabbage. Hollow out space in the top of cabbage to hold small container of sterno. Stud the cabbage with toothpick speared sausages and shrimp. Guests grill their own. Serve with sauce.

BARBECUE SAUCE

1 c. catsup
½ c. chili sauce
2 T. prepared horseradish
1 t. Worcestershire sauce
¼ t. Tabasco sauce

Combine all ingredients, mixing well. Heat and serve.

PICK-EM-UPS

Cocktail Prunes
Remove pits from extra large prunes. Fill with one of the following:

Sharp cheese spread
Peanut butter mixed with crisp bacon
Ham and cream cheese spread
Cream cheese mixed with chopped nuts
Whole blanched almond

COCKTAIL SAUSAGES

Cocktail wieners or frankfurters cut in 1-inch pieces
¼ c. mustard
½ c. currant jelly

Heat mustard and jelly in a saucepan. Add wieners and heat, covered, about 10 minutes. Serve in a chafing dish. Makes 2 to 3 dozen.

MEAT ROLL-UPS

8 thin slices of cooked meat:
  Salami
  Spiced ham
  Bologna
  Dried beef
  Boiled ham
  Roast beef
  Turkey ham

Spread filling on meat slices and roll up tightly. Chill thoroughly; cut into bite-sized pieces, or shape each slice into a cone. Makes 30 to 36.

FILLING

4 oz. cream cheese
  Grated onion
  Worcestershire sauce or mustard
  Horseradish
  Tabasco

Combine all ingredients according to taste; mix together well.
Note: For variation, use any prepared cheese spread.

Pastries

ROQUEFORT ROLL-UPS

1 8-oz. pkg. cream cheese
1 8-oz. pkg. Roquefort or blue cheese
½ c. mayonnaise
1 T. Worcestershire sauce
2 T. minced onion
1 c. butter, melted
Loaf of thinly sliced sandwich bread, crusts removed

Mix together cheeses and seasonings. Spread on bread slices, roll up jelly-roll fashion; dip in melted butter and bake on a cookie sheet in a 350° oven for 15 to 18 minutes. Cool slightly and cut into thirds. Makes 4 to 6 dozen.

MINIATURE CREPES

2 eggs
1 c. water
⅔ c. flour
½ t. salt
2 T. melted butter
½ pt. sour cream
1 2½ to 4-oz. jar red or black caviar

Beat eggs with half of the water. Stir in flour and salt. Add remaining water and butter. Spoon into a hot greased frying pan, making crepes paper thin and not more than 3 inches in diameter. Spread with sour cream and caviar; roll up. To serve, heat in a 300° oven for 3 to 5 minutes until just warm. Makes 36 crepes.

ARTICHOKE BALLS

¼ c. butter
1 small onion, minced
1 15-oz. can artichoke hearts, drained and minced
1 clove garlic, minced
½ c. grated Parmesan cheese
½ c. toasted bread crumbs
½ t. salt

Melt butter; sauté onion, artichoke, and garlic until onion is shiny. Remove from heat. Add cheese, salt, and bread crumbs to artichoke mixture. Form into 3 to 4 dozen bite-size balls. Bake in a 300° oven for 8 to 10 minutes. Makes 3 to 4 dozen Artichoke Balls.

QUICHE FOR A CROWD

2 cans green chiles
1 20-oz. pkg. Muenster or Monterey Jack cheese, diced
6 eggs, beaten
12 crackers, crushed
1 c. sour half and half

Rinse chiles, remove seeds, drain, and chop. Mix all ingredients together. Pour into a greased 11 x 13-inch casserole. Bake in a 350° oven for 50 to 60 minutes until bubbly and slightly brown. Remove from oven; cool for 15 minutes. Cut into 1-inch squares and serve warm. Serves 4 to 6.

Pictured opposite:
Miniature Crepes

MINIATURE QUICHE

2 c. flour
1 8-oz. pkg. sharp Cheddar cheese, grated
½ lb. margarine or butter
Dash of cayenne

Cream together cheese, butter and cayenne. Add flour and mix into a smooth dough. Wrap and chill for an hour or freeze for 30 minutes. Then form into 48 1-inch balls and press into miniature muffin tins. Place ½ teaspoon filling in center of each quiche then 1 tablespoon custard. Bake in a 400° oven for 12 to 15 minutes. Cool 5 minutes and remove from tins. Serve warm. You may freeze and reheat. Makes 48 Quiche.

CUSTARD MIX

4 eggs
1 c. milk
2 T. flour *plus* ¼ t. salt

Mix together well.

DENVER FILLING

1 c. chopped salami
½ onion, minced
1 T. butter

Sauté onion in butter. Stir in salami.

MUSHROOM FILLING

1 4-oz. can mushrooms, sliced
½ onion, minced
1 T. butter

Sauté mushrooms and onion in butter.

SHRIMP 'N CHEESE FILLING

48 baby shrimp
4 oz. of blue cheese crumbled

Mix together well.

SPINACH FILLING

1 pkg. frozen chopped spinach
½ onion, minced
1 T. butter

Cook spinach; drain well. Sauté onion in butter; stir in spinach.

ARTICHOKE SQUARES

2 jars marinated artichoke hearts, chopped
1 bunch green onions, sliced
2 T. vegetable oil
1 clove garlic, minced
1 c. grated Cheddar cheese
½ t. Worcestershire sauce
¼ t. Tabasco sauce
4 eggs, beaten
½ c. crushed soda crackers
Minced parsley

Drain the artichoke hearts, saving the oil. Sauté onion in oil. Combine all ingredients except crackers and parsley; put into a greased 8-inch square pan. Sprinkle with cracker crumbs and parsley. Bake in a 325° oven for 35 to 40 minutes. Chill for several hours. Cut into small squares and serve. Makes sixteen 2 x 2-inch squares.

PIZZA HORNS

1¼ c. flour
¼ t. salt
⅓ c. yogurt or sour cream
3 T. melted margarine
1 lb. lean ground beef
1 T. minced onion
½ c. pizza sauce
¼ t. oregano
1 T. minced parsley
1 egg, slightly beaten

Stir yogurt and margarine into flour and salt. On a lightly floured surface, knead gently to form a smooth dough. Add more flour if needed. Cover and let rest 30 minutes. Sauté meat and onion until browned; drain. Add pizza sauce, oregano, and parsley and stir; cool. Divide dough into thirds. Roll out each third to a 9-inch circle. Cut each circle into 8 triangles. Place a heaping teaspoon of pizza filling on the wide end of each triangle. Roll up each triangle from the wide end. Brush each triangle with slightly beaten egg. Prick tops with fork. Bake in a 400° oven for 10 to 12 minutes or until golden brown. Serve hot. Makes 24.

SESAME PUFFS

1 c. water
½ c. butter or margarine
½ t. salt
1¼ c. flour
4 eggs
⅓ c. sour cream
¼ c. sesame seed
1 lb. ground smoked ham
1 T. dill weed
¼ c. mayonnaise
1 T. mustard

Bring water, butter, and salt to a boil. Remove from heat and add flour all at once. Stir with a wooden spoon until mixture forms a ball. Add eggs, one at a time, beating well after each addition. Add sour cream and sesame seed, beating until smooth. Drop dough by rounded tablespoons onto a greased cookie sheet. Bake in a 425° oven for 12 minutes. Prick each puff with a fork and continue baking for 3 more minutes. Remove from cookie sheets and cool on wire racks. Combine remaining ingredients, adding more mayonnaise if necessary. Cut slice off top of each puff and remove any soft dough inside. Fill with ham mixture, or any filling of your choice. Replace tops and chill until serving time. Makes about 30.

TIROPETAS

½ lb. Feta cheese, crumbled
1 6 to 8-oz. pkg. cottage cheese
⅛ t. salt
3 eggs
2 pkgs. frozen chopped spinach, thawed and drained (optional)
1 t. minced onion (optional)
½ t. nutmeg (optional)
¼ lb. butter, melted
1 lb. phylo dough (20 sheets)
1 T. chopped parsley

Blend cheeses well. Add eggs, salt, parsley and optional ingredients, if desired. Working with 1 sheet of dough at a time, while keeping remainder refrigerated and covered with a dampened towel, cut phylo dough lengthwise into 2-inch strips. Brush strips with melted butter. Place 1 teaspoon of filling at end of strip, folding over end to make a triangle. Continue folding strip from side to side forming triangles, until all is folded. Place seam side down on a baking sheet. Brush tops with melted butter and bake in a 400° oven for 10 to 15 minutes until golden brown. May be frozen unbaked. Makes abut 10 dozen.

CHEESY TOMATO BREAD

1 large loaf of French bread, sliced in half lengthwise
Butter, softened
1 8-oz. can tomato sauce
Salt and pepper
¼ t. garlic powder
¼ t. basil
¼ t. oregano
2 c. grated Mozzarella cheese
1 c. grated Parmesan cheese

Butter cut surfaces of bread; spread with tomato sauce. Top with mixed seasonings. Sprinkle with Mozzarella, then with Parmesan. Place on baking sheet and bake in a 350° oven for 8 to 10 minutes. Cut bread diagonally into 1½-inch thick slices; serve hot. Serves 8 to 12.

PUFFED SHRIMP

1 egg white
Salt
⅓ c. mayonnaise
1 T. finely chopped celery
2 t. chopped chives
½ t. prepared mustard
¼ t. cream-style horseradish
1 4½-oz. can shrimp, drained and rinsed
16 squares of bread, buttered

Beat egg white with dash of salt until soft peaks form. Fold in all ingredients except the shrimp. Spread bread with egg white mixture and top each slice with a shrimp. Bake on an ungreased cookie sheet in a 375° oven for 8 to 10 minutes. Serve warm. Makes 16.

HERB TOAST

1 loaf thin sliced bread, cut into squares
  or fingers
½ c. butter, melted
¼ t. dill
¼ t. basil
¼ t. thyme
¼ t. marjoram

Add seasonings to butter. Dip bread pieces into butter. Bake in a 300° oven for 20 to 30 minutes until crisp and brown. Store covered. Makes 4 squares or 3 triangles per slice of bread.

PARMESAN CHEESE CRACKERS

¾ c. grated Parmesan cheese
¾ c. margarine or butter, softened
½ t. salt
1½ c. flour
¾ c. chopped walnuts

Cream together cheese and margarine. Add flour and salt; mix to form dough. Blend in nuts. Form into 2 rolls about 1 inch in diameter. Roll in waxed paper; refrigerate for one hour. Slice into thin wafers and bake on an ungreased cookie sheet in a 350° oven for 12 to 15 minutes. Sprinkle lightly with salt while warm. Makes 4 to 6 dozen.

CANADIAN BACON PASTIES

6 frozen patty shells, thawed
6 slices Canadian bacon, cut ¼-inch thick
6 slices Swiss or Cheddar cheese
  Prepared mustard

On lightly floured surface, roll each shell to a 9-inch circle. Spread bacon with mustard and top with cheese slice. Moisten edges of patty shell and fold two opposite sides to center, overlapping a little. Then fold other two sides to center, pinching edges to seal. Repeat 5 more times. Prick tops. Place on ungreased baking sheet. Bake in a 400° oven for 20 to 25 minutes or until golden. Makes 6 pasties.

MINIATURE CREAM PUFFS

½ c. water
¼ c. butter or margarine
⅛ t. salt
½ c. flour
¼ c. finely grated Cheddar cheese
  (optional)
2 eggs

Combine water and butter in a saucepan; bring to a boil. Add salt and flour all at once; stir quickly until mixture forms a ball. Remove from heat. Add cheese, if desired. Beat in 1 egg at a time, beating well until mixture is like velvet. Refrigerate mixture for 1 hour. Place 1 scant teaspoonful on a lightly greased cookie sheet; mound with tip of spoon. Bake in a 400° oven for 15 to 18 minutes until puffed and golden brown. Split cream puffs in half and fill with desired filling. Makes abut 4 to 5 dozen.

MEAT FILLING

1½ c. chopped cooked chicken, shrimp, or
  crab meat
2 T. minced celery or water chestnuts
1 t. minced onion
  Seasoned salt to taste
3 to 4 T. mayonnaise

Combine all ingredients, mixing well; fill puffs.

CUCUMBER FILLING

1 c. chopped cucumber
1 3-oz. pkg. cream cheese, softened
½ t. grated onion
½ t. salt
  Dash of pepper
2 to 3 T. mayonnaise

Combine all ingredients, mixing well; fill puffs.

CREAM CHEESE AND OLIVE FILLING

1 8-oz. pkg. cream cheese
½ t. instant chicken bouillion
1 T. minced onion
½ c. chopped ripe olives
2 T. mayonnaise

Combine all ingredients mixing well; fill puffs.

Pictured opposite:
Miniature Cream Puffs

MUSHROOM TURNOVERS

1 8-oz. pkg. cream cheese, softened
1 c. margarine or butter
2 c. flour
4 4-oz. cans of mushrooms, minced, and
  drained
½ onion, minced
3 T. butter
2 T. flour
¼ t. salt
¼ t. pepper
1 T. dry sherry
¼ c. sour cream

Cream together cheese and butter; add flour and form into a dough. Divide into 3 balls. Wrap each in waxed paper and chill at least 1 hour. Sauté mushrooms and onion in butter. Stir in flour, salt, pepper, and sherry. Cook until well blended. Remove from heat. Stir in sour cream and allow mixture to cool. Roll dough to a ⅛-inch thickness on lightly floured board. Cut out 3-inch circles. Place 1 teaspoon of filling on each, fold in half, stretching dough and crimping the edges. Bake in a 375° oven for 15 to 20 minutes until golden brown. Before baking, brush each with an egg wash of 1 egg yolk mixed with 1 tablespoon water. Makes about 40 to 48 turnovers.

BLUE CHEESE WEDGES

English muffins, split in half
Butter or margarine
Blue cheese crumbled

Spread muffin halves with butter; sprinkle with crumbled blue cheese and broil until bubbly. Cut into wedges.

MUSHROOM BALLS

1 8-oz. pkg. cream cheese
¼ lb. butter or margarine
1 c. flour
  Pinch of salt
1 lb. fresh firm mushroom caps, washed
  and dried
  Butter
  Salt, pepper, and garlic powder to taste
1 egg, beaten

Cream together cheese and butter until well blended. Add flour and salt; mix well to form a dough. Chill for 1 hour. Sauté mushroom buttons, rounded sides down first, in small amount of hot butter. Turn over and brown second side. Don't cook more than 2 to 3 minutes. Season with salt, pepper, and garlic powder. Let cool.

Roll out dough to 9 x 12-inches and cut into 3-inch squares. Place mushrooms on each piece of dough and enclose, pinching ends, and rolling gently to form a ball. Place balls on lightly greased baking sheet and brush with beaten egg. Bake in a 425° oven for 20 minutes or until golden brown. Makes about 24.

HAM PINWHEELS

1½ c. flour
1 c. grated Cheddar cheese
½ c. butter, softened
2 T. water
8 thin slices cooked ham
½ c. minced onion
¼ c. milk

Mix together flour, cheese, butter and water until dough forms. Divide dough into 2 equal balls. Roll each ball into a 10 x 14-inch rectangle. Cut each rectangle into four 5 x 7-inch pieces. Place 1 slice ham on each rectangle; sprinkle with minced onion. Roll jelly-roll fashion. Place each roll on a cookie sheet; brush with milk. Bake in a 450° oven for 10 to 12 minutes until golden brown. Remove and cut each roll into 4 or 5 pinwheels. Serve hot. Makes 32 to 40 Ham Pinwheels.

CROSTINI

1 loaf thin-sliced bread, slightly stale
Butter

Cut bread slices into 2-inch squares or circles. In a frying pan, melt butter and brown bread on 1 side only. Before serving, spread the untoasted side with 1 of the following spreads:

ANCHOVY AND MOZZARELLA

8 thin slices of Mozzarella cheese, cut into 1-inch squares
8 anchovy fillets

Place cheese on crostini; lay anchovy fillet on top of cheese. Broil on baking sheet 4 inches from heat for 1 minute or until cheese is golden. Makes 8.

ANCHOVY AND OLIVES

1 can anchovies, drained
3 pimiento-stuffed olives

Finely chop olives and anchovies. Blend well. Spread on crostini. Makes 8.

ANCHOVY AND PARMESAN

1 can anchovy fillets with capers, drained
2 T. Parmesan cheese, grated
2 t. lemon juice

Mash anchovy fillets to a paste. Add cheese and lemon juice, mixing well. Spread on crostini. Makes 6 to 12.

ANCHOVY AND TUNA

1 can tuna fish
3 anchovies, chopped
1 T. lemon juice
2 T. tomato paste
Dash of Tabasco sauce

Combine all ingredients, blending well. Spread on crostini. Makes 12 to 20.

PIGS-IN-A-BLANKET

1 can crescent roll dough
2 T. mustard
2 T. pickle relish, drained (optional)
24 cocktail wieners

Separate 1 can of dough into 8 triangles. Spread with mustard and relish. Cut each triangle into 3 small triangles. Place a wiener on the wide end of each triangle. Roll up and place on an ungreased cookie sheet. Bake in a 375° oven for 10 to 12 minutes. Serve hot. Makes 24.

SPICY BISCUITS

1 lb. sharp Cheddar cheese, grated
1 lb. hot bulk sausage
3 c. biscuit mix

Melt cheese in top of a double boiler. Add sausage; stir until sausage is thoroughly cooked. Add to biscuit mix; blend well. Form into 1-inch balls. Bake in a 450° oven for 15 to 20 minutes. Makes 3 to 4 dozen.

CHEESE BALLS

1 5-oz. jar sharp Cheddar cheese spread
¼ c. butter
½ t. salt
½ c. flour
Dash of red pepper
¾ c. sesame seed

Cream cheese with butter. Add flour, salt, and red pepper. Mix until well blended. Form into 1-inch balls, and roll in sesame seed. Chill for at least 2 hours. Bake on greased cookie sheet in a 400° oven for 10 to 12 minutes. Makes about 3 dozen.

KNISHES

3 c. flour
1 t. baking powder
½ t. salt
1 c. water
1 egg, slightly beaten
 Vegetable oil
 Filling of choice
1 egg yolk mixed with 1 T. flour

Combine flour, baking powder, and salt in a large bowl. Add water, egg, and 1 tablespoon oil. Stir with wooden spoon until dough forms. Turn out on a lightly floured surface and knead until smooth and elastic, about 5 minutes, using only enough additional flour to keep dough from sticking. Cover dough and let rest 30 minutes. Divide dough into fourths and roll out one-fourth of dough on lightly floured surface to a 12-inch square. Cut in half to make 2 6-inch wide strips. Brush lightly with oil. Spoon filling down center of strip. Bring 1 side of pastry over filling, then roll up to enclose filling completely, pinch ends together. Place on a lightly greased cookie sheet, seam side down. Score with a knife at 1-inch intervals; do not cut through. Brush with egg yolk wash. Bake in a 375° oven 30 minutes or until golden brown. Cut into 1-inch pieces. Serve warm. Makes about 8 dozen.

Potato Filling

2 medium-size potatoes, cooked and
 mashed
2 T. vegetable oil
¾ c. finely chopped onion
¾ t. salt
⅛ t. pepper
1 T. minced parsley

Sauté onion in oil until tender, not brown. Combine all ingredients, mixing well. Makes enough filling for 24 Knishes.

Kasha Filling

1 c. cooked Kasha
¾ c. finely chopped onion
2 T. vegetable oil
¾ t. salt
¼ t. pepper

Sauté onion in oil until golden brown. Stir into Kasha with salt and pepper. Makes enough filling for 24 Knishes.

Cheese Filling

1 3-oz. pkg. cream cheese
½ c. small-curd cottage cheese
1 egg yolk
1 t. sugar
¼ t. salt
¼ t. vanilla

Beat all ingredients together until smooth. Makes enough filling for 24 Knishes.

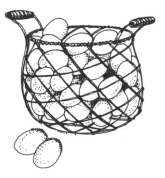

SPINACH PARMESAN APPETIZER PIE

4 green onions, snipped
4 T. butter or margarine
¼ lb. mushrooms, chopped
1 pkg. frozen spinach, thawed, drained
1 clove garlic, minced
¼ t. tarragon
3 T. minced parsley
4 eggs
½ c. milk
1 t. salt
¼ t. pepper
½ c. shredded Parmesan cheese

Sauté onions in butter for 3 minutes; add mushrooms and sauté 5 minutes. Stir in spinach, garlic, tarragon, and parsley. Simmer over medium heat, stirring constantly until liquid evaporates. Beat eggs with milk, salt, and pepper; add cheese. Combine with sautéed vegetables and pour into a lightly buttered 9-inch pie pan. Bake in a 375° oven for 35 to 40 minutes or until a knife inserted in center comes out clean. Cut in wedges and serve on individual plates with forks. Makes 6 to 9 servings.

Pictured opposite:
Spinach Parmesan Appetizer Pie

BACON ROLL UPS

10 slices white bread, crusts removed
½ lb. hot sausage, cooked and drained
1 8-oz. pkg. cream cheese, softened
10 slices bacon, cut in quarters

Cut bread slices into 4 fingers. Spread with mixture of sausage and cream cheese. Place each bread strip on top of a bacon strip; roll jelly-roll fashion. Secure with a toothpick. Bake in a 400° oven for 15 to 20 minutes until brown and crispy. Makes 40 Bacon Roll Ups.

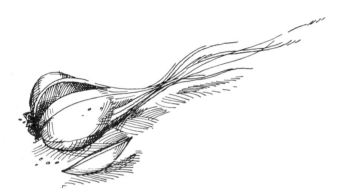

ASPARAGUS ROLLS

1 T. lemon juice
1 T. minced onion
Salt to taste
½ c. butter or margarine, softened
25 slices white bread, crusts removed
1 15-oz. can white asparagus spears, drained
¼ c. melted butter

Stir lemon juice and onion into butter; season to taste with salt. Roll bread slice flat with rolling pin, spread 1 teaspoon of butter mixture on one side of bread. Place an asparagus spear on one end and roll up tightly. Brush rolls with melted butter and place on ungreased baking sheet. Bake rolls in a 350° oven for 30 minutes, turning every 10 minutes to brown evenly. May be frozen after baking and reheated for 20 minutes at 350°. Makes 25 rolls.

DEVILED TOAST

½ c. butter, softened
1 t. Worcestershire sauce
½ c. sesame seed
1 loaf very thin-sliced bread, crusts removed

Mix together butter, Worcestershire sauce, and sesame seed. Spread on bread slices. Cut each slice into quarters or fingers. Bake in a 325° oven for 25 to 30 minutes until crisp and golden brown. Makes 5 to 6 dozen.

DEVILED BLUE CHEESE NIBBLES

1 8-oz. pkg. refrigerator biscuits, cut into quarters
¼ c. butter
¼ c. blue cheese
1 t. Worcestershire sauce

Arrange biscuits in a cake pan so they touch each other. Melt butter and cheese, add Worcestershire sauce. Pour cheese mixture over biscuits. Bake in a 400° oven for 12 to 15 minutes until golden. Serve hot. Makes 40.

EGG CUPS

4 green onions, sliced
¼ lb. mushrooms, minced
2 T. butter
2 slices smoked salmon, minced
6 eggs
4 T. cold water
Freshly ground pepper
12 Toast Cups

Sauté onions and mushrooms in butter. Add salmon, and warm through. Beat eggs with cold water until light. Pour over onion mixture; add pepper to taste and scramble lightly. Spoon into toast cups. Makes 12.

TOAST CUPS

Trim 12 slices of white bread. Butter both sides. Fit slices into muffin tins, pressing sides and bottom gently. Toast in a 400° oven for 5 to 8 minutes or until golden brown.

Nuts

VIRGINIA PEANUTS

1 to 2 lbs. shelled peanuts
¼ c. butter
Salt

Soak peanuts in water to cover for 24 hours; drain. Place on a non-stick cookie sheet; dot with butter. Roast in a 325° oven, stirring occasionally for 30 to 40 minutes. Remove and sprinkle with salt. Makes 4 to 8 cups.

STUFFED PECANS

1 lb. large pecan halves
1 3 to 4-oz. pkg. sharp Cheddar cheese spread
2 T. minced onion
Few drops Worcestershire sauce

Mix cheese and seasoning until smooth. Place a dollop between 2 nut halves. Chill and serve. Makes about 4 cups.

SNAPPY MIX

¼ lb. margarine
2 t. Worcestershire sauce
¼ to ½ t. Tabasco sauce
2 cloves garlic, crushed
4 to 6 c. popped corn
1 8 to 12-oz. pkg. corn chips
2 c. miniature pretzels
1 3-oz. can chow mein noodles
1 c. toasted soybeans (optional)

In a saucepan, melt margarine; add sauces and garlic. Mix remaining ingredients in a large roasting pan and pour spicy mixture over all until well-coated. Bake in a 250° oven for 1 hour stirring several times. Cool and store in airtight containers. Makes about 8 cups.

SAUTÉED NUTS

2 c. almonds, walnuts or pecans
4 T. butter
1 t. salt
1 t. ginger, curry powder, or garlic powder

Combine nuts and butter. Place in shallow pan in a 350° oven and bake for 30 minutes or until golden brown. Stir occasionally. Drain on absorbent paper and sprinkle with salt and seasoning. Makes about 2 cups.

Seafood

CURRIED TUNA SANDWICHES

1 7-oz. can water packed tuna
½ c. mayonnaise
1 t. lemon juice
¼ t. curry powder
¼ t. prepared horseradish
¼ t. salt
12 slices white bread cut in circles
   Softened butter or margarine

Drain and flake tuna. Combine all ingredients, except bread and butter. Spread each bread round with butter and tuna mixture. Tops may be decorated with sprig of parsley, bit of pimiento or olive slice. Makes 12 open-faced sandwiches.

TUNA-CHEESE BITES

1 6½-oz. can tuna
1 c. shredded Cheddar cheese
¼ c. butter, softened
2 T. lemon juice
1 T. minced onion
1 t. Worcestershire sauce
3 drops Tabasco sauce
30 toast rounds

Drain and flake tuna. Cream together cheese and butter. Add seasonings and tuna, mixing thoroughly. Spread each toast round with about 2 teaspoonfuls of the mixture. Place on a cookie sheet; broil about 4 inches from burner for 3 to 4 minutes or until lightly browned. Makes 30.

HERRING 'N SOUR CREAM

1 8 to 16-oz. jar herring in wine sauce
¼ c. mayonnaise
½ pt. sour cream
   Juice of ½ lemon
½ green pepper, chopped
1 t. celery seed
1 t. sugar
4 green onions and tops, sliced

Rinse and drain herring. Combine all ingredients; marinate for up to 3 weeks in refrigerator. Serve with crackers. Makes 2 to 3 cups.

TUNA BALLS

2 13-oz. cans tuna
2 3-oz. pkgs. cream cheese, softened
1 T. lemon juice
2 T. horseradish
¼ t. Tabasco sauce
1 c. snipped parsley

Drain and flake tuna. Cream the cheese; add lemon juice, horseradish, Tabasco sauce, and tuna. Shape tuna-cheese mixture into small balls; roll in parsley. Chill several hours. Makes about 40.

Pictured opposite:
Herring 'N Sour Cream

TUNA PINWHEELS

6 slices thin sliced bread, crusts removed
  Butter or margarine
1 6-oz. can tuna or shrimp
¼ c. mayonnaise

Drain and mash tuna. Mix in mayonnaise. Butter bread and spread with tuna mixture. Roll bread up jelly-roll fashion. Wrap in plastic wrap; chill several hours or overnight. Slice to desired thickness and serve. Makes 2 dozen.

TUNA-DILL SPREAD

1 8-oz. pkg. cream cheese
1 13-oz. can tuna
1 T. dry sherry
1 T. lemon juice
½ t. garlic powder
½ t. dill weed
⅛ t. white pepper

Rinse and drain tuna. Combine all ingredients; beat until light and fluffy. Serve on toast or crackers. Makes about 2 cups.

CRAB STUFFED MUSHROOM

1 7½-oz. can crab meat
3 green onions, snipped
¼ c. grated Parmesan cheese
½ c. mayonnaise
12 jumbo mushroom caps, washed and dried
½ c. butter or margarine
  Parmesan cheese

Drain crab meat; remove cartilage. Mix crab meat, onion, and ¼ cup Parmesan cheese with mayonnaise. Lightly sauté mushroom caps in butter. Remove from pan and drain. Stuff caps with crab mixture. Place in an ungreased shallow pan. Bake in a 325° oven for 5 minutes. Sprinkle caps with Parmesan cheese and broil for 3 minutes. Makes 12.

CRAB MEAT PUFF

1 6-oz. can crab meat
1 3-oz. pkg. cream cheese, softened
¼ c. mayonnaise
1 t. minced onion
1 t. salt
⅛ t. pepper
1 T. snipped parsley
  Toast rounds

Combine all ingredients except toast rounds. Mound crab meat mixture on toast; broil until bubbly. Makes about 1 cup.

KING CRAB DIP

4 oz. whipped cream cheese with chives
¼ c. milk
1 10½-oz. can cream of celery soup
1 T. dry sherry
1 7½-oz. can Alaska king crab *or*
1 pkg. frozen king crab

Blend cream cheese, milk, and celery soup. Heat in saucepan, stirring until smooth; add sherry. Add crab and heat through. Serve warm in a chafing dish with toast or crackers. Makes 8 to 12 servings.

KING CRAB SANDWICH

1 7¾-oz. can king crab meat
1 T. mayonnaise
1 t. soy sauce
⅛ t. garlic powder
⅛ t. pepper
1 egg white, stiffly beaten
  Bread rounds, toasted on 1 side

Remove membrane from crab meat; set aside chunks of meat. Combine mayonnaise, soy sauce, garlic, and pepper. Fold in beaten egg white. Heap on untoasted side of bread round. Top with crab chunk; broil 2 minutes until puffy and golden. Serves 8.

CRAB STUFFED MUSHROOMS

24 large mushroom caps
    Juice of 1 lemon
½ lb. crab meat
½ c. mayonnaise
¼ c. minced celery
    Dash of Tabasco
½ c. minced parsley

Toss mushroom caps in lemon juice; set aside. Mix together crab meat, mayonnaise, celery, and Tabasco. Fill each cap with crab mixture. Chill and serve. Sprinkle with parsley just before serving. Makes 24.

CRAB DIP

½ lb. crab meat
1 T. snipped chives
½ c. mayonnaise
1 c. grated Cheddar cheese
¼ c. chili sauce
1 T. sherry

Mix together all ingredients. Heat over low heat until cheese melts. Serve with melba toast or French bread chunks. Serves 4 to 6.

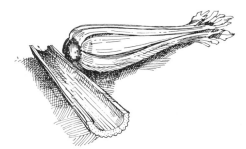

HOT CRAB DIP

1 6 to 8-oz. can crab meat, drained and
    flaked
2 T. lemon juice
1 c. sour cream
¼ c. mayonnaise
1 t. Worcestershire sauce
    Dash of Tabasco sauce
¼ c. snipped chives or parsley

Combine all ingredients except parsley or chives, mixing well. Heat to steaming; serve hot with melba toast or crackers. Serves 6 to 8.

CRAB MEAT DIP

1 8-oz. pkg. cream cheese, softened
⅛ t. salt
1 T. grated or minced onion
2 t. lemon juice
½ t. Worcestershire sauce
¾ c. sour cream or sour half and half
2 6½-oz. cans crab meat, minced

Combine all ingredients, mixing well; chill. Serve with crackers. Makes 2 cups.

HOT SHRIMP RAREBIT

1 10-oz. can tomato soup
1 c. grated Muenster cheese
½ lb. minced cooked shrimp
1 T. Worcestershire sauce

Melt soup and cheese together over low heat. Add shrimp and Worcestershire sauce. Serve hot with chunks of French bread. Serves 6 to 8.

PINK SHRIMP DIP

1 8-oz. pkg. cream cheese, softened
¼ c. mayonnaise
3 T. chili sauce
1 T. lemon juice
¼ t. Worcestershire sauce
    Dash of Tabasco sauce
1 can tiny shrimp, rinsed and drained

Combine all ingredients, blending well. Chill several hours. Serve with crackers or raw vegetables. Makes 1½ cups.

SHRIMP ROUNDS

24 cooked medium shrimp
½ to 1 c. Italian salad dressing
24 melba rounds, buttered
24 thin slices cucumber
    Dash of paprika

Marinate shrimp in salad dressing for 6 to 8 hours. Top melba toast with 1 slice cucumber and 1 shrimp. Sprinkle with paprika. Makes 24.

SHRIMP REMOULADE

1½ lbs. hot cooked shrimp
4 T. vegetable oil
2 T. olive oil
½ t. white pepper
½ t. salt
1 t. snipped parsley
½ t. horseradish
1 celery heart, minced
2 T. tarragon vinegar
4 T. brown mustard
½ c. snipped green onions

Combine all ingredients except shrimp; whip with a fork or whisk until well blended. Pour over hot shrimp. Shrimp should be hot so it will absorb the flavor of the marinade. Refrigerate in marinade. Serve chilled in individual seafood shells or on a serving dish. Makes 8 to 10 servings.

SEAFOOD COQUILLE

1 lb. scallops
3 T. snipped scallions
½ c. butter or margarine
1 lb. small cooked shrimp
3 T. flour
2 c. yogurt or sour cream
1 T. lemon juice
   Dash of Tabasco sauce
   Salt and pepper to taste
1 4-oz. can mushroom pieces, drained
12 patty shells
½ c. bread crumbs
½ c. grated Parmesan cheese

Put scallops in a saucepan and cover with water. Bring water to a boil and simmer scallops for 3 to 5 minutes or until they are firm. Drain. Sauté scallions in skillet with butter, adding the flour and blending well. Add shrimp, scallops and yogurt; blend well over low heat. Stir in seasonings and then the mushrooms. Spoon into individual shells; sprinkle with bread crumbs and cheese. Put shells on a cookie sheet; place under the broiler until the cheese browns. Makes 12 servings.

SHRIMP

5 c. water *or* 2 c. beer plus 3 c. water
2 T. horseradish
1 bay leaf
2 T. Worcestershire sauce
3 to 5 lbs. shrimp

In a large kettle, bring water to a rolling boil. Add horseradish, bay leaf, and Worcestershire sauce. Add shrimp and boil for 5 to 7 minutes. Drain immediately. Cool and shell shrimp. Chill shrimp; place on a bed of cracked ice. Spear with toothpicks to dip in sauce. Serves 15 to 20.

SHRIMP SAUCE

2 c. chili sauce
¼ c. horseradish
1 T. Worcestershire sauce
   Juice of ½ lemon
1 T. vinegar

Combine all ingredients and mix well.

SHRIMP PATÉ

3 c. cooked shrimp, minced
2 T. lemon juice
2 T. horseradish
¼ c. chili sauce
½ c. mayonnaise

Combine all ingredients. Chill and serve with cucumber or zucchini slices or crackers. Makes 4 cups paté.

SPANISH SAUCE FOR SHRIMP

1 c. mayonnaise
½ c. catsup
¼ c. chili sauce
½ c. chopped pimiento-stuffed olives
1 T. brandy
½ t. prepared mustard
½ t. Worcestershire sauce
½ t. lemon juice
   Dash of freshly ground pepper

Mix all ingredients together and chill. Makes about 1¾ cups.

Pictured opposite:
Seafood Coquille

HOT SHRIMP DIP

¼ c. butter
1 small onion, minced
½ lb. chopped cooked shrimp
½ c. grated processed Swiss cheese
¼ c. cocktail sauce

Sauté onion in butter. Add shrimp, cheese, and cocktail sauce. Cook over low heat until cheese melts. Serve hot with crackers. Serves 4 to 6.

SHRIMP BUTTER

¼ lb. butter or margarine, softened
1 4½-oz. can shrimp
¼ t. dill weed
2 t. lemon juice
Freshly ground pepper to taste

Wash and drain shrimp; chop. Blend all ingredients together and chill. Bring to room temperature 30 minutes before serving. Serve on crackers or bread. Makes about 1 cup.

SHRIMP DE JONGHE

2 lbs. shrimp, cooked and cleaned
¼ c. butter
¾ c. cold butter
1 clove garlic, minced
¾ c. dry sherry
½ c. minced parsley
1½ c. lightly toasted bread crumbs
¼ c. grated Parmesan cheese
¼ c. melted butter

Sauté shrimp lightly in ¼ cup butter. Place in 8 individual ramekins or shells. Beat cold butter until light and gradually add the garlic, sherry, parsley, and bread crumbs. Spoon bread mixture over the shrimp, spreading with a knife. Sprinkle with grated Parmesan and drizzle with melted butter. Bake in a 350° oven for about 30 minutes. May be prepared early in the day, refrigerated, brought to room temperature, and then baked. Serves 8.

SHRIMP-CHEESE CANAPES

30 bread rounds
1 c. chopped cooked shrimp
½ c. grated American or Cheddar cheese
1 T. minced celery
1 T. minced onion
3 T. mayonnaise
¼ t. dry mustard
¼ t. lemon juice
¼ t. Worcestershire sauce

Toast bread rounds on one side. Mix remaining ingredients together; spread on untoasted side of bread. Place 4 inches beneath broiler; broil for about 4 minutes. Makes 30 canapes.

ANCHOVY MELBA

¼ c. butter or margarine, softened
1 T. anchovy paste
24 slices of melba toast

Combine butter and anchovy paste, mixing well. Spread thinly on melba toast. Makes 24 appetizers.

DEVILED SHRIMP

2 lbs. shrimp, cooked and still warm
1 lemon, thinly sliced
1 red onion, thinly sliced
½ c. fresh lemon juice
¼ c. vegetable oil (olive oil may be used)
1 T. wine vinegar
1 garlic clove, minced
½ bay leaf
1 T. dry mustard
¼ t. cayenne
1 t. salt
Freshly ground pepper

Put shrimp, lemon and onion slices in a serving bowl. Combine lemon juice, oil, vinegar, spices, and herbs, and mix together well. Pour over the shrimp mixture. Cover and chill at least 2 hours, stirring once or twice.

PUFFY SHRIMP

1 can crescent roll dough
1 4½-oz. can shrimp
1 egg white
⅓ c. mayonnaise
1 T. finely chopped celery
2 t. snipped green onions or chives
½ t. mustard
½ t. cream-style horseradish

Wash and drain shrimp. Separate dough into 8 triangles. Cut each in half to form 16 triangles. Place on an ungreased cookie sheet. Beat egg white until soft peaks form. Fold mayonnaise, celery, onion, mustard, and horseradish into egg white. Spread mixture on triangles; top with 2 shrimp. Bake in a 375° oven for 15 to 18 minutes. Serve warm. Makes 16.

SARDINE DIP

1 c. creamed cottage cheese
1 3¾-oz. can sardines, undrained, mashed
1 T. lemon juice
1 T. minced onion
Dash of Tabasco sauce
¼ t. pepper

Combine all ingredients, mixing well. Chill and serve with crackers or rye bread. Serves 6 to 8.

SARDINE PASTE

1 8-oz. pkg. cream cheese, softened
½ t. salt
2 T. lemon juice
1 t. garlic powder
2 3¾-oz. cans sardines (boneless and skinless), mashed
⅛ t. Tabasco sauce

Combine all ingredients, mixing well. Spread on toast rounds. Makes about 2 cups.

CAVIAR BALL

¼ t. bouillon crystals
1 t. hot water
1 8-oz. pkg. cream cheese
¼ t. minced onion
1 T. mayonnaise
2 4-oz. jars red or black caviar

Dissolve bouillon in hot water. Cream together cream cheese, bouillon, onion, and mayonnaise; shape into a ball. Frost completely with the caviar. Place on a bed of endive or romaine. Serve with rye saltines or melba toast. Serves 8 to 12.

HALIBUT VINAIGRETTE

Prepare this appetizer at least 2 days before serving.

2 lbs. halibut steak, ½ inch thick
1 t. salt
¼ c. salad oil
1 large Spanish onion, thinly sliced
2 T. olive oil
2 cloves garlic, minced
¾ c. white wine vinegar
1 t. paprika
1 t. salt
½ t. freshly ground pepper

Sprinkle halibut steak on both sides with 1 teaspoon salt; let stand 15 minutes. In a large skillet, heat salad oil and sauté halibut 5 minutes on each side. Place on a dish and refrigerate. Sauté onion in olive oil until tender. Stir in garlic, vinegar, paprika, salt, and pepper; cool. Remove skin and bone from halibut and break into chunks. Arrange fish and onion mixtures in layers in a glass bowl. Refrigerate, covered, for at least 2 days. It keeps in refrigerator for 2 weeks. Serves 8.

CHILI CLAM DIP

1 8-oz. pkg. cream cheese, softened
1 8-oz. can minced clams and juice
1 bottle chili sauce
1 T. lemon juice

Mix together all ingredients well. Serve with corn chips or crackers. Serves 4 to 6.

CLAM FONDUE

2 T. butter
1 T. vegetable oil
¼ c. minced onion
½ green pepper, diced
½ lb. Cheddar cheese, shredded
4 T. catsup
1 T. Worcestershire sauce
Dash of Tabasco sauce
2 8-oz. cans chopped clams, drained
2 T. dry sherry
1 loaf French or Italian bread, cubed

In top of double boiler, chafing dish, or fondue pot, heat butter and oil. Sauté onion and green pepper until soft. Add a small amount of cheese at a time with catsup, Worcestershire sauce, and Tabasco sauce. Stir constantly until cheese melts. Just before serving, add clams and sherry. Dip cubes of bread in fondue. Serves 8 to 10.

ARTICHOKE-CLAM PUFFS

2 10-oz. pkgs. frozen artichoke hearts
1 8-oz. pkg. cream cheese, softened
¼ t. Tabasco sauce
2 T. sherry
1 6½-oz. can drained minced clams
3 T. grated Parmesan cheese, or paprika

Cook artichokes according to package directions until just barely tender. Drain and place on broil-and-serve platter. Beat cheese with Tabasco and sherry; stir in clams. Spoon mixture onto cut sides of artichokes. Sprinkle with Parmesan or paprika; broil until browned. Makes about 36.

ROASTED OYSTERS

Oysters
Melted butter

Place oysters on a cookie sheet in 350° oven for a few minutes until they pop open. Finish opening and serve with melted butter for dipping.

SCALLOPED OYSTERS

1½ c. coarse cracker crumbs
½ c. grated Parmesan cheese
¼ c. melted butter or margarine
½ t. salt
Dash of pepper
1 pt. drained fresh oysters
¼ c. dry sherry
½ c. yogurt or sour cream
1 T. butter or margarine
8 patty shells

Combine crumbs, cheese, ¼ c. butter, salt, and pepper in a skillet. Stir until well mixed. Spread half of the crumb mixture on the bottoms of 8 shells. Spoon oysters over crumbs. Combine the sherry and yogurt and spoon on top of the oysters. Top with remaining crumbs. Dot with bits of butter. Place shells on a cookie sheet and bake in a 375° oven for 20 minutes until crumbs are golden brown. Serves 8.

OYSTERS ON THE HALF SHELL

Oysters
Lemon wedges

Open fresh oysters, and place on a large tray of cracked ice. Serve with cocktail picks and lemon wedges, and bowls of horseradish, catsup, and vinegar.

Pictured opposite:
Oysters on the Half Shell

SALAD NICOISE

Salad greens to line a platter
2 6½-oz. cans tuna fish, drained
1 can sardines, drained, optional
12 pitted ripe olives
3 hard-boiled eggs, quartered
1 green pepper, cut in strips
12 cherry tomatoes
1 red onion, sliced in thin rings
8 to 10 anchovy fillets, drained
1 jar marinated artichoke hearts,
   reserve juice
2 to 4 T. wine vinegar

Arrange tuna, sardines, olives, eggs, green pepper, cherry tomatoes, onion, anchovy fillets, and artichoke hearts attractively on the salad greens. Combine artichoke juice and vinegar; pour over vegetables. Serves 8 to 12.

CRAB MEAT HORS D'OEUVRES

15 slices white bread, crusts removed
6 oz. crab meat, flaked
1 small onion, grated
1 c. grated Cheddar cheese
1 c. mayonnaise
1 t. curry powder
½ t. salt

Cut bread into 4 squares. Combine remaining ingredients and spread on bread. Broil until golden and bubbly. Makes 60 hors d'oeuvres.

OYSTER CANAPÉS

Squares of thinly sliced dark
bread, buttered
Red or black caviar
1 can smoked oysters

Border each bread square with caviar. In the center, place 1 oyster. Cover oyster with a dollop of sour cream or mayonnaise.

ANCHOVY CANAPÉS

1 small tin anchovy fillets, drained
1 3-oz. pkg. cream cheese, softened
1 green onion, snipped
1 T. sour cream
   Pinch of curry powder
   Buttered bread rounds
1 t. minced parsley
   Paprika

Mash anchovies. Add to cream cheese together with onion, sour cream, and curry powder. Beat until smooth. Spread on rounds of buttered bread. Sprinkle with parsley and lightly with paprika. Chill. Serves about 6.

SMOKED FISH CANAPÉS

Smoked whitefish, carp, trout or other
smoked fish
Butter, softened
Paprika
Parsley, minced

Mash fish in proportion of 1 teaspoon fish to 2 tablespoons butter. Spread on bread rounds and sprinkle with paprika and minced parsley.

NOVA SCOTIA SALMON AND ONION CHEESECAKE

Butter
½ c. fine bread crumbs
3½ 8-oz. pkgs. cream cheese, softened (28 oz.)
4 large eggs
⅓ c. heavy cream
½ c. chopped onion
½ green pepper, chopped
2 T. butter
¼ lb. Nova Scotia salmon, diced
½ c. grated Gruyere cheese
3 T. grated Parmesan cheese
Salt and pepper

Butter the inside of an 8 x 8 x 3-inch cheesecake pan. Sprinkle the bottom and sides with crumbs. Mix cream cheese, eggs, and cream with electric mixer until smooth. Set aside. Sauté onion and green pepper in 2 tablespoons butter. Fold the salmon, Gruyere cheese, Parmesan cheese, sautéed onion, and green pepper into the cheese cake mixture. Add salt and pepper to taste. Pour batter into prepared pan; tap gently to level mixture. Set pan into a larger pan (so edges do not touch); add 2 inches of boiling water to larger pan. Bake in a 300° oven for 1 hour and 40 minutes. Turn off oven and let cake remain in oven for 1 hour longer. Lift cake out of water; place on rack to cool at least 2 hours before unmolding. Makes 12 to 20 servings.

BACON BLUE CHEESE CHEESECAKE

½ lb. bacon, cooked and chopped
½ c. finely chopped onion
½ lb. blue cheese, crumbled
Salt and freshly ground pepper to taste
2 to 3 drops Tabasco sauce

Sauté onion in 1 tablespoon bacon fat until soft. To the basic cheese mixture, add bacon, onion, blue cheese, salt, pepper, and Tabasco sauce, blending thoroughly. Pour into pan and bake as directed above.

CRUNCHY SALMON SPREAD

16 rounds of bread or toast, buttered
1 1-lb. can salmon, drained and flaked
1 8-oz. can water chestnuts, drained and chopped
1 small onion, minced
1 stalk celery, minced
½ c. mayonnaise
2 T. soy sauce
1 T. lemon juice

Combine all ingredients, except bread. Spread salmon mixture on bread or toast rounds. Sprinkle snipped parsley on top. Makes 16 rounds.

SALMON NEWBURG

8 T. butter
6 T. flour
4 c. cream
5 T. grated Parmesan cheese
1 T. paprika
1 t. dry mustard
Salt to taste
Dash of Tabasco sauce
6 egg yolks, beaten
4 T. brandy
4 T. dry sherry
6 c. salmon, drained and flaked

Melt butter in a saucepan and stir in flour. Cook for 7 minutes without letting flour brown. Gradually add warm cream, stirring constantly until sauce is thick and smooth. Add Parmesan, paprika, mustard, salt, and Tabasco. Pour the sauce slowly over beaten egg yolks, stirring constantly. Add brandy and sherry. Stir in salmon; heat thoroughly. Place in chafing dish. Serve with toast rounds or patty shells. Serves 24.

SCANDINAVIAN SALMON

1 T. salt
1 T. sugar
1½ t. whole peppercorns, crushed
1 T. dill weed
1 lb. raw salmon fillets

Mix together salt, sugar, pepper, and dill. Place fish on a large piece of heavy foil. Cover with seasonings. Close foil; place on tray or in a shallow dish. Weight down with 3 to 4 unopened heavy cans. Refrigerate 48 hours. Scrape off seasonings, slice thin and serve with toast and lemon wedges. Serves 10 to 12.

SALMON SPREAD

1 1-lb. can salmon, drained and flaked
1 unpeeled cucumber, grated
1 3-oz. pkg. cream cheese
½ c. mayonnaise
1 T. dry white wine
¼ t. pepper
¼ t. tarragon
¼ c. minced parsley
¼ c. snipped chives

Remove skin and bones from salmon. Mix together all ingredients except parsley and chives. Spoon into serving bowl, sprinkle with parsley and chives. Serve cold with crackers. Serves 12 to 16.

DILLY SALMON SPREAD

1 15½-oz. can salmon
1 c. sour cream or sour half and half
½ c. chopped celery
2 T. lemon juice
1 t. Worcestershire sauce
½ t. dill weed
¼ t. salt

Drain and flake salmon. Add sour cream, celery, and seasonings. Mix thoroughly and chill. Serve with chips, crackers or vegetables. Makes 2½ cups.

CURRIED SALMON SPREAD

1 1-lb. can salmon, drained and flaked
1 stalk celery, minced
2 green onions, snipped
¼ c. mayonnaise
¼ c. sour cream
1 T. lemon juice
1 t. curry powder
Dash of pepper

Remove skin and bones from salmon. Mix together all ingredients well. Serve with toast rounds or crackers. Serves 12 to 16.

NOVA PINWHEELS

1 lb. smoked salmon
1 8-oz. pkg. cream cheese, softened
2 T. sour cream, mayonnaise, or yogurt

Blend together cheese and sour cream. Spread mixture on individual strips of salmon; roll up jelly-roll fashion. Cut in ½ inch slices. Place pinwheel flat on buttered party rye slices.

SALMON MOUSSE

2 T. gelatin
¼ c. cold water
1 15½-oz. can salmon
1 10¾-oz. can tomato soup
1 8-oz. pkg. cream cheese, softened
1 c. mayonnaise
1 green pepper, finely chopped
1 c. chopped celery
1 small onion, grated
1 T. Worcestershire sauce
½ t. salt
¼ t. white pepper

Dissolve gelatin in water. Drain and flake salmon. Heat soup and cream cheese over low heat until cheese is dissolved. Add softened gelatin and stir until well blended. Add remaining ingredients and mix well. Place in a well-greased fish mold; chill overnight in the refrigerator. Unmold on bed of endive or leaf lettuce. Serve with toast. Serves 12 to 16.

Pictured opposite:
Salmon Mousse

Vegetables

PEPPER CRESCENTS

6 medium green peppers
1 4-oz. pkg. blue cheese, softened
1 8-oz. pkg. cream cheese, softened
1 8-oz. pkg. Cheddar cheese spread, softened
2 T. mayonnaise
1 t. mustard

Wash green peppers, cut each in half lengthwise and remove seeds. Blend cheeses, mayonnaise, and mustard together. Spoon into pepper shells. Chill until firm; slice each shell lengthwise into crescents. Makes 24 crescents.

RATATOUILLE

4 T. olive oil
1 large onion, chopped
1 clove garlic, minced
1 green pepper, chopped
1 medium eggplant, chopped
3 ripe tomatoes, chopped
2 zucchini, chopped
½ t. basil
½ t. thyme
1 t. salt
1 T. lemon juice

Heat olive oil, add vegetables and seasonings, except lemon juice. Simmer slowly until thickened, 20 to 40 minutes. Sprinkle with lemon juice, chill. Serve with crackers. Makes 24 to 36 servings.

CORSICAN COMBO

2 6¾-oz. cans pitted ripe olives, drained
1 pt. cherry tomatoes
¼ c. minced fresh parsley

Wash and stem tomatoes. Marinate olives and tomatoes in marinade for 12 to 24 hours. Just before serving, garnish with parsley. Serves 8 to 10.

MARINADE

½ c. wine vinegar
1 c. olive oil
1 clove garlic, cut
1 bay leaf
1 t. basil

Combine all ingredients, mixing well.

STUFFED CELERY

1 stalk celery
1 4-oz. pkg. blue cheese, crumbled
1 c. yogurt or sour cream
¼ c. finely snipped green onions or chives
1 T. brandy

Combine all ingredients except celery, and chill until of spreading consistency. Cut celery into 2-inch pieces, fill with blue cheese/yogurt mixture, and serve cold. Makes 6 to 7 dozen.
Note: For variation, stuff celery with sharp cheese spread and sprinkle with chopped nuts.

CARROT STIX PROVENCALE

1 lb. carrots, cut into sticks
1¼ c. sauterne
¼ c. water
1 clove garlic, minced
1 t. seasoning salt
1 t. sugar
2 T. olive oil
⅛ t. dry mustard
1 bay leaf
2 T. snipped parsley

Bring all ingredients except carrots and parsley, to a boil; simmer for 5 minutes. Add carrots and simmer for 6 minutes longer. Cool, refrigerate, stirring in snipped parsley.

MIDDLE EAST SPREAD

1 1-lb. eggplant, unpeeled and diced
1 onion, chopped
2 to 3 T. vegetable oil
1 green pepper, chopped
1 red pepper, chopped
1 clove garlic, minced
1 t. salt
Pepper to taste
½ of a 15-oz. can tomato sauce with tomato bits

Salt and drain eggplant. Sauté onion in oil until golden brown. Add eggplant and sauté. Add peppers, garlic, salt, pepper, and tomato sauce. Cover and simmer until tender, about 10 minutes. Stir and chill for about 1 hour before serving. Add more salt if desired. Serves 4 to 6.

COCKTAIL BEETS

2 1-lb. cans small whole beets, drained
1 8-oz. pkg. cream cheese, softened
2 T. horseradish
1 T. mayonnaise

Combine cream cheese, horseradish and mayonnaise, mixing well. Scoop center out of beets and fill with cream cheese mixture. Serves 4 to 6.

PICKLED CARROT STIX

1 lb. carrots
¾ c. vinegar
¾ c. water
½ c. sugar
1 t. mixed whole pickling spice

Peel carrots; cut into sticks. Combine remaining ingredients and bring to a boil; simmer for 5 minutes. Place carrots in a dish, cover with hot liquid. Cool and refrigerate for a few days before serving. Serves 10.

COCKTAIL TOMATOES

12 cherry tomatoes
24 tiny cooked shrimp
¼ c. plain yogurt
1 T. minced onion
½ t. dried dill weed
⅛ t. salt

Scoop out centers of cherry tomatoes; invert and drain. Drain and wash shrimp. Combine yogurt, onion, dill, and salt. Fill tomato with the yogurt mixture, top with 2 shrimp each. Makes 12 Cocktail Tomatoes.

ARTICHOKE PRETTIES

1 10-oz. pkg. frozen artichoke hearts, cooked, drained, chilled
½ c. sour cream
½ c. red or black caviar
½ t. lemon juice
1 T. minced onion

Mix sour cream, caviar, lemon juice, and onion together. Spoon a little mixture into the cavity of each artichoke heart. Makes 4 to 6 servings.

TOMATO ROUNDS

36 rounds of thin white bread, buttered
36 slices of ripe tomato
½ c. mayonnaise
2 T. minced fresh basil

Top bread with tomatoes; garnish with mayonnaise spiced with fresh basil. Makes 36 rounds.

CUCUMBER SANDWICHES I

1 large cucumber, peeled
1 8-oz. pkg. cream cheese, softened
½ t. garlic salt
½ t. Worcestershire sauce
1 t. salt
¼ c. snipped green onion stems or snipped chives
30 rounds or fingers of white bread, buttered

Cut cucumber in half lengthwise; remove seeds. Dice and drain in a strainer for at least 1 hour. Mix cream cheese, garlic salt, Worcestershire sauce, and salt until well blended. Stir in drained cucumber and snipped onion. Spread on buttered bread rounds. Make open faced or closed sandwiches. Refrigerate covered with waxed paper and a damp cloth, until serving time. Makes about 2½ dozen.

CUCUMBER SANDWICHES II

48 thin rounds of pumpernickel, buttered
1 large cucumber
Minced chives

Score cucumber and slice thin. Marinate cucumber slices in marinade for at least 3 hours. Drain and place one slice of cucumber on each bread round. Top with a sprinkle of minced chives. Makes 48 sandwiches.

MARINADE

1 medium onion, minced
1 c. vinegar
Salt and pepper to taste

Combine all ingredients and mix well.

ONION SANDWICHES

48 slices of party pumpernickel, buttered
1 sweet red onion, minced
1 c. mayonnaise
1 c. minced parsley

Combine onion and mayonnaise. Spread on bread; garnish with parsley. Chill. Makes 48 sandwiches.

CUCUMBER RING

1 envelope unflavored gelatin
½ c. cold water
½ t. salt
4 c. creamed cottage cheese
2 3-oz. pkgs. cream cheese, softened
½ c. mayonnaise
1 medium cucumber
1 green onion, snipped
⅔ c. finely chopped celery

Soften gelatin in water. Add salt. Heat and stir over low heat until gelatin is dissolved. Beat cheeses together; add mayonnaise and gelatin. Pare and seed cucumber and grate. Stir in cucumber, onion, and celery. Pour into a lightly oiled 6-cup ring mold. Chill 6 to 8 hours or overnight. Garnish with cherry tomatoes and radishes. Serve with crackers. Serves 12.

STUFFED CUCUMBER

1 cucumber
1 3-oz. pkg. cream cheese, softened
1 T. mayonnaise
1 T. snipped green onion or chives
Snipped parsley

Combine cream cheese, mayonnaise, and green onion. Score cucumber with fork lengthwise. Cut in half and remove seeds with spoon. Fill cavity with cheese mixture, packing tightly. Chill several hours. Slice ¼-inch thick and sprinkle tops with snipped parsley. Makes 6 to 10 servings.

Pictured opposite.
Tomato Rounds
Cucumber Sandwiches I
Cucumber Sandwiches II

ENA'S IKRA

3 to 4 medium zucchini
2 to 3 T. vegetable oil
1 medium onion
1 tomato
1 t. vinegar
   Salt and pepper to taste

Peel and slice zucchini. Sauté zucchini in oil until golden brown. Process zucchini, tomato and onion in food processor or put through meat grinder. Add vinegar, salt, and pepper. Serve with toast. Makes 10 to 12 servings.

MUSHROOM TIDBITS

1 8-oz. pkg. cream cheese, softened
1 T. snipped green onions or chives
1 T. butter or margarine, softened
1 3-oz. can chopped mushrooms, drained
¼ t. garlic powder

Combine all ingredients, mixing well. Spread on crackers. Sprinkle with paprika. Broil 3 to 5 minutes. Makes about 36.

MUSHROOMS FLORENTINE

2 pkgs. frozen chopped spinach
1 t. instant chicken bouillon
36 large mushrooms
4 T. butter or margarine
¼ t. garlic powder
¼ t. dry mustard
¼ t. seasoned salt
   Parmesan cheese, grated

Clean mushrooms, separate stems and caps. Cook spinach as directed on package, adding chicken bouillon to the water. Drain well. Chop mushroom stems and sauté in butter. Combine spinach and seasonings. Lightly sauté mushroom caps in butter or margarine until slightly browned; drain. Fill caps with spinach mixture and sprinkle with Parmesan cheese. Place in a shallow pan and bake in a 375° oven for 15 minutes. Makes 36 appetizers.

WATER CHESTNUTS AND BACON

1 8-oz. can water chestnuts, drained
½ lb. bacon
½ c. soy sauce

Cut slices of bacon just long enough to encircle and overlap water chestnuts. Secure the bacon with a toothpick. Place in a bowl of soy sauce for several hours. Remove from sauce and broil until crisp. Makes 32 servings.

MARINATED MUSHROOMS I

1 lb. small mushrooms, cleaned and dried
½ c. olive oil
2 T. lemon juice
2 T. vinegar
1 t. salt
½ t. freshly ground pepper
¼ t. thyme
1 t. tarragon

Combine all ingredients and simmer over low heat for 5 to 10 minutes. Cool; refrigerate in marinade overnight. Bring to room temperature before serving. Makes 32 to 38 mushrooms.

MUSHROOM CAPERS

18 to 24 large mushrooms, washed and dried
⅓ c. fine dry bread crumbs
1 T. lemon juice
⅛ t. garlic powder
⅛ t. rosemary
⅛ t. marjoram
¼ t. salt
¼ c. almonds, finely chopped
1 T. capers, minced
   Butter
   Parsley

Chop mushroom stems and combine with remaining ingredients. Spoon mixture into mushroom caps. Place in a greased shallow baking pan. Dot each mushroom with butter and bake in a 350° oven for 20 minutes. To serve, sprinkle with snipped parsley. Makes 18 to 24.

MUSHROOM CAPS

12 large mushroom caps, washed and dried
1 3-oz. pkg. cream cheese, softened
½ t. curry powder or garlic powder
12 parsley sprigs

Combine cream cheese and curry powder. Fill mushroom caps with seasoned cream cheese. Garnish with a small sprig of parsley. Serves 6.

MUSHROOM CAVIAR

½ lb. mushrooms, minced
4 T. butter
2 T. minced onion
2 T. lemon juice
1 T. Worcestershire sauce
3 T. mayonnaise
½ t. salt
Dash of pepper

Sauté mushrooms in butter for about 5 minutes. Add onion, sauté for 5 more minutes. Remove from heat, cool slightly, drain. Add remaining ingredients. Mix well. Chill and serve with toast. Makes 1 to 1½ cups.

MARINATED MUSHROOMS II

1 lb. mushrooms, washed and dried
Snipped parsley

Pour vinaigrette dressing over mushrooms and allow to marinate for several hours. Pour off dressing. Sprinkle mushrooms with snipped parsley and serve on platter with toothpicks. Makes 32 to 38 mushrooms.

VINAIGRETTE DRESSING

2 T. red wine vinegar
6 T. olive oil
2 t. prepared mustard
2 t. lemon juice
1 t. salt
¼ t. freshly ground pepper

Combine all ingredients, mixing well.

MUSHROOM PATÉ

½ lb. mushrooms, sliced
2 T. margarine
1 8-oz. pkg. cream cheese, softened
1 t. minced onion
1 t. Worcestershire sauce
¼ t. garlic powder
2 slices white bread, cubed

Sauté mushrooms in margarine until tender. In blender or food processor, blend all ingredients until well mixed. Spoon into small bowl; cover and refrigerate until chilled. Serve with toast rounds. Makes 1½ cups.

HOT MUSHROOM CAPS

1 lb. mushrooms
2 T. butter or margarine
Garlic powder and pepper to taste

Clean and dry mushrooms. Separate caps and stems. Chop mushroom stems fine; sauté quickly in butter. Fill caps with seasoned sautéed stems and place in buttered baking dish. Heat in a 425° oven for 8 minutes. Serves 4 to 6.

VEGETABLES VINAIGRETTE

1 cucumber
3 carrots
½ head cauliflower
½ lb. string beans
1 lb. mushrooms, sliced
6 T. tarragon vinegar
½ c. vegetable oil
4 T. olive oil
4 T. lemon juice
1 t. sugar
1 T. salt
1 T. dill weed (optional)

Score cucumber and slice ¼ inch thick. Slice carrots in sticks or circles. Separate cauliflower and clean string beans. Combine vinegar, oils, lemon juice, sugar, salt, and dill weed; mix until blended. Pour over vegetables; marinate in refrigerator for up to three days. Serves 10 to 12.

A Gourmet Touch
for the Gourmet on the Go

This main section contains a combination of recipes from the two best-selling gourmet treats—*Gourmet on the Go* and *Gourmet Touch*. It provides the perfect answer for the busy gourmet who has neither the time nor inclination to spend on elaborate menu preparation. Herein are elegant meals that the busy cook will find easy to prepare, fun to serve and, most of all, delicious to eat. The authors have also included tempting dishes to please the meat-and-potatoes man as well as the most discriminating gourmet. Bachelor, career woman, busy homemaker, all will feel like a French chef when preparing and serving the recipes in this section.

Contents

SOUPS AND STEWS

TOMATO BOUILLON

Mmm good, now it's better!

1 10½-oz. can tomato soup
1 10½-oz. can beef bouillon
1 soup can water
¼ c. dry sherry
½ t. sugar

Blend all together and heat just to boiling. Serves 2 to 4.

CONSOMMÉ MADRILENE

Feel a little warmer inside.

2 c. water
3 t. beef or chicken instant bouillon
1 T. tomato paste
1 T. lemon juice
1 T. dry red wine
¼ t. sugar
Lemon slices for garnish

Mix together all ingredients except lemon slices. Bring to a boil and simmer for a few minutes until piping hot. Garnish with lemon slices. Makes 2 to 4 servings.

CREAM OF AVOCADO SOUP

A dish for a grand occasion.

1 large avocado
Lemon juice
1 t. salt
Dash pepper
4 t. chopped chives *or* ¼ t. dill weed
1 c. plain yogurt
1½ c. light cream

Cut avocado into quarters. Cube ¼ of a quarter; toss with lemon juice, cover and refrigerate. In blender or food processor, blend until smooth the remaining avocado, salt, chives, pepper, yogurt, cream and 2 teaspoons lemon juice. Cover and refrigerate until well chilled. Add avocado cubes to soup cups; fill with soup and serve. Serves 6.

CREAM OF ARTICHOKE SOUP

Serve this most delicate soup either hot or chilled and with a thin slice of lemon floating on each serving.

1 12-oz. can artichoke hearts, drained and rinsed
1 14-oz. can chicken broth
1 T. lemon juice
½ to ¾ t. salt
Dash pepper
1 c. light cream
Thin lemon slices (optional)

Rinse and drain artichokes. Place in blender with broth. Puree at high speed 30 seconds. Place in saucepan with lemon juice, salt and pepper. Heat just to boil. Remove from heat. Stir in cream. Reheat if necessary. *Do not boil.* Float lemon slice on top.

VICHYSSOISE

Classic, but simple.

1 lb. leeks or green onions
½ c. chopped onion
4 T. butter or margarine
2 c. cubed potato
½ t. salt
Dash white pepper
3½ c. instant chicken broth
2 c. milk
1 c. light cream
Dash nutmeg
½ c. snipped chives

Slice leeks crosswise, using white parts only, into ¼-inch slices. Melt butter in large saucepot and sauté leeks and onion over medium heat until just golden. Stir with wooden spoon. Add potato, salt, pepper and chicken broth and bring to boiling. Reduce heat and simmer, covered, for 30 to 45 minutes until potatoes are soft. Remove from heat. Put into blender or food processor 2 cups at a time and blend until smooth. Stir in milk and cream and chill covered for 6 hours. Serve well chilled topped with nutmeg and chives. Makes 8 servings.

FRESH MUSHROOM SOUP

Fresh mushrooms with a hint of vermouth are smashing.

- 1 lb. mushrooms, cleaned and sliced
- 6 T. butter or margarine
- 1 onion, finely chopped
- ½ t. sugar
- 3 T. flour
- 3 c. chicken broth
- ½ c. dry vermouth
- 2 to 3 T. fresh parsley, chopped or snipped

Melt butter in a saucepan. Sauté onions sprinkled with sugar until golden. Add mushrooms and stir for a few minutes. Sprinkle with the flour and cook for a few minutes. Add chicken broth, stirring until slightly thickened. Just before serving, stir in vermouth and heat until steaming hot. Garnish each bowl with parsley. Makes 4 to 6 servings.

SUMMER GAZPACHO

There are as many varieties of Gazpacho as there are districts in Spain. Here's one we like.

- ¼ t. pepper, freshly ground
- ½ small onion, sliced
- 1 small green pepper, seeded and sliced
- 3 ripe tomatoes, peeled, seeded and quartered
- 1 large cucumber, peeled, sliced and seeded
- 1 clove garlic
- ½ t. basil
- 1 t. salt
- 2 T. olive oil
- 3 T. wine vinegar
- ½ c. chilled chicken broth

Place all ingredients in blender and blend until mixed, but not smooth. Chill well before serving. Pass small bowls of additional chopped cucumber, chopped chives and croutons for help-yourself garnishes. Makes 4 servings.

SWEET AND SOUR CABBAGE BORSCHT

- 1½ lbs. brisket or soup meat
  Marrow bones
- 4 qts. water
- 1 medium-size cabbage, shredded
- 1 8-oz. can tomato sauce
- 1 1-lb. can tomatoes
- 1 beet, sliced (optional)
- 2 small onions, sliced
- 1 piece sour salt or juice of 1 lemon
  Salt and pepper to taste
  Brown sugar to taste (¼ to ½ c.)
- 1 1-lb. can sauerkraut (optional)

Boil meat and bones in water, skimming off foam and particles that come to top. Add remaining ingredients and simmer covered, for about 1 to 2 hours. Season to taste. Serves 8 to 10.

SABETA

The Spanish have their own tasty version of bouillabaisse.

- 1 onion, chopped
- 1 stalk celery, chopped
- 1 green pepper, chopped
- 1 clove garlic, minced
- 1 28-oz. can tomatoes
- 1 can water
- ½ c. dry vermouth
- 2 chicken legs with thighs or 2 chicken breasts
- ¼ c. chopped parsley
- 1 t. sugar
- 2 t. salt
- ½ t. basil
- 1 small bay leaf
- 1 6-oz. pkg. flounder, cod or haddock
- 1 can chopped or whole clams and juice
- 1 can shrimp, rinsed and drained

In a large soup pot or Dutch oven, combine all ingredients except flounder, clams and shrimp. Bring to a boil and simmer for 45 minutes to an hour. Remove chicken; skin and bone it. Put chicken back into pot. Add fish cut into chunks (may be partially frozen), bring to a simmer and cook 15 to 20 minutes. Just before serving, add clams, clam juice and shrimp; return to simmer and serve piping hot with crusty garlic bread. Makes 6 to 8 servings.

CRAB BISQUE

At your next cocktail party make one for the road, a steaming tureen of this delicious bisque. Your guests will thank you for it.

- 1 can tomato soup
- 1 can green pea soup
- 1 can consommé
- 2 soup cans milk
- 2 6-oz. pkgs. frozen Alaska crabmeat, thawed and drained
  Salt and pepper to taste
  Few drops of Worcestershire sauce
- 2 T. sherry

About 20 minutes before serving, mix together tomato soup, pea soup, consommé, milk, salt, pepper and Worcestershire sauce. Simmer for 10 minutes over low heat. Then add the crabmeat and simmer for 10 more minutes. Just before serving stir in the sherry. Makes 6 to 8 servings.

WINTER GAZPACHO

We call this recipe Winter Gazpacho because it has canned tomatoes. It's a touch of summer to brighten the dreary winter.

- 2 large cans whole tomatoes
- 1 cucumber, peeled and finely chopped
- 1 green pepper, finely chopped
- 1 small onion, finely chopped
- 6 stalks celery, finely chopped
- 6 sweet pickle slices, finely chopped
- 3 T. pimiento, chopped
- 3 T. capers
- 2 T. wine vinegar
- ¼ t. dry mustard
- 3 T. salad oil
- 3 T. olive oil
- ½ t. salt
- ¼ t. pepper, freshly ground
  Few drops of Tabasco

Drain tomatoes, save juice. Place tomatoes, oils, mustard, vinegar, salt, pepper and tabasco in blender and blend at low speed for about 1 minute. Tomatoes should be in small pieces. Pour into the tomato juice and stir in cucumber, green pepper, onion, celery, pickle, pimiento and capers. Chill until very cold. Makes 4 to 8 servings.

COOL AS A CUCUMBER SOUP

An overture to an elegant dinner; serve in old-fashioned glasses.

- 1 c. sour cream
- 1 cucumber, peeled, seeded and sliced
- ¼ t. dry mustard
- ½ t. instant chicken bouillon
- 1 T. snipped chives or 1 green onion
  Salt and pepper to taste

Put all ingredients into a blender and blend only until cucumber is finely chopped, not smooth. Chill and serve. Garnish with a sprinkle of dill or chives if desired. Makes 2 to 4 servings.

NEW ENGLAND CLAM CHOWDER

You don't have to dig clams to dig this chowder—everything is out of a can!

- 1 can cream of celery soup
- 2 cans cream of potato soup
- 2 cans minced or chopped clams
- 2 soup cans milk
- 3 slices bacon, fried and crumbled (optional)
- ½ small onion, minced
  Dash of marjoram

Mix all the ingredients together, heat until piping hot and serve. Makes 4 to 6 servings.

QUICK ONION SOUP

The rich aroma and homemade taste of onion soup need not take hours. A few minutes to combine the ingredients, 30 minutes in the oven and voila!

- 3 large onions, sliced thin
- 3 cans consommé
- ⅛ lb. butter
- ¼ c. red wine
- 1 c. grated Swiss or Parmesan cheese
- 1 c. croutons

Melt butter and sauté onions until clear. Add consommé and wine. Pour into oven casserole, sprinkle with cheese and bake in a preheated 350° oven for 30 minutes. To brown the cheese, broil for a minute after cooking. Pass the croutons. Serves 4.

Pictured opposite: Winter Gazpacho

VEGETABLE SOUP

The aroma of vegetable soup on a winter's day brings a feeling of warmth and hungry anticipation. It must simmer for several hours and really tastes best on the second day.

 1 lb. chuck
 1 or 2 pieces of short rib (or a soupbone)
 2 large cans tomatoes
 3 cans water (or enough to cover vegetables)
 1 or 2 small turnips, peeled and diced
 ¼ head cabbage, shredded
 2 medium onions, chopped
 2 t. salt
 ½ t. pepper
 2 t. thyme
 1 bay leaf (optional)
 ¼ to ½ c. Burgundy wine
 3 to 4 c. assorted fresh vegetables (or 2 pkgs. frozen mixed vegetables)

Brown meat, add vegetables, liquids and seasonings, simmer slowly for 3 to 5 hours. After soup has chilled, fat may be easily removed.

SAILOR'S STEW

Piping hot sailor's stew tastes delicious on a cold day.

 ½ lb. bacon, cut up
 2 onions, chopped
 1 can corn
 1 can peas
 1 can kidney beans
 1 can tomatoes
 Salt and pepper to taste

Sauté bacon and onions and pour off fat. Add remaining ingredients and simmer until thick. Makes 4 to 6 servings.

QUICK SENEGALESE SOUP

Chicken curry soup: cold for a hot day, hot for a cold day.

 2 10½-oz. cans cream of chicken soup
 1 soup can light cream
 2 t. curry powder
 4 to 6 thin lemon slices

Combine soup, cream and curry powder and mix until smooth; use a blender if desired. Serve hot or cold garnished with lemon slices. Makes 4 to 6 servings.

COLD SPINACH SOUP

Keep your cool in the summer.

 1 pkg. frozen chopped spinach
 2 T. instant chicken bouillon
 ¼ pt. sour half and half
 3 c. water
 Salt to taste

Partially thaw spinach; break into small chunks. Put into a blender with half of the water and blend. Add remaining water and seasonings and mix again. Add sour cream and blend. Chill thoroughly and serve garnished with chopped hard-cooked egg or diced cucumber. Serves 4.

FRENCH PUMPKIN SOUP

If you can't bear to throw away the jack-o'-lantern, the French have a delightful solution.

 1 fresh pumpkin, peeled
 (or 6 c. canned pumpkin, without spices)
 3 c. heavy cream
 ½ t. salt
 ¼ t. white pepper

Cut the pumpkin into pieces, remove seeds and stringy parts. Drop into boiling salted water and cook until tender, about 30 minutes. Drain and put through a food mill. Season to taste with salt and pepper. Add cream, blend well, heat and serve.

If using canned pumpkin, blend pumpkin, salt, pepper and cream. Heat and serve. Makes 4 to 6 servings.

LEMON SOUP

This is a proper start for a Greek dinner.

 6 c. chicken broth
 ⅓ c. raw rice
 2 egg yolks
 Juice of 1 lemon

Bring chicken broth to a boil and add rice. Simmer for 30 minutes or until rice is tender. Beat egg yolks and lemon juice until frothy, and slowly stir into 1 cup of the broth. Pour this mixture back into the rest of the soup, stirring constantly. Reheat to just below the boiling point and serve immediately. Serves 6.

BEEF BURGUNDY

Classically French in origin, but simplified in our presentation, this dish gains in flavor as it cooks. It may be prepared in advance, then refrigerated or frozen.

2 lbs. lean stew beef, cut into cubes
2 T. flour
2 T. butter
1 T. olive oil
1 t. salt
¼ t. pepper
2 c. beef consommé
1 c. Burgundy wine
1 medium onion, chopped
1 carrot, sliced
1 clove garlic, minced
1 bay leaf
¼ t. thyme
1 jar small whole onions
    (or ½ pkg. frozen)
1 can sliced mushrooms
1 T. snipped parsley

Toss the meat in flour, salt and pepper and brown in fat. Add consommé, wine, onion, carrot, garlic, bay leaf and thyme. Simmer 2½ to 3 hours until meat is tender. Add parsley, onions and mushrooms just before serving and simmer until hot.

If more liquid is needed during cooking, add consommé and wine in proportions of 2 parts consommé to 1 part wine. Makes 4 to 6 servings.

GLAZED CORNED BEEF, HAM OR CANADIAN BACON

Glistening with a pineapple glaze, corned beef never dressed like this before.

1 corned beef, ham or Canadian bacon, cooked
8 to 10 whole cloves
2 t. mustard
½ c. brown sugar
½ c. bread crumbs
1 medium can crushed pineapple, drained

Place meat in foil-lined roasting pan. Score top and stud with whole cloves. Mix mustard, brown sugar, bread crumbs and pineapple together and coat top of the meat. Bake in a preheated 325° oven 45 to 60 minutes until heated through. Watch for scorching. Add a little water if necessary.

LONDON BROIL

For years well-known restaurants have used flank steaks to create a gourmet treat. The secret lies in the marinade and in the cooking and cutting techniques. Try both of these: one with an Oriental touch, the other with a French flair. They are deliciously different, each with its own distinctive flavor.

ORIENTAL

1 or 2 flank steaks
2 cloves garlic, minced
¼ c. chopped crystallized ginger
¼ c. lemon juice
¼ c. soy sauce
¼ t. pepper

FRENCH

1 or 2 flank steaks
½ c. vegetable oil
½ c. Burgundy wine
2 T. minced onion
1 clove garlic, minced
1½ t. salt
5 drops Tabasco

Score both sides of the steaks in a diamond pattern about ⅛-inch deep. Combine all ingredients in a large, shallow baking dish. Coat steaks with the marinade and turn four times during a 2-hour period of marinating in the refrigerator. Remove steak from the marinade and broil for 7 minutes on each side. To serve, cut steak diagonally into thin slices. Makes 4 to 6 servings.

ONE-RIB BEEF ROAST

Small families can enjoy prime rib of beef.

3 to 4-lb. rib roast
2 T. butter
1 clove garlic, minced
  Salt and pepper to taste

Mix minced garlic with softened butter and spread on both sides of the roast. Place roast on rack in shallow pan. Broil 3½ to 4 inches from heat until brown. Turn and brown other side. Sprinkle with salt and pepper and roast in a 350° oven about 9 minutes per pound for a medium-well-done roast. Makes 4 servings.

BOEUF EN BROCHETTE

½ c. soy sauce
2 T. brown sugar
2 T. salad oil
1 t. ground ginger
1 t. dry mustard
¼ t. pepper
2 cloves garlic, minced
1½ lbs. top sirloin, 1 inch thick, thinly
  sliced
  Canned water chestnuts
  Cherry tomatoes
  Small whole onions (cooked)
  Mushrooms
  Green pepper, cut into 1-inch squares
  Small, cooked potatoes

Combine first seven ingredients; mix well. Add meat and water chestnuts; let stand 2 hours, drain and reserve marinade. Thread meat on skewers, accordion style, alternating with remaining vegetables. Broil over hot coals 5 to 6 minutes, turning frequently and basting with marinade; or broil in oven 3 to 5 inches from heat until crispy brown.

Note: Thin strips are easier sliced if meat is partially frozen.

BOEUF AU GINGEMBRE

Let us introduce roast eye of round to you; it's a splendid entree.

4 to 5-lb. eye of round roast
4 slices gingerroot
3 slices garlic
3 T. salad oil
¾ c. soy sauce
½ c. dry white wine

Make slashes in roast and tuck into each a sliver of garlic or ginger. Combine oil, soy sauce and wine. Put roast and sauce into a sealable plastic bag overnight. Remove roast from bag and place in a greased shallow roasting pan. Place in a preheated 450° oven for 30 minutes, 45 minutes for a larger roast. Turn off heat, leaving roast in the oven for an additional 20 minutes. Remove from oven and let stand 10 minutes before slicing. Serves 6 to 8.

MEXICAN POT ROAST

Pot roast with a robust chili flavor. Serve over rice.

¾ to 1 lb. chuck roast or lean stew beef
  Salad oil
1½ c. water
1½ t. salt
½ t. sugar
¼ t. pepper
1 t. chili powder
⅛ t. ground cumin
⅛ t. dried ground chili peppers
1 28-oz. can tomatoes
1 large onion, chopped
½ green pepper, chopped
1 or 2 carrots, sliced

Brown meat in a little oil. Add water, seasonings and vegetables. Cover and simmer for 1½ to 2 hours. Remove cover; cut meat into bite-size pieces and simmer for an additional 30 minutes until thickened. Taste for spicy flavor, adding more chili powder if desired. Serves 4.

BRAISED SHORT RIBS

The answer to inflation.

3½ to 4 lbs. beef short ribs
1¼ c. beef bouillon
1 T. flour
1 T. butter or margarine
1 clove garlic, minced
2 T. dry sherry
  Salt
  Pepper

Brown short ribs in shallow baking pan in a 450° oven for 15 minutes; pour off fat. Lower oven temperature to 350°, cover pan with foil and cook until meat is tender, 1½ to 2 hours. Skim off excess fat. Brown the flour slowly in a skillet and mix in butter, forming a paste. Stir this into beef stock, stirring until thickened. Add garlic, sherry, salt and pepper to taste. Pour over ribs and bake, uncovered, another 15 minutes. Makes 6 servings.

Pictured opposite:
Boef en Brochette

STEAK DIANE

Make like a maitré d—prepare and flame this dish at your dinner table.

4 tenderloin or rib-eye steaks, (¼- to ½-inch thick)
4 T. butter
4 T. snipped chives
4 T. snipped parsley
1 t. Dijon mustard
1 t. Worcestershire sauce
¼ t. salt
¼ t. pepper
½ c. dry vermouth
¼ c. brandy

In a large chafing dish or electric frying pan, melt 2 tablespoons of the butter and brown steaks quickly, turning once. Remove to platter. Add remaining butter, chives, parsley, mustard, Worcestershire sauce, salt and pepper and bring to a light boil. Add vermouth and simmer, stirring occasionally for 2 to 3 minutes. Heat brandy in a small saucepan (do not boil). Return steaks to skillet. Pour heated brandy over steaks and flame. Serve as soon as flame dies, spooning sauce over the steaks.

BEEF STROGANOFF

Traditional Russian Stroganoff, with a little wine for additional zest, is easy, quick and delicious.

2 to 2½ lbs. beef (tenderloin, sirloin or flank steak)
3 T. flour
½ t. salt
¼ t. pepper
3 T. fat
3 onions, thinly sliced
½ c. tomato juice
1 can consommé
½ t. sugar
½ c. sour cream
½ lb. sliced mushrooms
3 T. Burgundy wine (optional)

Cut meat in thin strips. Toss in flour, salt and pepper. Brown meat and onions in 3 tablespoons hot fat. Add tomato juice, consommé and sugar. Reduce heat and simmer until meat is tender. Blend in sour cream, mushrooms and wine. Heat but do not boil. Serve over buttered noodles, rice or mashed potatoes. Makes 4 to 6 servings.

STUFFED STEAK

Try this succulent and mouth-watering way to dress up a steak.

1 3-lb. sirloin steak, cut 1¼-inch thick
2 T. butter or margarine
1 8-oz. can mushrooms, drained
2 green onions, chopped
1 T. flour
2 T. snipped parsley
1 T. lemon juice
1 T. Worcestershire sauce
Salt and pepper to taste

Cut a pocket in the steak with a sharp knife. The pocket should be the length of the steak and almost all the way from side to side.

Melt butter and sauté onions and mushrooms until onions are soft. Stir in flour, then add lemon juice and Worcestershire sauce and stir until thickened. Add parsley.

Fill the pocket in the steak with the stuffing. Put three or four toothpicks along the edge to keep the pocket closed.

Broil for 10 to 12 minutes on each side. Salt and pepper to taste. Makes 6 to 8 servings.

HAMBURGER STROGANOFF

Dinner on the double.

1 lb. ground chuck
½ lb. mushrooms, sliced (or 1 can, drained)
2 small onions, chopped
3 T. butter
2 T. flour
1 can beef consommé
1 T. tomato paste or catsup
1 t. Worcestershire sauce
½ t. salt
⅛ t. pepper
1 c. sour cream
Paprika

Sauté meat, onions and mushrooms in butter. Drain excess fat. Sprinkle with flour, stir lightly, add consommé and stir until smooth and slightly thickened. Add tomato paste, Worcestershire sauce, salt and pepper. Simmer and stir for 10 minutes. Just before serving stir in sour cream (do not boil). Sprinkle with paprika. Serve over noodles, rice or toasted English muffins. Serves 4.

DAUBE DE BOEUF

Blackberry stew is wonderful and just a little different.

    3 to 4 lbs. top round, cut in 1-inch cubes
      Flour, salted and peppered
    ⅛ c. vegetable oil
    ½ c. blackberry wine
    1½ c. water
    ½ pkg. dry onion soup mix
    1 6-oz. can tomato paste
    2 T. brown sugar
    ½ lb. fresh, sliced mushrooms *or* can of
      mushrooms, drained
    2 T. butter
      Parsley

Dredge meat in seasoned flour and brown in heated oil in Dutch oven or electric frying pan. Mix together wine, water, soup mix, tomato paste and brown sugar. Pour over meat. Bring to a boil, lower heat, cover and simmer for 1½ to 2 hours until meat is very tender. Sauté mushrooms in butter and add to beef. Garnish with parsley and serve with kasha, rice or noodles. Serves 6 to 8.

IN-THE-OVEN STEW

A pot you'll love not watching, *Boeuf a la mode*. Season, place in the oven and forget it.

    2 lbs. chuck, cubed
    2 onions, quartered
    2 stalks celery, quartered
    4 potatoes, pared and quartered
    2 carrots, peeled, quartered
    ¼ c. dry bread crumbs
    1 t. salt
    ½ t. pepper
    1 t. thyme
    1 1-lb. can tomatoes and juice
    1 t. Worcestershire sauce
    ¾ c. dry red wine
    ½ pkg. frozen peas
    1 4-oz. can mushrooms

In a large casserole with a cover, combine all ingredients except peas and mushrooms. Place in a 325° oven for 3 hours. Add peas and mushrooms and cook, uncovered, for an additional 30 minutes. Makes 4 to 6 servings.

GROUND BEEF ROULADE

A welcome change; meat roll, cheesey and saucy.

    1½ lbs. ground round
    1 t. salt
    1 t. minced parsley
    1 t. dehydrated onion
    1 egg, lightly beaten
    ½ c. bread crumbs
    1 clove garlic, minced (optional)
    2 T. dry vermouth
    6 oz. shredded mozarella cheese
    1 15-oz. can tomato sauce and bits

Combine all ingredients except vermouth, cheese and tomato sauce. Mix lightly and press onto a 14 x 10-inch rectangle of waxed paper. Sprinkle with cheese and roll up, jelly-roll fashion. Place seam side down in a rectangular pan. Combine tomato sauce with vermouth and spread half of sauce over the roll and bake in a 375° oven for 45 minutes. Spread remaining sauce over roll and bake 10 minutes longer. Makes 4 to 6 servings.

TSIMMES

The joy of Jewish cooking, traditional and basic.

    2 lbs. beef brisket or chuck roast
      Shortening
    1 onion, chopped
    ¼ c. flour
    1 t. salt
    ¼ t. pepper
    1 qt. boiling water
    1 lb. carrots, sliced
    2 to 3 sweet potatoes, peeled
    2 to 3 large white potatoes, peeled
    1 c. prunes, pitted
    1 c. brown sugar

Brown meat slowly in a little fat in a Dutch oven (browning both sides). Add onion and cook until transparent. Remove from heat. Stir flour into drippings until smooth; add salt and pepper. Gradually stir in boiling water. Reduce heat and simmer, covered, for 1 hour. Preheat oven to 350°. Add carrots, potatoes, prunes and brown sugar and bake for two hours; remove cover during last 15 minutes of baking. Serves 8.

BEEF AND PEPPERS

Inexperienced western chefs will become masters of Oriental cookery with Beef and Peppers, which is eating at its best.

1½ lbs. beef (tenderloin, sirloin or flank steak)
1 clove garlic, minced
½ t. ginger
1 T. soy sauce
1 t. vegetable oil
2 t. cornstarch
   Vegetable oil
2 sliced Bermuda or sweet onions
2 green peppers, quartered
2 tomatoes, quartered
1 t. sugar
1 c. canned bouillon (or consommé)
1 T. cornstarch
1 t. soy sauce
¼ c. cold water
2 T. sherry

Cut meat diagonally into thin strips while partially frozen. Combine garlic, ginger, 1 tablespoon soy sauce, 1 teaspoon oil and 2 teaspoons cornstarch. Add beef, toss lightly. Sauté small amounts of meat in hot oil quickly until done. Remove meat and keep warm.

Add oil to pan, heat, sauté onions and green peppers for about 2 to 3 minutes. Add stock, bring to a boil. Blend 1 tablespoon cornstarch and the water together. Add to hot mixture with 1 teaspoon soy sauce and the sugar. Cook, stirring constantly, about 2 minutes. Add meat, sherry and tomatoes to sauce. Warm thoroughly and serve with rice. Makes 4 servings.

BEEF WELLINGTON

Uncomplicated and unforgettably delicious.

- 1 beef tenderloin
- 3 T. butter or margarine
- Salt
- Pepper
- Garlic, minced
- 2 pkgs. refrigerated crescent rolls
- 1 egg white, beaten

Season meat. Turn thin tail of beef under and tie with string. Place butter in a pan and roast beef in a 425° oven for about 40 minutes. Meanwhile, make Duxelles and set aside. Remove beef from oven and cool. Open rolls as per directions on package and carefully unroll dough; but do not separate rolls. On a lightly floured sheet of waxed paper, arrange dough pieces to form a rectangle. Pinch perforations together to make 1 piece of dough. Place Duxelles on the dough. Place fillet, top side down, on top. Bring edges of dough together down the center of the fillet. Brush edges of dough with egg white and pinch to close, forming a smooth seam. Place seam down in shallow pan or on a cookie sheet. With remaining dough cut flowers or leaves; moisten with egg white and arrange over top of dough. Brush entire surface with egg white. Bake in a 400° oven for about 25 minutes or until crust is browned. Makes 6 to 8 servings.

DUXELLES

- ½ lb. mushrooms, cleaned and chopped
- 2 T. butter + 1 T. salad oil
- ¼ c. minced onion
- ¼ c. sherry

Put the mushrooms in a dish towel, a few at a time and squeeze out the moisture. In a skillet, heat butter and oil; sauté onions. Add mushrooms and sherry and cook until dry. Season with salt and pepper. Makes about 2/3 cup.

ROAST BONELESS SIRLOIN STRIP

For that can't-miss occasion.

- 1 whole strip sirloin
- Salt and pepper to taste

Score light covering of fat on top of meat, season and place on rack in a shallow baking pan. Place in a 325° oven until internal temperature reaches 125° for rare. A 5-pound roast will take about 1 hour. Let roast stand in warm place outside of oven for 10 to 15 minutes before carving. Serve with oven-browned potatoes. Serves 8.

ENTRECOTE BUERRE DE MOUTARDE

Sirloin steak grilled with a spicy onion and mustard sauce.

- 1 3½ to 4-lb. sirloin, or other steaks, 1½ inch thick
- ½ c. butter or margarine
- ½ t. dry mustard
- ½ t. freshly ground pepper
- ½ t. garlic powder
- ½ t. salt
- 2 T. snipped parsley
- ¼ c. minced green onion
- 2 t. Worcestershire sauce

Heat together butter and seasonings in saucepan until butter melts. Place steak on rack and broil 3 to 4 inches from heat: 10 to 12 minutes on each side for rare, 14 to 16 minutes each side for medium, brushing with butter mixture. Serves 4 to 6.

MADRAS BEEF AND FRUIT CASSEROLE

One of the most imaginative of beef dishes.

- 2 lbs. lean stew beef
- 3 T. butter or 2 T. salad oil
- 2 c. water
- Juice and rind of 1 lemon
- 2 c. mixed dried fruit
- 1 T. cinnamon or 2 t. curry

In a heavy skillet, brown meat in butter or oil. Stir in water, dried fruit, lemon juice and rind, cinnamon or curry. Pour into a covered casserole. Place into a 325° oven for 1½ hours. Serves 4.

OYSTER BEEF AND PEPPERS

Oyster Sauce may be purchased at Oriental food stores if not available at your supermarket.

1½ lb. flank steak or tenderloin of beef, frozen
2 T. soy sauce
1 t. brandy
½ t. salt
Dash pepper
2 T. cornstarch
2 T. salad oil
1 green pepper, sliced
3 green onions, snipped
½ c. chicken broth
2 T. Oyster Sauce
1 T. cornstarch
3 T. cold water

When the meat is slightly thawed, slice in very thin strips, cutting across the grain. Combine soy sauce, brandy, salt and pepper to make a marinade. Marinate meat slices for 15 minutes. Dust the meat with 2 tablespoons cornstarch and brown in oil. Remove meat from pan and sauté green onions and pepper. Combine broth, Oyster Sauce, cornstarch and cold water. Return meat to pan; add Oyster Sauce mixture. Cook until sauce is clear. There should be just enough gravy to hold the meat together. Makes 4 servings.

SZECHUAN BEEF

Variation on a quickie theme.

1½ lbs. flank steak
4 T. soy sauce
2 T. dry sherry
1 t. sugar
Peanut oil
2 green peppers, sliced
4 green onions, sliced
1 c. thinly sliced celery
1 t. salt
1 t. red pepper flakes (more if desired)
1 t. cornstarch
2 T. water
2 T. sherry
1 T. soy sauce
Cooked rice

Slice meat into thin strips, cutting across the grain. Combine 4 tablespoons soy sauce, 2 tablespoons sherry and sugar; add meat and stir, coating pieces well. Heat oil in skillet over moderately high heat and stir fry green pepper and onion for 1 minute. Remove vegetables and set aside. Add more oil and stir fry meat until lightly browned. Return vegetables to pan, add celery, salt and red pepper flakes. Stir fry 4 minutes. Mix cornstarch with water, 2 tablespoons sherry, and 1 tablespoon soy sauce. Add to pan and cook until sauce is thickened and smooth. Serve over hot rice. Makes 4 servings.

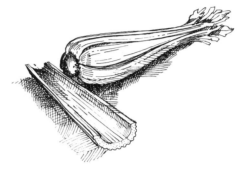

BEEF AND PEA PODS

Serve this colorful main dish family-style, right from the wok as would the Chinese, and accompanied by a bowl of rice.

1½ lbs. boneless sirloin or flank steak, partially frozen and cut in thin strips
1 clove garlic, minced
½ t. ginger
1 T. soy sauce
1 t. salad oil
2 t. cornstarch
2 medium onions, sliced
1 c. beef broth
1 T. cornstarch
1 t. sugar
1 t. soy sauce
¼ c. cold water
1 pkg. frozen pea pods, thawed
2 T. sherry

Combine garlic, ginger, 1 tablespoon soy sauce, oil and 2 teaspoons cornstarch. Add beef and toss lightly. Stir fry small amounts of meat in hot oil in wok or skillet until done. Remove meat and keep warm. Stir fry onions for a minute or two. Add stock and bring to a boil. Blend 1 tablespoon cornstarch, sugar, soy sauce and water; add to stock. Cook until thickened and clear. Add meat, pea pods and sherry and heat through. Serves 4.

BRISKET OF BEEF

Prepare this brisket the day before you serve it and be a relaxed hostess as it heats in the oven. It holds beautifully for hours and can be covered lightly with foil if it starts to dry out.

    1 5-lb. brisket of beef
    2 t. salt
    ¼ t. pepper
    2 onions, sliced
    4 stalks celery
    1 c. catsup
    1 8-oz. can beer

Place beef in roaster, fat side up. Season with salt and pepper. Place onions, celery and catsup over the beef. Put ¼ cup water in bottom of pan. Roast in a preheated 350° oven uncovered, basting until well browned. Cover. After about 3 hours, pour the beer over the beef, recover and cook until tender. Remove meat from gravy. Strain gravy and chill until fat rises and solidifies. Remove layer of fat.

Slice chilled meat and reheat in gravy. Add ½ cup water if necessary. If a thicker gravy is desired, place cooked onions and celery in a blender with the skimmed gravy and blend until smooth. Serves 8.

ROAST BEEF TENDERLOIN

For that special dinner, be extravagant and roast a whole beef tenderloin.

    1 4-to 4½-lb. beef tenderloin
    ½ c. vegetable oil
    ½ c. Burgundy wine
    2 T. grated onion
    1 clove garlic, minced
  1½ t. salt
    5 drops Tabasco (optional)

Combine all ingredients and allow beef to marinate in refrigerator at least 2 hours. Remove from sauce. Preheat oven to 450°. Place meat in a shallow pan and brush with marinade. Bake for 15 minutes. Reduce temperature to 350°. Baste with marinade occasionally and continue baking for 35 minutes for medium rare, or less time for rare. Serve garnished with sautéed mushroom caps and sprigs of parsley. Makes 6 servings.

SPEEDY SAUERBRATEN

Be a kitchen wizard and use your leftover roast beef to make this taste-tempting German entrée.

    2 T. butter
    1 small onion, chopped
    ¼ c. celery, chopped
    ½ c. dark raisins
    2 T. catsup
    1 T. cider vinegar
    ¼ c. crumbled gingersnaps
    ¼ t. dry mustard
    ½ c. water
    1 can bouillon
    1 T. cornstarch
       Sliced roast beef

Sauté onion and celery in butter for 5 minutes. Add raisins, vinegar, catsup and gingersnaps mixed with dry mustard. Add water and stir. Dissolve cornstarch in 2 tablespoons of the bouillon. Add with remaining bouillon and cook, stirring constantly, until clear. Add sliced beef to the sauce, cover and simmer for 15 minutes. Serve on a bed of noodles. Sprinkle with poppy seeds if desired. Makes 2 to 4 servings.

TEN-MINUTE SUKIYAKI

Be a minute miser. Using your electric frying pan, cook and serve at the table, Japanese-style.

    3 T. vegetable oil
    1 medium sliced onion
    4 large sliced mushrooms
    ½ lb. thinly sliced beef
    ¼ lb. fresh spinach
    3 5-inch pieces celery,
       thinly sliced
    4 T. soy sauce
    2 T. sugar
    ½ can consommé
    4 scallions

Sauté onion in oil, add mushrooms and meat, cook 2 minutes. Add spinach and cook 1 minute; add celery and cook 1 minute. Cut scallions lengthwise into thin pieces. Add to mixture. Then add soy sauce, cook 1 minute. Add sugar and consommé and cook 2 minutes. Add thinly sliced rare roast beef, if desired, and cook 10 minutes. Makes 2 to 3 servings. Repeat as often as necessary.

SPAGHETTI SAUCE

Spaghetti sauce need not simmer all day long. This one will be ready before you have finished setting the table and cooking the pasta.

- 1 lb. ground chuck (optional)
- 3 T. olive oil
- 1 medium onion, chopped
- 2 cloves garlic, minced
- 1 1-lb. can tomatoes
- 1 6-oz. can tomato paste
- ¼ t. oregano
- ⅛ t. thyme
- ⅛ t. basil
- ½ c. sweet vermouth

Brown meat, drain fat. Sauté onions and garlic in olive oil until golden. Add meat and remaining ingredients. Simmer until smooth and thick, about 35 minutes. Serve over cooked spaghetti (makes enough for 1 pound). Sprinkle with grated parmesan cheese. Serves 4.

Cook the pasta (spaghetti) until al dente (slightly chewy) — about 8 to 10 minutes in rapidly boiling water (check package for directions).

LASAGNE

- 1 lb. ground round or chuck
- 1 clove garlic, minced
- 1 T. parsley flakes
- 1 T. basil
- 1½ t. salt
- 1 1-lb. can tomatoes
- 2 6-oz. cans tomato paste

Brown meat, drain fat. Add next 6 ingredients. Simmer about 30 minutes, stirring occasionally.

- 1 pkg. lasagne noodles, cooked and rinsed in cold water
- 3 c. small curd, creamed cottage cheese
- 2 eggs, slightly beaten
- 2 T. parsley flakes
- 2 t. salt
- ½ t. pepper
- ½ c. grated Parmesan cheese
- 1 lb. mozzarella cheese, sliced thin

Combine cottage cheese, eggs, parsley flakes, salt, pepper and Parmesan cheese. Place half of the cooked noodles in a 13 x 9-inch baking dish. Spread half of the cheese mixture, half of the mozzarella, half of the meat sauce over the noodles. Repeat layers, ending with meat sauce. Decorate top with triangles of mozzarella. Bake in a preheated 375° oven for 30 minutes. Let stand 10 to 15 minutes before serving. Cut into squares if desired. Makes 8 to 10 servings.

POLYNESIAN
SWEET-SOUR MEATBALLS

Enjoy meatballs with the flavor of the Islands.

1 lb. ground round
1 egg
2 T. flour
½ t. salt
   Dash of pepper
3 T. vegetable oil
1 c. chicken bouillon
2 large green peppers, cut in small pieces
4 slices canned pineapple, cut in pieces
3 T. cornstarch
½ c. sugar
1 T. soy sauce
½ c. vinegar
½ c. pineapple juice

Shape meat into 16 balls. Combine egg, flour, salt and pepper to make a smooth batter. Heat oil in a large skillet. Dip meatballs in batter and fry until brown on all sides. Remove from pan and keep warm. Pour out all but 1 tablespoon of fat. Add ½ cup of the bouillon, the green peppers and the pineapple. Cover and cook over medium heat for 5 minutes.

Blend cornstarch, sugar, soy sauce, vinegar, pineapple juice and remaining bouillon. Add to skillet and cook, stirring constantly, until mixture comes to a boil and thickens. Return meatballs to sauce and heat. Serve with rice. Yield: 4 servings.

MEAT BLINTZES

A hostess with flair will appreciate a dish hearty enough to stand alone on the menu.

1 lb. ground beef (sautéed and drained) or cooked chicken or leftover roast, ground
1 egg
1 T. instant minced onion
1 t. salt
¼ t. pepper

Make blintzes (see bread section). Mix above ingredients together. Place 1 heaping teaspoonful on each blintz and fold envelope-style. Brown blintzes as directed in recipe and serve with applesauce or sour cream. Makes 22 to 24 blintzes.

Note: These blintzes may be frozen and thawed in refrigerator before browning.

MOUSSAKA

Traditionally, Moussaka is made with ground lamb. Ground beef may be substituted for lamb, or use half beef and half lamb.

1 eggplant, peeled and sliced
1 lb. ground chuck
1 medium onion, chopped
1 clove garlic, minced
1 1-lb. can tomatoes
½ t. oregano
1 t. salt
⅛ t. pepper
1 T. olive oil
½ c. cottage cheese
2 eggs, slightly beaten
   Nutmeg

Sauté meat, onion and garlic until meat is brown. Drain well. Add tomatoes, oregano, salt, pepper. Simmer 10 minutes.

Brush eggplant slices with olive oil and broil for 5 minutes on each side. Make layers of eggplant and meat sauce in a greased casserole. Top with cottage cheese and eggs beaten together. Sprinkle with a little nutmeg. Bake in a preheated 350° oven for 2 hours. Serves 4.

STUFFED PEPPERS

A natural for summer menus when peppers are plentiful.

6 green peppers
3 T. chopped onion
2 T. butter
1 lb. ground chuck
½ c. cooked rice
½ t. salt
¼ t. pepper
2 8-oz. cans tomato sauce
¼ c. sherry
½ c. sour cream
¼ lb. sharp Cheddar cheese, grated or shredded

Remove stem ends and seeds from peppers. Sauté onion in butter, add meat and brown. Mix in rice, salt and pepper and 1 can tomato sauce. Fill peppers and arrange in a baking dish. Combine sour cream, the remaining can of tomato sauce and the sherry and pour over peppers. Bake in a preheated 350° oven 45 to 60 minutes. Sprinkle with the cheese and bake another 15 minutes. Makes 4 to 6 servings.

MEAT LOAF WELLINGTON

An old friend takes on a new look. Dress your meat loaf in style with a flaky brown crust.

- 2 eggs
- 1 can cream of mushroom soup
- 1 c. dry bread crumbs
- 1 T. mustard
- 3 lb. lean ground beef
- 2 T. instant minced onion
- 2 t. salt
- 2 t. Worcestershire sauce
- 2 T. catsup
- 1 can refrigerated crescent roll dough

Combine all ingredients except dough and press mixture into a loaf pan. Bake in a preheated 350° oven for 1½ hours. Cool in pan for 5 minutes. Drain off fat and invert meat loaf onto a cookie sheet.

Separate roll dough into 4 rectangles. Overlap slightly on a pastry cloth or floured board to form a large rectangle. Roll out to form a 10 x 15-inch rectangle. Drape over meat loaf, covering all visible sides. Trim excess dough; it can be used to make a braided design on top. Brush top and sides with slightly beaten egg white. Bake in a preheated 325° oven for 15 to 20 minutes or until golden brown. Yield: 6 to 8 servings.

BEEF BISTRO

A Spanish dish, full flavored but not spicy hot.

- 1½ lbs. boneless top round
- 1 green pepper, chopped
- 1 onion, chopped
- 2 ribs of celery, sliced
- 1 clove garlic, minced
- 1 can sliced mushrooms
  (or ½ lb. fresh mushrooms)
- 1 can tomato soup
- 1 jar stuffed olives, drained and sliced
- ½ c. Burgundy wine

Trim meat, then cut in strips or cubes and brown in fat. Add green pepper, onion, celery, garlic, mushrooms and soup and simmer, covered, for 45 to 60 minutes. Add wine and olives 10 to 15 minutes before serving. Add ⅓ cup water if there is insufficient sauce. Yield: 4 servings.

FILLED CABBAGE

Double the recipe while you have the kettle on. It improves with age (make a day ahead). It can also be frozen.

- 1 head cabbage
- 1 lb. ground chuck
- 4 T. raw rice
- 4 T. grated onion
- 2 T. catsup
- 1 egg
- 1 t. salt
- ½ t. pepper
- 1 large can tomatoes
- 1 can tomato soup
- ¼ c. white raisins
  Juice of 1 lemon
- ½ c. brown sugar
- 1 medium onion, sliced
- ½ t. salt

Cut a wedge from the core of the cabbage. Place in a large pot of boiling water, core side down. Simmer until the leaves separate. Put 12 large leaves back into the water for about a minute until slightly soft. Lift out and cut away the thick part of each leaf.

In a bowl mix ground chuck, rice, grated onion, catsup, egg, 1 teaspoon salt and the pepper. Put a twelfth of meat mixture on each leaf, fold in the sides and roll up. Mix tomatoes, tomato soup, lemon juice, sugar and remaining salt.

Line a shallow casserole with some shredded cabbage and onion slices. Spoon in half of the tomato mixture, then filled cabbage rolls. Cover with remaining shredded cabbage, onion slices and tomato mixture. Bake covered in a preheated 350° oven for 1 hour. Uncover, add raisins, baste and bake 2 more hours, basting occasionally. Makes 4 to 6 servings.

VEAL LOUISA

A perfect dish for dinner or buffet supper. Serve in a chafing dish, along with a bowl of rice or noodles.

- 2 lbs. lean veal
- 1 t. paprika
- 1 t. salt
- ¼ t. pepper
- 3 T. flour
- 2 T. vegetable oil
- 2 T. butter
- 1 clove garlic, minced
- ½ onion, chopped fine
  (or 2 T. instant minced onion)
- 1 c. chicken broth or instant bouillon
- ½ c. Sauterne
- ½ to 1 c. sour cream

Cut veal into strips. Dredge in flour, paprika, salt and pepper. Sauté in butter and oil over medium heat until brown. Add garlic, onion, broth and wine. Cover and simmer gently for 20 minutes, until tender. Just before serving, stir in sour cream. Serve over rice or noodles. Makes 4 to 5 servings.

VEAL A LA BOLOGNESE

Veal chops reach their zenith by adding ham and cheese and this smooth sauce.

- 6 veal chops, steaks or cutlets
- 1 egg (beaten with 2 T. water)
- 1 c. bread crumbs
- ½ c. grated Parmesan cheese
- ½ t. salt
  Black pepper, freshly ground
- ½ c. butter
- 6 slices of salami or cooked ham
- 1 c. milk
- 1 c. tomato sauce

Dip meat into egg mixture and then into bread crumbs which have been combined with 2 tablespoons of the cheese, the salt and the pepper. Sauté in butter for 10 minutes. Top meat with salami or ham and sprinkle with remaining cheese. Combine milk and tomato sauce and pour over meat. Cover and simmer for 25 minutes. Makes 6 servings.

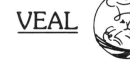

VEAL A LA FRANCAISE

Celebrate the happy marriage of veal, wine and herbs at your dinner table.

- 5 lbs. veal rump, boned and rolled
- 1 t. salt
- ¼ t. pepper
- 3 c. dry white wine
- 1 T. lemon-pepper marinade
- 1 clove garlic, slivered
- 1 bay leaf
- ½ t. rosemary
- ½ t. tarragon

Place meat in a large roasting pan. Blend seasonings into wine and pour around meat. Cover loosely with foil and bake in a preheated 350° oven for 2½ to 3 hours. Baste every 15 minutes and recover with foil. When meat is cooked, remove from oven and make the following sauce.

SAUCE

- 2 c. meat juices (add wine if necessary)
- 2 lbs. mushrooms, washed and sliced
- ⅛ lb. butter or margarine
- 1 T. flour
- ¼ c. cold water

Sauté mushrooms in butter, drain and set aside. Skim fat from meat liquid. Blend flour with water, add meat juices, place in a saucepan and cook until slightly thickened, stirring constantly. Stir in mushrooms, pour sauce over veal in roasting pan, return to oven and cook 30 minutes longer. Serve sliced thin with sauce. Makes 8 to 10 servings.

ESCALOPES DE VEAU

With almost no effort on your part you can enhance the delicate flavor of veal.

- **2 lbs. veal, cut in thin slices**
- **½ c. chopped onion**
- **1 T. butter**
- **½ t. salt**
- **¼ t. pepper**
- **¼ c. consommé**
- **½ c. dry white wine**
- **¼ c. bread crumbs**
- **3 T. melted butter**
- **½ c. grated Swiss cheese (⅛ lb.)**

Sauté onion in butter until golden. Place in casserole, add veal slices, salt, pepper, consommé and wine. Combine crumbs with melted butter and cheese and top casserole with this mixture. Bake, uncovered, in a preheated 350° oven for 1 hour. Makes 4 servings.

VEAL, HAM AND CHEESE

For those who don't like fancy cooking!

- **4 veal cutlets, ¼ inch thick**
- **4 T. butter or margarine**
- **¼ c. dry sherry**
- **4 thin slices of prosciutto or cooked ham**
- **½ lb. Port du Salut or Swiss cheese cut in 4 slices**

In a large skillet over medium high heat in hot butter, cook veal cutlets until lightly browned on both sides. Use more butter if needed. Remove skillet from heat; add sherry and stir to release brown bits in skillet. Arrange veal cutlets in one layer; cover each with slice of ham and slice of cheese to fit. Cover skillet and cook over low heat 5 to 10 minutes. Makes 4 servings.

VEAL PICCATA

- **4 veal scallops, pounded thin**
- **Flour**
- **Salt and pepper**
- **6 T. butter**
- **2 T. olive oil**
- **3 T. lemon juice**
- **2 T. snipped parsley**
- **1 8-oz. pkg. green noodles**

Prepare noodles according to package directions. Lightly dust veal with flour seasoned with salt and pepper. Heat 4 tablespoons butter and oil in a large skillet over medium heat until bubbly. Quickly brown veal on both sides. Remove veal from pan to warm platter. Add lemon juice, parsley and remaining butter to skillet, stirring until just heated. Arrange veal on noodles and pour butter over all. Garnish with lemon slices. Serves 2 to 4.

VEAL VERONIQUE

Subtle combination of grapes with wine to enchance the delicate flavor of veal.

- **6 veal chops (rib, loin or shoulder)**
- **1 T. salad oil**
- **1 T. butter**
- **½ c. chicken broth**
- **½ c. dry white wine or Sauterne**
- **1 T. cornstarch**
- **¼ c. water**
- **Snipped parsley**
- **1 T. chopped green onion or chives**
- **1 c. halved green grapes**
- **1 T. lemon juice**

Brown chops in oil and butter. Add broth and wine; cover and simmer over low heat for 30 minutes or until meat is tender. Remove chops to a warm platter. Combine cornstarch and water and stir into pan juices along with parsley and onion. Cook and stir until mixture thickens and bubbles. Stir in grapes and lemon juice. Pour sauce over chops and serve. May be garnished with lemon slices and clusters of parsley. Makes 4 to 6 servings.

VEAL PAPRIKASH

Veal and sour cream go so well together; the combination superb.

- **2 lbs. veal, cubed**
- **¼ c. flour**
- **½ t. salt**
- **¼ t. pepper**
- **4 T. safflower or corn oil**
- **2 t. paprika**
- **2 onions, sliced**
- **1 c. instant chicken bouillon**
- **½ to ¾ c. sour cream**

Coat veal lightly with flour, salt and pepper. Heat oil in skillet and brown veal; add onions and cook until just tender. Stir in paprika. Add chicken bouillon, cover and simmer gently 20 minutes until veal is tender. Just before serving, stir in the sour cream and heat through. Do not boil. Serve with noodles. Makes 4 servings.

Note: A substitute for sour cream is sour half and half.

VEAL VERMOUTH

Chill the wine and light the candles; it's as romantic as a night in Venice.

1½ lbs. thin veal steak
2 T. flour
¼ c. butter
1 clove garlic, minced
½ lb. mushrooms, sliced
½ t. salt
  Dash of pepper
1 T. lemon juice
⅓ c. dry vermouth
2 T. snipped parsley

Flatten veal to ¼-inch thick. Cut into 2-inch squares and flour. Melt butter and sauté veal, a little at a time, until golden brown on both sides. Return all meat and the garlic to the skillet and heap mushrooms on top. Sprinkle with salt, pepper and lemon juice. Pour on vermouth, cover and cook over low heat for 20 minutes or until veal is fork tender. Add a little more vermouth if needed. Sprinkle with parsley just before serving. This dish can be prepared ahead and reheated in the oven. Serves 4.

LAMB

LAMB CHOPS A LA GRECQUE

Shoulder chops need help, and here is the way to make them tender and succulent.

- 4 to 6 shoulder lamb chops, round bone
- 1 1-lb. can whole tomatoes
- 1 onion, chopped
- 1 green pepper, cut in square chunks
- 1 t. salt
- ½ t. sugar
- 1 t. dried oregano
- 1 clove garlic, minced

Score fat around edges of chops to prevent curling. Brown both sides well under broiler. Drain off all fat. In the broiler pan, combine tomatoes, onion, green pepper, salt, sugar, oregano and garlic. Place chops on top and bake in a preheated 350° oven 30 to 45 minutes, until chops are tender.

Sliced zucchini may be added during the last 10 minutes of baking if desired. Makes 4 to 6 servings.

GLAZED LAMB CHOPS

An unusual way to serve lamb, using the less expensive shoulder chops.

- 4 to 6 large shoulder lamb chops, ¾-inch thick
  Salt and pepper to taste
- 2 T. vegetable oil
- ½ t. curry powder
- ½ c. orange juice
- 2 T. lemon juice
- 4 T. honey
- 1 11-oz. can mandarin oranges, drained

Sprinkle chops with salt and pepper. Score fat around edges of chops to prevent curling. Brown both sides well under broiler. Drain off all fat. Place in oiled baking pan. Combine curry powder, orange juice, lemon juice and honey. Pour over chops and bake in a preheated 350° oven 30 to 45 minutes. Add oranges to sauce for last 5 minutes to warm them. Yield: 4 to 6 servings.

LAMB PILAF

For a taste of the Middle East, throw caution to the winds and proceed as directed.

- 2 T. butter or margarine
- 3 lbs. boned lamb
- 1 large onion, sliced
- ½ t. cinnamon
- ½ t. freshly ground pepper
- 2 c. raw white rice
- 1 c. white raisins
- 2 t. salt
- 1 can consommé
- 2 c. water
- ¼ c. lemon juice
- 1 c. slivered almonds
- 3 T. snipped parsley

Cut lamb in 1-inch cubes. Melt butter and sauté lamb over high heat until brown. Remove lamb as it browns and drain on paper toweling. After all lamb is browned, lower heat to medium and sauté onion, cinnamon and pepper for 3 to 5 minutes.

In a buttered casserole, sprinkle about ½ cup rice to cover bottom. Make layers of rice, raisins, meat and onions. Repeat until all are used up. Sprinkle top with salt. Combine consommé and water and pour over the mixture in the casserole. Cover and bake in a preheated 400° oven 60 minutes. Remove cover, sprinkle with lemon juice and almonds and bake for 10 more minutes. Add parsley just before serving. Makes 8 to 10 servings.

GIGOT A LA MOUTARDE

Leg of lamb roasted in the French manner will find its way to your table often after you've tried it.

- 1 6 to 8-lb. leg of lamb
- ½ c. Dijon mustard
- 2 T. soy sauce
- 1 t. rosemary or thyme
- 1 garlic clove, slivered
- ¼ t. ginger
- 2 T. vegetable oil

Blend mustard, soy sauce, herbs and ginger in a bowl. Beat in oil to make a creamy mixture. Make 4 shallow slashes in the meat with a sharp knife and tuck into each a sliver of garlic. Brush lamb liberally with sauce and let stand for 1 to 2 hours. Roast on a rack in a preheated 350° oven for 1¼ to 1½ hours. Makes 4 to 6 servings.

COTELETTES D'AGNEAU PORTUGAISE

The secret is in the marinade which makes lamb shoulder tender and succulent.

- 2 to 4 shoulder lamb chops, slashed on fat side
- 2 T. salad oil
- 2 T. red wine vinegar
- 2 T. minced dehydrated onion
- 1 clove garlic, minced
- 1 t. Dijon mustard
- 1 t. salt
- ½ t. thyme
- ½ t. basil

Mix together all seasonings. Pour over lamb chops and cover tightly. Marinate for 1 hour or overnight, turning meat a few times. Take lamb from refrigerator 1 hour before you plan to broil it. Remove from marinade and broil 4 to 5 inches from heat until brown; turn and repeat. Serves 1 to 2.

LAMB ON SKEWERS

Don't just sprinkle the flavor on; let it marinate. Cook in or cook out.

- 2½ lbs. boned leg of lamb, cut in 1½-inch cubes
- ½ t. salt
- ½ t. freshly ground pepper
- 1½ T. finely snipped parsley
- ¼ t. each thyme, oregano and rosemary
- 1 clove garlic, minced
- ½ c. salad oil
- 1 c. Burgundy wine
  Whole fresh mushrooms
  Green peppers, cut in pieces
  Onions, quartered

Place lamb cubes in a large bowl. Combine first seven ingredients and pour over lamb. Cover and refrigerate overnight. Reserve marinade and thread mushrooms, lamb, green pepper and onion on skewers. Broil on a grill 6 inches above medium-hot coals for 15 minutes, turning skewers frequently and brushing with marinade. Or broil 4 inches from heat in oven, turning and basting until done. Serves 4 to 6.

BUTTERFLIED LEG OF LAMB AU DIABLE

Elegant, extravagant and easy to carve with the bone removed.

- 1 6 to 7-lb. leg of lamb, boned and butterflied
- 1 clove garlic, crushed
- ½ c. salad oil
- ¼ c. red wine
- ½ c. chopped onion
- 2 t. Dijon mustard
- 2 t. salt
- ⅛ t. fresh ground pepper
- ½ t. oregano
- ½ t. basil
- 1 bay leaf, crushed

Put the lamb, fat side down, in shallow pan. Combine all seasonings and pour this marinade over the lamb. Cover pan tightly and refrigerate overnight, turning meat at least once. Take lamb out of refrigerator 1 hour before you cook it. Make incisions in meat so it lies flat. Place meat and marinade in broiler pan, fat side up, and broil 4 inches from heat for 10 minutes. Turn, baste and broil 10 minutes on the other side. Lower temperature to 425° and roast lamb about 15 minutes. Test with a sharp knife; meat should be pink and juicy. Remove meat from marinade and transfer to a hot platter. Bits of brown onion may be scraped off if you like. Carve lamb into thin slices. Serves 6 to 8.

OVEN IRISH STEW

B'gosh and b'gorra, it cooks itself!

- 2 lbs. lamb stew meat or shoulder chops
- 1 20 to 24-oz. pkg. frozen stew vegetables
- 1 medium onion, chopped
- 1 10-oz. can beef broth
- 2 T. flour
- 1 t. crushed marjoram

Place meat and vegetables in a baking dish. Mix beef broth, flour and marjoram; pour over meat and vegetables. Cover and bake in a 350° oven for 2 to 2½ hours. Makes 4 to 6 servings.

POULTRY

ROAST DUCK WITH ORANGE SAUCE

1 4- to 5-lb. duckling, cleaned
1 large whole onion, peeled
½ c. orange juice

Pull out all loose fat from cavity and from inside of neck. Place onion in cavity. Roast duck on a rack in a preheated 350° oven for 2½ to 3 hours. Prick skin with fork to drain fat. When bird begins to brown baste every 15 to 20 minutes with orange juice.

SAUCE

1 T. duck drippings
1 c. orange juice
¼ c. orange peel, julienned
¼ c. currant jelly
¼ c. brown sugar
1½ T. cornstarch
(dissolved in ¼ c. cold water)

Boil julienned orange peel 5 minutes, then drain. In a saucepan combine all ingredients and cook until thick and clear. Pour ¼ cup sauce over duck and serve remaining sauce at the table. Do not slice duck. Serve in quarters.

CHICKEN VERMOUTH

This recipe is economical and delicious as well as low in calories.

4 whole chicken breasts
¼ c. butter
1 clove garlic, minced
1 t. salt
¼ t. pepper
½ lb. mushrooms, sliced
1 T. lemon juice
¾ c. dry vermouth
¼ c. snipped parsley

Simmer chicken breasts in water to cover until tender enough to remove from bones. Sauté in butter. Add garlic, salt, pepper and lemon juice. Heap mushrooms on top, pour on vermouth, cover and cook for 20 to 30 minutes or until chicken is fork tender. Add a little more vermouth if needed. Sprinkle with parsley just before serving. Makes 6 servings.

CHICKEN ALMOND

With an Oriental touch, chicken quickly becomes exotic.

3 c. cooked chicken
3 T. vegetable oil
2 c. celery, cut in ½-inch slices
2¼ c. chicken stock
3 T. soy sauce
4 T. cornstarch
1 t. sugar
½ c. water
2 cans Chinese vegetables
½ c. whole almonds
2 T. sherry
1 or 2 pkgs. frozen Chinese pea pods, thawed, drained and dried (optional)

Heat chicken in hot oil until golden brown. Add celery, chicken stock and soy sauce. Cook a few minutes. Mix together cornstarch, sugar and water. Add to chicken mixture and simmer until thickened. Add Chinese vegetables, almonds and sherry. Simmer just until mixture is heated through. If desired, add pea pods and stir into hot mixture. Do not overcook. Serve over Chinese noodles or rice. Serves 6 to 8.

CHICKEN COUNTRY CAPTAIN

1 frying chicken, cut up
½ c. flour
½ t. salt
⅛ t. pepper
¼ c. butter
1 medium onion, diced
½ green pepper, diced
1 clove garlic, minced
1½ t. curry powder
½ t. thyme
1 1-lb. can stewed tomatoes
½ c. currants
Toasted slivered almonds

Dredge chicken in seasoned flour. Brown in butter. Remove. Sauté onion, green pepper and garlic in drippings until soft. Add curry powder and cook for 2 to 3 minutes. Add tomatoes, thyme and currants. Cook 2 to 3 minutes. Put chicken in baking dish. Pour sauce over chicken and bake at 350° for 45 minutes, or until chicken is tender. Garnish with almonds.

CURRIED CHICKEN, TURKEY OR LAMB

Create a sensation with a spicy, steaming bowl of curry and a bowl of fluffy rice surrounded by small bowls of assorted condiments. Have at least four condiments — salty, sweet, crunchy and spicy. Everyone will want to sprinkle some of each over the top of the curry.

5 T. butter
1 onion, chopped
2 tart apples, chopped
4 T. flour
2 t. curry powder
2 cans beef consommé
  (or chicken broth for chicken or turkey)
1 c. water
  Juice of 1 lemon
4 c. cooked, cubed lamb, chicken or turkey
  (leftovers may be used)
  Cooked rice

Melt 2 tablespoons of the butter and sauté onion and apples until tender. Add the rest of the butter and blend in the flour and curry powder. Stir in consommé, water and lemon juice, cook until slightly thickened. Add meat and simmer for 30 to 45 minutes. Cook ahead and reheat if desired. Serve with rice and assorted condiments, such as bacon cooked and crumbled (or bacon substitute), chutney (see accompaniments), coconut, chopped peanuts, slivered toasted almonds, snipped green onions, chopped hard-cooked egg, raisins, mandarin oranges, chopped green pepper. Makes 8 servings.

CHICKEN SAUTERNE

Rich repast; creamy sauce with a hint of white wine—a variation of *coq au vin blanc*.

    3 to 4 whole chicken breasts
    1 t. salt
    1 pkg. frozen peas with onions
    2 T. butter
    ½ lb. small mushrooms
    3 T. butter
    3 T. flour
    1 T. instant minced onion
    ½ t. salt
    ½ t. celery salt
    ½ t. paprika
    ½ t. dried oregano
    2 T. chopped pimiento
      Few drops Tabasco
    1 c. instant chicken broth
    ½ c. dry Sauterne or dry white wine
    1 c. light cream

Place chicken breasts in a large saucepan. Cover with water; add salt and simmer about 30 minutes or until tender. Remove skin and bones, leaving chicken in large pieces. Cook frozen peas as directed. Sauté mushrooms in 2 tablespoons butter. Remove from pan. Melt another 3 tablespoons butter, stir in flour and seasonings. Stir in chicken broth and wine and simmer until thickened. Cool slightly and stir in cream, mushrooms, peas and chicken. Reheat, but do not boil. Serve over toasted English muffins. Serves 4 to 6.

CHICKEN A L'ORANGE

    2 fryer chickens, quartered or cut
      in pieces
    1 t. salt
    ½ t. pepper
    ½ c. butter or margarine
    1 clove of garlic, minced

Melt butter; add salt, pepper, and garlic. Pour over chicken and bake in a preheated 350° oven for 1 hour and 15 minutes. While chicken is baking, prepare Sauce which will be enough for 2 to 3 chickens.

SAUCE

    1 c. red currant or plum jelly
    ⅛ t. ginger
    1 T. dry mustard
    1 6-oz. can frozen orange juice
    4 T. sherry
    1 1-lb. can pitted bing cherries,
      drained (optional)

In saucepan, melt jelly over low heat. Blend in ginger, mustard and orange juice concentrate. Stir all together and add sherry. Sauce may be poured over the chicken, adding the cherries if desired, and baked in a 375° oven for 15 minutes. If you like, reserve some sauce to heat and pass at the table.

Note: For very festive occasions, heat ½ cup brandy and carefully ignite and pour over the chicken. Using the cherries, it is then called Chicken Jubilee.

CANTONESE CHICKEN

With pineapple and green pepper.

    4 chicken breasts (2 whole)
    3 T. dry sherry
    4 T. soy sauce
    ½ t. ground ginger
    1 clove garlic, minced
    2 T. salad oil
    1 to 2 c. pineapple chunks
    1 green pepper, seeded and cut in small
      squares
    3 T. cornstarch
    ½ c. sugar
    1 T. soy sauce
    ½ c. vinegar
    ½ c. pineapple juice
    ½ c. chicken broth

Skin and bone chicken breasts; cube or slice. Combine sherry, 4 tablespoons soy sauce, ginger and garlic; marinate chicken in mixture for 60 minutes. Heat oil in skillet or wok and fry chicken until golden brown. Remove to platter. Stir fry pineapple and green pepper for about 2 minutes, adding another drop of oil if necessary. Combine cornstarch, sugar, 1 tablespoon soy sauce, vinegar, pineapple juice and chicken broth. Stir until smooth, then pour into pan. Stir constantly until mixture comes to a boil and thickens. Add chicken to sauce and heat thoroughly. Serve with rice. Serves 3 to 4.

POULET A LA MARENGO

Chicken, the cook's best friend and a real budget buy, comes up smiling again.

- 1 broiler-fryer, cut in pieces
- ¼ c. vegetable oil
- ½ c. chopped onion
- 1 t. salt
- ⅛ t. pepper
- ¼ t. oregano, crushed
- 1 clove garlic, minced
- 2 tomatoes, peeled and quartered
- ½ c. dry white wine
- 1 3-oz. can sliced mushrooms
  Parsley

Brown chicken slowly in hot oil. Add onion; cook until onion is soft. Drain fat, season with salt and pepper. Add oregano, garlic, wine and broth drained from mushrooms. Scrape bottom of pan to loosen browned bits. Cover and cook over low heat until chicken is tender, about 35 minutes. Add tomatoes and mushrooms to chicken. Continue cooking for 5 minutes. Garnish with parsley. Makes 4 servings.

CHICKEN DIVAN

A very special way to use leftover chicken or turkey.

- 1 lb. cooked asparagus spears or broccoli (fresh or frozen)
  Sliced cooked chicken or turkey
- 1 can cream of chicken or celery soup
- ¼ c. light cream
- ½ c. dry Sauterne
- ½ c. grated Parmesan cheese
- 1 T. butter, cut into dots
  Paprika

Place cooked vegetable on the bottom of a greased shallow, flat-bottomed casserole. Lay chicken slices on top, overlapping them. In a saucepan, mix soup, cream, wine and half of the cheese. Cook over low heat until smooth and well blended, stirring constantly. Pour sauce over the chicken, covering completely. Top with Parmesan cheese, dot with butter, sprinkle lightly with paprika and bake in a preheated 450° oven until golden brown on top, about 15 minutes. Serves 4.

HAWAIIAN CHICKEN

Say aloha to this Hawaiian chicken dish; you may want to go native.

- **Chicken breasts or 1 fryer**
- ¾ c. vinegar
- 1 c. sugar
- 2 T. cornstarch
- 1 T. mustard
- 1 T. Worcestershire sauce
- 1 13¼-oz. can pineapple chunks and juice
- 1 green pepper, cut in ¼-inch strips
- 1 tomato, quartered
- 2 T. sherry

Cut fryer in pieces to serve 4 to 6. Prepare sauce while chicken is baking. In a saucepan, stir vinegar into cornstarch and sugar and cook until clear. Then add mustard, Worcestershire sauce and pineapple juice, stirring until well blended. About 15 to 20 minutes before serving time, add pineapple chunks, green pepper, tomato and sauce to the chicken and broil on center rack in oven until chicken is glazed and hot. Five minutes before serving, stir in the sherry.

SHERRIED CHICKEN RISOTTO

Everybody will want second helpings of this dish.

- 1¼ c. raw rice
- 1 can cream of mushroom soup
- 1 can cream of chicken soup
- ¼ c. melted butter or margarine
- ¼ c. dry sherry
- 10 to 12 pieces of chicken (legs, thighs and breasts)
- ½ c. slivered almonds
- ⅓ c. grated Parmesan cheese

Lightly butter a 3-quart baking dish and sprinkle rice over the bottom. In a bowl combine soups, butter and sherry. Spread 1½ cups of soup mixture over the rice. Place chicken in single layer on top of soup. Spread the remaining soup mixture over chicken. Bake covered in a preheated 350° oven for 1 hour. Remove cover and bake 1 hour longer. Sprinkle with almonds and cheese the last 15 to 20 minutes of baking time. Makes 4 to 6 servings.

POULET AU CITRON

1 to 2 chickens, quartered
2 t. grated lemon peel
½ c. lemon juice
2 cloves garlic, minced
2 t. dried thyme
1½ t. salt
1 t. black pepper
3 to 4 T. melted butter or margarine
1 to 2 lemons, sliced for garnish
    Chopped parsley

Wash and dry chicken well. Arrange pieces in single layer in a shallow baking dish. Combine lemon peel and juice with garlic, thyme, salt and pepper. Spoon over chicken, turning to coat well. Refrigerate in marinade for several hours, turning a couple of times. Remove from marinade; place chicken in a shallow baking dish and brush with melted butter. Bake, covered, in a 375° oven for 25 minutes. Remove cover; brush with remaining marinade and bake, uncovered, for an additional 40 minutes or until chicken is browned and cooked through. Garnish with lemon and parsley. Serves 4 to 8.

MANDARIN CHICKEN

12 dried Chinese mushrooms
1 c. warm water
1 piece gingerroot, sliced
2 cloves garlic, minced
¼ c. sesame oil
1 3½ lb. chicken, cut up
6 t. soy sauce
1 6-oz. can bamboo shoots
½ c. dry sherry
¼ c. brandy
2 t. cornstarch
½ t. sugar
1 T. cold water

Soak mushrooms in warm water until soft. Drain, reserving liquid. Cut off and discard stems; slice caps. In a large skillet over high heat, stir fry gingerroot and garlic in oil for a few seconds. Add chicken and cook for 5 minutes. Remove pan from heat; add soy sauce and cook over moderate heat for another few minutes. Add ¾ cup mushroom liquid, mushrooms and drained bamboo shoots. Bring to a boil; add sherry and simmer, covered, for 20 minutes or until chicken is tender. Add heated brandy, ignite and shake pan gently until flames go out.

Transfer chicken to a warm oven pan. Combine cornstarch and sugar with cold water. Stir into brandy mixture. Simmer for a few minutes until sauce is thickened. Pour over chicken. Serves 4 to 6.

CHICKEN DEL PRADO

Serve with a bowl of buttered, cooked spaghetti.

2 fryers, cut up
½ c. flour
1½ t. salt
½ t. pepper
½ c. salad oil
2 cloves garlic, minced
1 large onion, diced
2 ribs celery, sliced
1 green pepper, cut in strips
½ lb. mushrooms, sliced
1 t. crushed thyme
¼ t. cayenne pepper
1 bay leaf
1 14-oz. can Italian plum tomatoes
1 c. dry white wine
2 T. tomato paste
8 to 10-oz. cooked, drained spaghetti

Combine flour, salt, pepper and dust chicken. Save any flour mixture left. Brown chicken, a few pieces at a time in oil in a large skillet. Place browned chicken in large casserole. In same skillet with no more than 2 tablespoons of leftover oil, sauté garlic, onion, celery, green pepper and mushrooms until just tender and crisp. Add leftover flour mixture, thyme, cayenne and bay leaf. Stir to coat vegetables. Add plum tomatoes and liquid, wine and tomato paste. Stir to blend. Bring to a boil and pour over chicken in casserole. Cover and bake in a 350° oven for 60 minutes or until chicken is tender.

ROCK CORNISH GAME HEN

4 Cornish hens
1 12-oz. jar apricot or peach preserves
1 c. creamy French dressing
½ pkg. onion soup mix

Mix together preserves, dressing and dry soup mix. Spoon over hens. Place on a foil-lined pan and bake in a 350° oven for 1 hour and fifteen minutes or until tender. Hens may be cut in half and baked the same way, cut side down.

 # PORK

PORTUGUESE PORK TENDERLOIN

You will earn special commendations for tenderloin in this fragrant wine sauce.

- 2 lbs. pork tenderloin
- 2 T. flour
- 3 T. butter
- 1 onion, sliced
- ⅔ c. dry white wine
- ½ lb. sliced mushrooms
- ⅛ t. rosemary
- 2 T. lemon juice
- 2 T. parsley, chopped

Season flour with salt, pepper, paprika. Roll tenderloins in seasoned flour. Sauté in butter until golden brown. Add sliced onion and mushrooms, sauté for a minute or two. Add wine and rosemary. Cover and cook over low heat for 45 to 60 minutes, until tenderloins are done. Add lemon juice and parsley just before serving. Makes 4 to 6 servings.

SCALLOPED PORK CHOPS

A pork chop treated well can hold its own in any company.

- 6 to 8 pork chops
- 1 T. mustard
- 1 T. vegetable oil
- 4 to 6 medium potatoes, peeled and sliced thin
- 1 small onion, chopped
- 1 can cream of celery soup
- 1 soup can milk
- 1 to 2 t. salt
- ¼ t. pepper
- ½ t. marjoram

Spread a little mustard on each chop and brown chops in oil. In a 2- to 3-quart casserole, arrange potatoes, onion and chops in layers. Mix soup, milk, salt, pepper and marjoram together and pour over potatoes and chops. Cover and bake in a preheated 350° oven for 1½ to 2 hours. Makes 4 to 6 servings.

CASSOULET

A traditional cassoulet calls for a pork roast, a lamb roast, homemade sausage and three days of roasting, cooking and blending. This one will simmer along in your electric frying pan and be ready in about an hour.

- 12 large uncooked Italian sausages
- 2 pkgs. frozen lima beans, thawed
- 3 fresh tomatoes (or 1 can)
- 1 large onion, chopped
- 2 cloves garlic, minced
  Salt and pepper to taste
- 1 bay leaf
- ½ t. sweet basil
- 2 t. sugar
- ⅓ c. chicken broth
- 5 T. chopped parsley
- 1 large bottle dry vermouth (or dry white wine)

Put sausages in a cold frying pan. Pour wine until it comes halfway up the sausages. Cover and steam for about 15 minutes. Remove cover and sauté the sausages until brown. Remove to platter.

Using a little of the sausage fat, sauté onion and garlic until golden. Add tomatoes, bay leaf, pepper, basil and sugar; simmer 3 minutes. Add chicken broth and ½ cup wine. Then add lima beans, sausages and 3 tablespoons of the parsley. Cover and cook for 45 minutes. Add salt and pepper to taste. Sprinkle with remaining parsley and serve. Makes 6 to 8 servings.

HAM STEAK CASSOULET

Baked beans, an old standby, is treated well with a few additions.

- 2 ham steaks, ¼ to ½ inch thick
- 2 1-lb. cans baked beans
- 1 medium onion, chopped
- ½ green pepper, chopped
- 1 T. wine vinegar
- ¼ t. dry mustard
- 3 T. catsup
- 3 T. brown sugar

In a large shallow baking dish, mix beans with onion, pepper, and seasonings. Top with ham steaks and bake in a 350° oven for 45 minutes until ham is browned and beans bubbly hot. Serves 4 to 6.

FLEMISH PORK CHOPS

Traditional to Northern France. Usually served with buttered noodles, but also good with baked potatoes.

6 pork chops, trim fat
2 T. margarine
1 large onion, chopped
¾ c. Burgundy
¾ c. chicken broth
½ t. salt
¼ t. pepper
½ t. basil
2 T. tomato paste
1 T. flour
2 T. butter

Brown pork chops in margarine. Remove chops and sauté onion in same pan. Mix Burgundy, broth and tomato paste together. Return chops to pan; season with salt, pepper and basil. Pour wine mixture over chops, cover, and simmer for 1 hour until chops are tender. Remove chops to platter. Mix butter and flour into a paste and stir into pan juices until they thicken. Pour over chops and serve. Serves 4 to 6.

PORK TENDERLOIN PEKING

2 pork tenderloins
½ t. salt
¼ t. pepper
½ t. ginger
½ t. garlic powder
2 T. salad oil
1 c. chicken broth
2 carrots, cut in julienne strips
1 medium onion, cut in rings
2 zucchini, sliced
1 stalk celery, sliced
2 T. soy sauce
1 T. sherry

Mix together salt, pepper, ginger and garlic powder. Pat onto tenderloins. Heat oil in large skillet and brown seasoned tenderloins. When they are golden brown, add chicken broth. Cover and simmer for 40 to 45 minutes until meat is tender and done. Add vegetables, soy sauce and sherry. Cook, uncovered, 10 to 15 minutes until vegetables are tender crisp. Serve with rice. Makes 4 to 6 servings.

SWEET-SOUR PORK

1½ lbs. lean pork, cut into bite-size pieces
3 T. salad oil
1 medium onion, chopped
1 green pepper, chopped
1 rib celery, sliced
1 clove garlic, minced
Salt
Pepper

Sauté onion, pepper and celery in oil for a few minutes. Remove from pan and set aside to use in Sauce. In the same pan, brown pork, seasoning with garlic, salt and pepper to taste. Prepare Sauce and pour over pork; cover and simmer for 45 minutes, or until tender and well done. Serves 4 to 6.

SAUCE

¾ c. sugar
¼ c. vinegar
1 T. soy sauce
1 T. lemon juice
1 T. catsup
1 T. cornstarch
¼ c. chicken broth

Combine sugar, vinegar, soy sauce, lemon juice and catsup. Mix well.

Before serving, dissolve cornstarch in chicken broth, stirring until mixture thickens and clears. Add onion, pepper, celery, and catsup mixture. Pour over pork. Serve hot with rice. Serves 4 to 6.

SPARERIBS ALOHA

3 lbs. meaty spareribs
1 13¼-oz. can pineapple chunks with juice
1 green pepper, cut into 1-inch pieces
3 T. brown sugar
1 T. cornstarch
3 T. vinegar
1 t. salt
¼ c. soy sauce
3 pieces preserved ginger, slivered

Cut spareribs into 2 or 3 rib sections and brown in a 350° oven for 1 hour, pouring off excess fat frequently. Add pineapple, juice and green pepper. Blend brown sugar, cornstarch, vinegar, salt and soy sauce; add ginger. Pour over ribs and bake for another 30 minutes, basting frequently. Serves 3 to 4.

FILLET OF SOLE VERONIQUE

An epicure's delight.

- 1 lb. sole or flounder fillets
  Salt
- 1 T. lime juice
- 1 t. dried parsley
- ¼ t. tarragon
- ½ clove garlic, minced
- ¾ c. white wine
- ¼ lb. seedless green grapes
- 1½ T. butter
- 1 T. flour
- 2 T. orange juice

Sprinkle fish fillets lightly with salt and lime juice. Place in lightly greased skillet. Sprinkle with parsley, tarragon and garlic. Add wine and simmer 12 to 15 minutes until fish flake easily and look milky white, not transparent. Add grapes the last 5 minutes. Remove from heat but keep warm on a separate platter.

In the original skillet, melt butter with remaining juices and blend in flour until smooth. Add orange juice and cook, stirring until mixture thickens. Add more wine if desired. Pour sauce over fillets. Serves 3 to 4.

POISSONS EN COQUILLE

- 2 lbs. fish fillets, cut in ½ x 2-inch strips
- 2 large onions, sliced
- ½ lb. fresh mushrooms, sliced
- 1 clove garlic, minced
- ¼ lb. butter
- 1½ t. salt
- ¼ t. white pepper
- 1 c. sour cream
- 2 t. Worcestershire sauce
- 1 t. mustard
  Buttered bread crumbs
  (or cooked egg noodles)
  Parsley to garnish

Sauté onions and mushrooms in half of the butter. Add garlic, cook for 1 minute. Remove from pan. Sauté fish until done in remainder of the butter. Return onions and mushrooms to pan. Blend seasonings with sour cream and stir gently into fish. Heat thoroughly. Serve in individual ramekins with toasted, buttered crumb topping or on a platter with cooked buttered noodles. Garnish with parsley. Makes 4 to 6 servings.

Pictured opposite:
Sole Gratinee, p. 96

SEAFOOD

FILLET OF SOLE FLORENTINE

Vary your fish repertoire. Top the delicate sole with creamy spinach.

- 2 lbs. sole or turbot fillets
- 2 T. butter or margarine, cut into dots
- ½ t. salt
- 2 10-oz. pkgs. frozen chopped spinach, cooked and drained
- 1 can cream of mushroom soup
- 3 T. sherry
- 1 T. melted butter or margarine
- 3 T. dry bread crumbs
- 2 T. grated Parmesan cheese

Wash, drain and dry the fish fillets. Arrange in a baking dish and dot with the butter or margarine. Sprinkle with salt, cover the dish with foil and bake in a preheated 350° oven for 15 minutes. Remove from oven and drain liquid.

Spread cooked spinach over the top of the fish. Blend soup with sherry and pour over all. Mix bread crumbs with melted butter and cheese and sprinkle over top. Bake uncovered for 20 minutes. Yield: 6 to 8 servings.

FILLET OF HADDOCK MARGUERY

The Friday fish fry, try it baked any day of the week.

- 2 lbs. fresh or frozen haddock, sole or turbot fillets, thawed and drained
- 1 can cream of celery or shrimp soup
- 1 can shrimp, washed and drained (optional)
- ¼ c. butter or margarine, melted
- ½ t. grated onion
- ½ t. Worcestershire sauce
- ¼ t. garlic salt
- 1 T. sherry
- 1¼ c. crushed crackers

Place fish fillets in a greased 13 x 9 x 2-inch baking dish. Combine soup and sherry. Spread fillets with soup and shrimp. Bake in a preheated 375° oven for 20 minutes. Combine butter and seasonings, mix with crumbs and sprinkle over fish. Bake 10 minutes longer. Serves 6 to 8.

EVERYMAN'S THERMIDOR AU GRATIN

Tastes like the real thing.

½ c. butter
½ c. flour
1 t. salt
Pinch cayenne
¼ t. dry mustard
2½ c. milk
¼ c. butter
½ lb. fresh mushrooms, sliced
1 T. minced onion
3 c. poached cod or haddock chunks
2 T. sherry
⅓ c. Parmesan cheese
½ c. bread crumbs

Melt butter over low heat. Add flour, salt, cayenne and mustard; stir until smooth. Add milk slowly; stir and cook until thickened and smooth. Remove from heat. Melt ¼ cup butter; sauté mushrooms and onion. Add mushrooms, onion, fish and sherry to sauce. Mix gently, then pour into a buttered casserole. Sprinkle with cheese and bread crumbs. Bake in a 350° oven for about 15 minutes until bubbly hot. Makes 6 servings.

POISSONS FLORENTINE

A breeze of a meal to make; delicious and beautiful.

1½ lbs. flounder fillets (or snapper or sole), fresh or frozen, thawed
1 10-oz. pkg. frozen chopped spinach, cooked and drained
1 egg, slightly beaten
2 T. minced onion
1 clove garlic, minced
½ t. salt
2 tomatoes
½ to ¾ c. grated Parmesan cheese
2 T. butter

Mix egg with spinach. In a greased 9 x 13-inch baking dish, layer fish fillets, spinach, onion, garlic, salt and slices of tomato. Top each tomato with 1 teaspoon cheese and a dot of butter. Bake in a 350° oven for 20 minutes until fish flakes easily and tomatoes and cheese are hot and bubbly. Makes 4 servings.

SOLE GRATINEE

Baked fish entree that will become a family favorite.

8 to 10 small fillets of sole, sprinkled with salt, pepper and paprika
1¼ c. dry vermouth
3 T. flour
3 T. softened butter
½ c. light cream
2 to 3 tomatoes, sliced
½ c. grated Swiss cheese
2 T. chopped parsley

Arrange fillets in 8 x 10-inch shallow baking dish; they will overlap. Pour 1 cup dry vermouth over and poach for 20 minutes in a 350° oven until fish flakes easily with a fork. When fish is done, pour poaching liquid into saucepan. Bring to a simmer. Combine flour and butter to make a paste and add to poaching liquid, stirring with a whisk until it thickens. Add remaining vermouth and cream; cook, stirring, until mixture coats spoon. Arrange sliced tomatoes on top of fish. Pour sauce over all. Sprinkle with cheese and parsley; broil 4 to 6 minutes until cheese melts and sauce bubbles. Serves 4.

SHRIMP CANLIS

Simple but delicious. Serve with hearty vegetable salad, garlic bread and dry white wine.

2 lbs. raw shrimp, shelled and deveined
2 T. olive oil
3 T. butter
1 large clove garlic, minced
½ t. salt
Dash pepper
1 t. Dijon mustard
Juice of 1 lemon
½ c. dry vermouth

Heat oil in large skillet. Add shrimp and sauté for a few minutes. Reduce heat. Add butter, garlic, salt, pepper and mustard, blending well. Add lemon juice and vermouth; cook for another 2 to 3 minutes, stirring gently and constantly. Makes 4 servings.

SALMON EN CROUTE

This wonderfully flexible dish can be used for brunch, lunch or dinner and served hot or cold.

PASTRY

½ lb. butter or margarine
2 c. flour
¼ t. salt
1 c. sour cream

Cream butter; cut in flour and salt. Add sour cream and form into a dough. Divide dough into 2 parts and wrap in waxed paper; chill 1 hour. Meanwhile make Salmon Filling.

SALMON FILLING

2 7¾-oz. cans salmon, drained, bones and skin removed
½ c. sour cream
2 T. dill weed
2 T. chopped parsley
2 ribs celery, chopped
½ medium onion, minced
4 eggs, hard-boiled and chopped
2 T. lemon juice
1 t. salt
¼ t. pepper

Combine all ingredients.

ASSEMBLY

Roll out each half of dough on lightly floured waxed paper, forming a 12 x 4-inch rectangle. Place 1 pastry rectangle on a lightly greased jelly roll pan. Spread with salmon mixture. Cover with remaining rectangle. With tines of fork, press edges together to seal. Roll out leftover dough; trim by crisscrossing strips. Brush top of dough with slightly beaten egg. Prick with tines of fork 4 times. Bake in a 350° oven for 35 to 45 minutes until golden brown. Slice and serve with the following sauce.

SAUCE

2 c. sour cream
2 T. dill
2 T. lemon juice
¼ c. mayonnaise

Combine all ingredients. Serves 4 to 6.

RED SNAPPER CREOLE

Economical extravaganza.

2 to 3 lbs. fish fillets (red snapper, pollock, cod, halibut)
⅔ c. chopped onion
½ c. chopped green pepper
½ c. chopped celery
2 T. butter
1 1 lb. 12-oz. can tomatoes
1 6-oz. can tomato paste
2 cloves garlic, minced
1 bay leaf
1 t. salt
¼ t. pepper
½ t. oregano
   Celery salt to taste
½ c. dry white wine, (optional)

Sauté onion, green pepper and celery in butter. Add tomatoes, tomato paste and seasonings; simmer about 20 minutes. Place fillets on greased pan and bake in a 350° oven for 20 minutes. Add wine to sauce, pour over fillets and return to oven for an additional 10 minutes until fish flakes easily. Serve with rice. Serves 6 to 8.

SHRIMP PAELLA

⅓ c. butter
2 T. olive oil
1 medium onion, sliced
½ lb. mushrooms, sliced
2½ c. hot chicken broth
¼ t. saffron
1 t. thyme
1 bay leaf
1 T. Worcestershire sauce
1 c. rice
½ c. chopped green pepper
½ c. chopped celery
1 lb. cooked shrimp
2 tomatoes, peeled, seeded and chopped

Melt butter in saucepan, add olive oil and heat. Sauté onion until golden, add mushrooms and sauté. Place in greased casserole, add broth, seasonings and rice. Cover tightly and bake in a 400° oven 25 minutes. Stir in celery, green pepper, tomato and half the shrimp. Arrange remaining shrimp on top. Cover and bake 15 minutes more. Serves 2 to 4.

IMPERIAL CRAB

Affluence and availability. You really must have fresh crab meat to do justice to this recipe.

- 4 T. butter or margarine
- 4 T. flour
- 2 c. milk
- 1 t. salt
- ⅛ t. pepper
- ½ t. celery salt
  Dash cayenne pepper
- 1 egg yolk, beaten
- 2 T. sherry
- 1 c. soft bread crumbs
- 1 lb. fresh crab meat, preferably backfin
- 1 t. chopped parsley
- 1 t. minced onion
- ¼ c. buttered bread crumbs
  Paprika

Melt butter over medium heat; add flour and blend. Gradually stir in milk, salt, pepper, celery salt and cayenne. Cook over low heat, stirring constantly, until thickened. Blend a little of the sauce into the egg yolk, stirring constantly; then blend it back into the sauce. Cook two minutes more; remove from heat. Add sherry, bread crumbs, crab meat, parsley and onion. Mix gently and pour into a greased casserole. Top with buttered crumbs and sprinkle with paprika. Bake in a preheated 350° oven for 30 to 35 minutes. Makes 4 to 6 servings.

BROILED FISH AU GRATIN

Fish ahoy!

- 1 lb. fish fillets
- 4 T. mayonnaise
- 2 green onions, snipped
- ¼ c. grated Parmesan cheese
- 1 T. lemon juice
- 2 T. melted butter or margarine
  Few drops of Tabasco

Pat fillets dry with paper towels. Place fish on oiled broiler rack. Broil 4 inches from heat for 8 to 12 minutes. Combine remaining ingredients and spread over fish. Broil until puffy and golden and fish flakes easily with a fork.

SHRIMP SUPREME

For the discerning Captain's Table.

- 1½ lbs. cooked shrimp
- 3 T. butter
- 3 T. flour
- 1½ c. milk
- 4 T. Worcestershire sauce
- ½ c. catsup
- 1 bay leaf
  Dash red pepper
  Juice of ½ lemon
  Salt
  Pepper

Melt butter, add flour. Slowly stir in milk and make a thick cream sauce. Add Worcestershire sauce, catsup, bay leaf, red pepper, lemon juice, salt and pepper to taste. Add cooked shrimp and heat to steaming. Serve with rice. Serves 4.

STIR-FRIED SHRIMP AND PEA PODS

Orient Express; all aboard in 5 minutes.

- 3 T. safflower or corn oil
- ½ t. ground ginger or ½ t. finely chopped fresh gingerroot
- 1 clove garlic, minced
- ¾ lb. uncooked shelled and deveined shrimp
- 1 6-oz. pkg. frozen or ½ lb. fresh pea pods
- ¼ to ½ c. sliced bamboo shoots (optional)
- ¼ c. instant chicken bouillon
- 1 T. soy sauce
- 1 t. sugar
- 1 T. dry sherry

Heat oil in wok or frying pan with ginger and garlic. Add shrimp and stir fry 1½ minutes. Add pea pods and bamboo shoots; stir fry 2 minutes. Add chicken bouillon, soy sauce, sugar and sherry and stir fry 2 minutes. Serve on hot cooked rice. Serves 2; to serve 4, double the shrimp.

Pictured opposite:
Stir-Fried Shrimp and Pea Pods

SALMON DIABLE

Stretch a can of salmon into a luncheon dish or appetizer.

½ c. sour cream
¼ c. mayonnaise
¼ c. sherry
1 T. lemon juice
1 T. Worcestershire sauce
½ t. dry mustard
2 eggs, slightly beaten
⅛ t. Tabasco sauce
¼ c. chopped celery (optional)
1 1-lb. can salmon, drained and flaked
⅓ c. cracker crumbs
¼ c. snipped parsley
1 T. snipped chives, fresh or frozen
Salt and pepper to taste
Paprika
Lemon slices

Mix together sour cream, mayonnaise, sherry, lemon juice, Worcestershire sauce, mustard, celery, eggs and Tabasco. Pour over the salmon, cracker crumbs, parsley, chives, salt and pepper. Stir gently until well blended. Spoon into 6 baking shells or a baking dish. Sprinkle with paprika and bake in a preheated 350° oven for 30 minutes. Garnish with lemon slices. Serve with the following sauce. Serves 4.

SAUCE

1 c. sour cream
1 t. mustard
1 t. horseradish
¼ t. salt
1 T. snipped chives

Combine and stir.

It is easier to slice meat, fish or fowl if they are partially frozen.

BOUILLABAISSE

This is an adaptation of a traditional fisherman's dish into which whatever was not sold of the day's catch was put into a stew. The idea is to have a variety of seafoods; the choice is yours. Substitutions are in order if you don't care for, or can't get, one of the listed seafoods or fish. It makes a complete meal.

⅓ c. olive oil
1 clove garlic, minced
2 medium onions, sliced
2 1-lb. cans tomatoes
2 lbs. frozen flounder fillets, thawed and cut into fingers
1 7½-oz. can crab meat, drained and cartilage removed (or ½ lb. fresh)
1 7½-oz. can chopped clams and juice
1 1-lb. pkg. frozen shrimp, thawed
1 t. bouillon crystals
1 bay leaf
½ c. chopped pimiento
¼ c. dried parsley flakes
½ t. thyme
½ t. saffron
1 c. dry white wine

Sauté onions and garlic in olive oil until golden. Add tomatoes, flounder, crab meat, clams, shrimp, bouillon crystals and bay leaf. Simmer 15 to 20 minutes. Add pimiento, parsley flakes, thyme, saffron and wine. Turn heat to low, cover, and let stand for about 10 minutes to absorb flavors. Makes 8 to 10 servings.

TUNA PATÉ

Tuna, the perennial sandwich filling, takes on a new look.

2 7-oz. cans water-packed tuna fish, drained and flaked
1 8-oz. pkg. cream cheese, softened
1 T. grated onion
3 T. chili sauce
1 t. Worcestershire sauce
2 T. snipped parsley
2 T. dry sherry

Blend together cream cheese, onion, chili sauce, Worcestershire sauce and parsley. Add tuna fish and sherry and mix well. Add salt to taste. Heap in a bowl or make into a ball. Serve with raw relishes or crisp crackers.

SHRIMP AND CRAB MEAT SUPREME

A quick seafood delight! Out of the freezer and onto the table in half an hour.

    1 lb. frozen shrimp
    1 6-oz. pkg. frozen crab meat
    1 pkg. white sauce mix
    1⅓ c. water
    ¼ c. white wine
    2 T. butter
    1½ c. coarse bread crumbs
    ¼ t. paprika
      Dash of cayenne pepper

Cook shrimp. Drain crab meat. Add sauce mix to water and bring to a boil. Simmer 1 minute. Add cayenne pepper. Add wine, butter, shrimp and crab meat. Pour into baking dish. Sprinkle crumbs and paprika over the top. Bake in a preheated 350° oven for 15 minutes. Makes 2 to 4 servings.

LOBSTER THERMIDOR

Try this when you're in the mood to splurge, or trim the food budget by using poached cod, haddock or pollock in place of lobster.

    ¼ c. melted butter
    ½ c. flour
    1 t. salt
      Pinch of cayenne pepper
    ¼ t. dry mustard
    2½ c. milk
    ½ lb. fresh mushrooms, sliced
    ¼ c. butter
    4 c. cooked lobster (bite-sized pieces)
    2 T. dry sherry
    ⅓ c. grated Parmesan cheese

To the melted butter, add flour, salt, cayenne and mustard, stirring constantly until smooth. Add the milk slowly, stirring constantly. Cook until thickened. Remove from heat. Sauté the mushrooms in the ¼ cup butter. Add mushrooms, lobster and sherry to the sauce. Mix well and pour into a buttered casserole. Sprinkle the top with Parmesan cheese. Bake in a preheated 400° oven about 15 minutes until bubbly. Makes 6 to 8 servings, but recipe may be cut in half.

Variation: Add ¼ to ½ cup grated Swiss cheese to cream sauce.

SHRIMP CURRY

Choose at least four of the condiments listed below. You should have a combination of sweet, crispy, salty and tangy to complement the distinctive flavor of the curry.

    1 lb. cooked, cleaned shrimp
    ¼ c. melted butter
    ¼ c. flour
    ½ t. salt
    1½ c. milk
    1 t. curry powder
    3 T. catsup
    ¼ c. sherry
      Dash of paprika

Blend flour, salt and melted butter over medium heat until smooth. Slowly stir in milk. Cook, stirring gently, until thickened. Blend in catsup and curry powder. Add shrimp and heat through. Just before serving, stir in sherry and sprinkle with paprika. Serve over hot rice with assorted condiments, such as chopped hard-cooked egg, raisins, crumbled bacon or bacon substitute, coconut, snipped green onions, chopped peanuts or chutney. Serves 4.

SHRIMP CREOLE

Creole is from New Orleans, where seafood is an everyday ingredient in their cuisine. This dish is so quick and easy you will want to serve it frequently.

    ⅔ c. chopped onion
    ½ c. chopped green pepper
    ½ c. chopped celery
    2 T. butter
    1 large can tomatoes
    1 8-oz. can tomato sauce
    2 cloves garlic, minced
    2 bay leaves
    1 t. salt
    ¼ t. pepper
    ½ t. oregano
      Celery salt to taste
    1½ lbs. cooked shrimp

Sauté onions, green pepper, celery in butter. Add tomatoes, tomato sauce and seasonings and simmer for about 40 minutes. Add cooked shrimp just before serving. Serve over cooked rice. Yield: 4 to 6 servings.

Note: Chicken and pork chops are delicious when baked in this sauce at 350° for 1 hour.

CASSEROLES, EGGS, AND PASTA

TURKEY TETRAZZINI, 1

Life saver for leftover turkey or chicken.

- 4 c. cooked turkey or chicken
- ½ lb. thin spaghetti, cooked and drained (break into small pieces before cooking)
- ½ lb. mushrooms, sliced
- 3 T. butter
- 1 10½-oz. can cream of chicken soup
- 1 10½-oz. can cream of mushroom soup
- 1 c. milk
- ½ c. chicken broth
- ¼ c. sherry
- ½ c. grated Parmesan or sharp Cheddar

Sauté mushrooms in butter. Combine soups, milk, broth and sherry; mix with mushrooms, turkey and spaghetti. Turn into a shallow greased casserole. Sprinkle with cheese and bake in a 350° oven for 30 minutes until piping hot. Makes 6 to 8 servings.

TUNA ORIENTAL

Sweet-sour sauce turns tuna to terrific!

- 1 13¼-oz. can pineapple chunks
- 2 2-oz. envelopes sweet and sour sauce mix
- 1 medium green pepper
- 2 ribs celery, sliced (optional)
- 2 6½-oz. cans tuna
- 1 can bamboo shoots
- 1 can sliced water chestnuts

Fifteen minutes before serving drain pineapple; set aside chunks. Add enough water to juice to make 2 cups liquid. In saucepan, heat sauce mix and juice until thickened, stirring occasionally. Add green pepper and celery and cook 5 minutes. Add tuna and pineapple chunks, bamboo shoots and water chestnuts; cook until thoroughly heated. Serve with rice. Makes 4 servings.

SPANAKOPITTA (SPINACH PIE)

Food for the gods.

- 2 pkgs. frozen, chopped spinach
- 2 T. butter
- 1 small onion, chopped
- ¼ c. chopped scallions
- 2 T. parsley
- 1 t. dill
- 1 t. salt
- ¼ t. pepper
- ¼ c. milk
- 3 eggs
- ¼ lb. feta cheese
- ½ lb. phylo pastry
- 1 c. melted butter

Thaw spinach and squeeze free of as much water as possible. Sauté onion in 2 tablespoons butter until a light golden brown. Add scallions and cook until they wilt. Add spinach and seasonings. Toss lightly. Remove from heat and add milk. Beat eggs lightly in another bowl and add feta cheese, coarsely crumbled. Add to spinach mixture, mix well. With a pastry brush, coat bottom and sides of an 11 x 7 x 2-inch baking dish with melted butter. Line with 8 sheets of phylo, brushing each sheet with melted butter. Do not trim overhanging sections. Pour in spinach mixture and fold overhanging sections back over filling. Top with 8 sheets of phylo, brushing each sheet with butter. Trim overlap. Brush top with butter and score into squares or diamonds. Bake in a 350° oven 45 minutes. Let stand 10 minutes before serving. Serves 4.

CLAM SPAGHETTI

- 1 lb. thin spaghetti, cooked and drained
- 4 T. butter
- 1 clove garlic, minced
- 1 t. basil
- 2 T. chopped parsley
- 1 c. dry white wine
- 1 T. lemon juice
- 3 cans chopped or minced clams and juice
- 1 c. grated Parmesan cheese

Melt butter; sauté garlic for a minute or so. Add basil, parsley, wine, lemon juice, clams and juice; heat just to a boil. Put spaghetti in large, deep soup bowls; sprinkle with half of the Parmesan cheese. Pour sauce over spaghetti and serve. Serves 4 to 6.

Pictured opposite:
Spanakopitta

GNOCCHI

Italian delight; serve with Veal Piccata or ham.

- 1 T. finely chopped onion
- 3 T. butter or margarine
- 2 10-oz. pkgs. frozen chopped spinach, thawed and drained
- ¾ c. ricotta cheese
- ⅔ c. flour
- 2 egg yolks
- 1 c. grated Parmesan cheese
- 1 t. salt
- ¾ t. pepper
- ¼ t. nutmeg
- 3 qts. broth or water
- ¼ c. melted butter
- ½ c. grated Parmesan cheese

Sauté onion in butter until golden. Add well drained spinach; sauté 5 minutes or until there is no liquid. Place spinach in large mixing bowl. Add ricotta and flour, mixing thoroughly. Beat in egg yolks, 1 cup grated Parmesan cheese, salt, pepper and nutmeg. Mix thoroughly. Shape mixture into small balls, quickly dusting hands with flour if they become sticky. Bring broth to boiling. Drop in all Gnocchi; again bring to a boil and cook 3 to 4 minutes. Drain in a colander and spoon into heated serving dish. Pour melted butter over and sprinkle with Parmesan. Makes 48 1-inch balls.

MANICOTTI

This stuffed pasta is no longer laborious to make. Stuff uncooked shells and bake.

TOMATO SAUCE

- 3 T. olive oil
- 1 small onion, chopped
- 1 clove garlic, minced
- 1 6-oz. can tomato paste
- 1 14-oz. can Italian plum tomatoes
- 2 c. water
- ½ t. salt
- ½ bay leaf
- ½ t. basil

Sauté onion and garlic in olive oil. Add remaining ingredients and cook over medium heat 45 to 60 minutes until thick. Remove bay leaf.

PASTA

- 2 c. shredded mozarella
- 1 c. ricotta or creamed cottage cheese
- ½ c. grated Parmesan cheese
- 2 beaten eggs
- ¼ c. snipped parsley
- ½ t. salt
  Dash pepper
- 12 manicotti shells

Combine 1 cup mozarella with ricotta and Parmesan cheese; add eggs, parsley, salt and pepper. Mix thoroughly. Stuff uncooked manicotti shells with cheese mixture. Pour ½ cup Tomato Sauce into oblong baking dish. Arrange stuffed manicotti in dish; pour remaining sauce over top. Sprinkle with remaining mozarella. Cover and bake in a 400° oven 40 minutes. Serves 3 to 4.

TORTILLA CASSEROLE

Mexican dinner in a dish. *Bueno!*

- 1½ lbs. ground chuck
- 2 T. salad oil
- 1 onion, chopped
- 1 stalk celery, chopped
- 1 green pepper, chopped
- 1 c. rice
- 1 can red kidney beans, drained (optional)
- 1 c. sliced olives, black or green
- 1 28-oz. can tomatoes
- 1 c. water
- 2 t. salt
- 2 to 3 T. chili powder
- ¼ t. pepper
- 1 T. Worcestershire sauce
- 1 c. grated Cheddar cheese
- 1 c. crumbled corn chips

Brown ground chuck in a skillet. Transfer to a large casserole. In same skillet, heat oil and sauté onion, celery, pepper and raw rice for a few minutes. Add to casserole. Pour beans, olives, tomatoes, water, salt, chili powder, pepper and Worcestershire sauce over meat and vegetables. Mix well. Top with corn chips and cheese. Cover and bake in a 375° oven for 60 minutes. Makes 6 to 8 servings.

TYROPITTA (CHEESE PIE)

Classic Greek dish.

- 1 lb. feta cheese *or* ½ lb. feta plus ½ lb. small curd cottage cheese
- 5 eggs
- ½ lb. phylo pastry
- ½ c. melted butter

Beat eggs lightly. Crumble cheese into small particles and add to eggs. With pastry brush, coat bottom and sides of 11 x 7 x 2-inch baking dish with butter. Cut phylo to fit if necessary and put 4 sheets into pan, brushing each with butter. Spoon in some of the cheese mixture. Top with 2 sheets of phylo, brushed with butter. Add another layer of cheese and another layer of phylo. Continue until cheese mixture is used. Top with 4 layers of phylo, brushing butter over each layer, and top with butter. Score and bake in a 350° oven for 45 minutes. Serves 4.

1-2-3 SOUFFLÉ

Traditional steps of separating, beating, cooking and folding are eliminated in this fabulous culinary delight. No last-minute fuss!

- 1 T. butter, softened
- 6 eggs
- ½ c. light cream
- ¼ c. Parmesan cheese, grated or cubed
- ½ t. mustard
- ½ t. salt
- ¼ t. pepper
- 11 oz. cream cheese, softened
- ½ lb. Cheddar cheese, shredded or cubed
- ½ c. cubed salami or ham (optional)

Butter a 5-cup soufflé dish. Combine cream, eggs, Parmesan cheese, mustard, salt and pepper in blender. Blend until smooth. Add cream cheese and Cheddar. When smooth, pour mixture into soufflé dish. Bake in a preheated 375° oven for 50 minutes. Top will be golden brown and slightly cracked. Serve immediately.

Note: Soufflé can be prepared and held for up to 2 hours at room temperature or refrigerated 3 to 4 hours longer. Allow 5 to 10 minutes additional baking time. Serves 2 to 4.

LAYERED CHEESE SOUFFLÉ

Even the most well-run households occasionally have some slightly stale bread, and that's just what is needed for this fluffy never-fail soufflé. It is a joy for breakfast, luncheon or dinner.

- 10 slices slightly stale white bread
- 6 eggs, beaten
- 2 c. milk
- ¾ t. salt
- 1 t. dry mustard
- 1 t. Worcestershire sauce
- 2 c. sharp Cheddar cheese, grated
  Tuna, shrimp, crab meat, or turkey slices (optional)
- 3 T. butter

Trim crusts off bread. Combine eggs, milk, salt, mustard and Worcestershire sauce, beating well. Grease an 11 x 13-inch pan and alternate layers of bread and cheese, ending with bread. If seafood or poultry is used add it to the cheese layer. Cover with the liquid mixture and refrigerate for 3 to 4 hours or overnight.

Bring to room temperature, dot with butter and bake in a preheated 350° oven 1 hour. Makes 4 to 6 servings.

Grilled ham or bacon goes well with this soufflé.

SOUFFLÉ OMELET

Be an omelet eggspert.

- 2 T. butter
- 3 T. flour
- ½ t. salt
- ¼ t. pepper
- 1 c. milk
- 4 eggs, separated
- 1 c. grated Swiss or Cheddar cheese (optional)

Melt butter over medium heat. Blend in flour, salt and pepper. Add milk and cook, stirring, until thick and smooth. Stir in cheese if desired. Beat egg whites until stiff. Beat egg yolks slightly and stir into white sauce. Fold into whites in two parts. Turn into ungreased 9-inch pie plate. Bake in a 400° oven for 15 minutes or until puffy and golden brown. Serve with Chinese Sauce or Mushroom Sauce (p. 137). Serves 2.

GHIVETCH

It is important to have a variety of shapes, colors and flavors in this beautiful vegetable mélange. Vary the amounts to suit your taste. Substitute eggplant for zucchini, cabbage for celery or add a sliced turnip. Increase the servings by adding another carrot, potato or tomato.

  2 medium carrots, thinly sliced
  2 small potatoes, cubed
  4 medium tomatoes, quartered
  1 Bermuda onion, sliced
  1 small head cauliflower (broken in floweretts)
  ½ green pepper, julienne strips
  ½ sweet red pepper, julienne strips
  ½ pkg. frozen green peas, thawed
  1 c. sliced fresh green beans
  1 rib celery, sliced
  3 small zucchini, sliced
  1 c. beef bouillon
  1 c. olive oil
  1 clove garlic, minced
  2 t. salt
  ½ bay leaf, crumbled
  ½ t. savory
  ¼ t. tarragon

Put all of the vegetables in an ungreased, shallow, 11 x 13-inch casserole dish. Heat bouillon, oil, garlic, salt, bay leaf, savory and tarragon to boiling and pour over vegetables. Cover casserole with heavy foil. Bake in a preheated 350° oven until tender, about 1 hour. The vegetables should be crisp and colorful. Makes 8 to 10 servings.

RED CABBAGE

A vegetable so good it steals the meal.

- 1 head red cabbage, shredded
- 1 T. shortening or bacon fat
- ½ c. vinegar or lemon juice
- 1 t. salt
- ¼ c. sugar
- 1 onion, chopped (optional)
- 1 or 2 tart apples, chopped (optional)
- ¼ c. currant jelly

Melt shortening; add cabbage, vinegar, salt, sugar, onion and apple. Simmer until tender, about 1½ hours. Just before serving, stir in jelly. Serves 4 to 6.

HONEY-ORANGE PARSNIPS

- 4 medium parsnips, peeled and sliced
- 3 T. butter or margarine
- 1 T. honey
- 1 t. grated orange rind
- 3 T. orange juice

Cook parsnips in a small amount of boiling water or in a steamer until crisp tender. Drain. Combine remaining ingredients; pour over parsnips and simmer, stirring occasionally, until sauce is reduced and parsnips are glazed. Makes 4 servings.

GREEN BEANS IN TOMATO SAUCE GUISO DE EJOTES

This most congenial vegetable is treated in the Spanish way.

- 1 T. olive oil
- ½ onion, chopped
- 1 8-oz. can tomato sauce
- 1 clove garlic, minced
- 1 t. salt
- ⅛ t. dried ground chili peppers
- 1 lb. fresh or 1 package frozen green beans
- 1 T. minced parsley

Sauté onion in oil for 5 minutes. Mix in tomato sauce, garlic, salt, chili peppers and green beans. Bring to a boil; cover and cook over low heat 20 to 30 minutes. Stir in parsley. Serves 2 to 4.

VEGETABLES

BROCCOLI AU GRATIN

Broccoli never had it so good!

- 1 T. butter
- 1 T. flour
- ¼ t. salt
- 1 3-oz. pkg. cream cheese
- 1 1-oz. pkg. blue cheese
- ½ c. milk
- 2 pkgs. frozen chopped broccoli, thawed
- ½ c. crushed crackers

Melt butter over low heat; blend in flour, salt and cheeses. Add milk, stirring until mixture thickens. Stir in broccoli and pour into a greased casserole. Top with cracker crumbs and bake in a 350° oven for 30 minutes. Serves 4 to 6.

GLAZED CARROTS

Good things from the good earth.

- 1 lb. carrots, scrubbed, peeled, cut in strips or slices
  Salt and pepper
- ½ c. orange marmalade
- ¼ c. butter
- 1 T. mint jelly (optional)

In a saucepan, cover carrots with water; add salt and pepper to taste. Cook until barely tender; drain. Melt butter with marmalade and jelly, stirring until all are blended. Add carrots and cook together for a few minutes. Serves 4 to 6.

BRUSSELS SPROUTS

Tangy, chilled Brussels sprouts make a nice side dish with ham or corned beef.

- 1 pkg. Brussels sprouts
- ½ c. chicken broth
- 2 T. tarragon vinegar
- 1 medium onion, chopped

Bring chicken broth to a boil. Add Brussels sprouts and simmer until tender. Drain and sprinkle with vinegar and onion. Chill 3 to 4 hours. Makes 2 to 4 servings.

RUTABAGA

This misunderstood vegetable will now be appreciated.

3 c. peeled, cubed rutabaga
2 T. butter or margarine
1 T. light brown sugar
2 T. soy sauce
1 T. lemon juice
1 t. Worcestershire sauce

Cook rutabaga in small amount of boiling water or steamer until tender crisp. Combine remaining ingredients; pour over drained rutabaga. Simmer until sauce is reduced and vegetables are glazed. Makes 4 servings.

SHERRIED ONIONS

Creamed onions, nicely dressed up with sherry and raisins.

1 20-oz. pkg. frozen onions, cooked according to directions
3 T. butter or margarine
3 T. flour
½ t. salt
Dash pepper
1½ c. milk
½ c. raisins
¼ c. sherry

Melt butter over low heat. Stir in flour, salt and pepper; cook, stirring constantly, until smooth. Gradually add milk and cook, stirring until thickened and smooth. Add onions, raisins and sherry; heat until steaming and serve. Makes 4 to 6 servings.

GREEN TOMATO SLICES

An early frost should cause no dismay. A harvest of green tomatoes makes this great dish.

¼ c. cornmeal
1 t. salt
⅛ t. pepper
1 t. sugar
4 green tomatoes cut into ½-inch slices
4 T. butter for frying

Combine cornmeal, salt, pepper and sugar. Dip very green, firm tomato slices into mixture to coat both sides; fry in hot butter a few at a time until golden. Add more butter as needed. Serves 4.

CORN FRITTERS

Who can resist a platter of hot, crisp corn fritters? In order for the supply to keep up with the demand, get a head start and keep them hot on a cookie sheet in a preheated 350° oven. They are at their best, however, hot off the griddle.

Fat or oil
¾ c. sifted flour
1 T. sugar
1 t. baking powder
½ t. salt
¼ t. pepper
2 eggs, beaten
¾ c. whole kernel corn, drained

Mix together flour, sugar, baking powder, salt and pepper. Add eggs and corn to the flour mixture, stirring well. Fry batter in 1 inch of hot, deep fat or oil using about 1 tablespoon batter for each fritter. Turn to brown the other side. Drain on paper toweling and serve piping hot with warmed syrup. Makes about 12 fritters.

RATATOUILLE

This versatile French vegetable casserole is delicious hot or cold. Prepare the day before, as it improves with age.

¼ c. olive oil
1 clove garlic, minced
2 onions, sliced thin
2 green peppers, seeded and sliced into strips
1 eggplant, peeled and cubed
5 small zucchini, cut into ½-inch slices
5 tomatoes, quartered
1 t. salt
1 t. thyme
⅛ t. freshly ground pepper
1 t. olive oil

Heat ¼ cup olive oil in a 2-quart saucepan. Add garlic and onions and cook 5 minutes over medium heat until the onions are transparent. Add the vegetables in layers, sprinkling each layer with salt, pepper and thyme. Sprinkle 1 teaspoon olive oil over the top. Simmer, covered, over low heat for 30 to 35 minutes. Remove cover and simmer for 10 more minutes to reduce the sauce. Yield: 6 to 8 servings.

ZUCCHINI FLORENTINE

Bring harmony to a garden medley.

- 3 5-inch zucchini, scrubbed and halved lengthwise
- 2 T. minced onion
- 2 pkgs. frozen chopped spinach, thawed
- ¼ c. grated Parmesan cheese
- 3 T. butter

Prepare zucchini by scooping out pulp leaving ¼-inch shells; mince pulp. Melt butter in skillet and sauté pulp and onion until tender. Squeeze water out of spinach. Add to zucchini mixture; keep warm while making sauce.

SAUCE

- 2 T. butter
- 2 T. flour
- 1 c. cold milk
  Dash nutmeg
- ¼ t. salt
- ¼ t. white pepper
- ¼ t. sugar

Melt butter in skillet; stir in flour. Stir for 3 minutes without browning. Add cold milk, nutmeg, salt, pepper and sugar. Stir until thickened. Add spinach-onion mixture to sauce. Arrange zucchini shells in buttered, shallow oven-proof dish. Divide filling among the shells, mounding it. Sprinkle each with 1 tablespoon Parmesan and bake in a preheated 350° oven for 30 minutes. You may brown top under broiler. Makes 6 servings.

ASPARAGUS ORIENTAL

Start fresh with spring vegetables.

- 1 T. salad oil
- 2 thin slices fresh gingerroot
- 3 c. fresh asparagus
- ½ t. salt
  Pepper to taste
- ¼ c. toasted almonds (optional)

Heat skillet or wok; add oil and gingerroot. When ginger is hot, remove. Slice asparagus, on a slant, in 1½-inch slices; add to oil. Sprinkle with salt and pepper and cover. Lift skillet slightly above heat and shake constantly while cooking. Cook 4 to 5 minutes until crisp tender. Add toasted almonds if desired. Serves 2 to 4.

PEA PODS

A dish in a dash.

- 1 T. salad oil
- 1 clove garlic, minced
- 1 10-oz. can bamboo shoots, drained
- 1 8-oz. can water chestnuts, drained and sliced
- 1 can mushrooms, drained
- 2 6-oz. pkgs. frozen pea pods, thawed
- 1 T. soy sauce
- 1½ t. instant chicken bouillon, dissolved in 1/3 c. water
- ½ t. sugar
- 2 t. cornstarch mixed in 2 T. cold water

In large skillet or wok heat oil. Add garlic, bamboo shoots, water chestnuts, mushrooms, pea pods and soy sauce. Stir fry for 1 minute. Add bouillon and sugar and cook over medium heat 2 minutes. Add cornstarch water mixture and stir 1 to 2 minutes until thickened. Sprinkle with slivered almonds if desired. Makes 6 to 8 servings.

EGGPLANT CASSEROLE

Infinite options.

- 1 t. sugar
- 2 t. dried oregano or basil, crushed
- ½ t. salt
  Dash pepper
- 1 large eggplant, thinly sliced
- 1 large can tomato sauce with bits or 3 to 4 tomatoes, sliced
- 1 large green pepper, sliced
- 1 medium onion, chopped
- 1 to 2 medium zucchini, thinly sliced
- ½ c. grated Parmesan cheese
- 8 oz. sliced mozzarella or Swiss cheese

Mix together sugar, oregano, salt and pepper and set aside. Place a layer of eggplant in a greased casserole, add a layer of tomatoes or sauce and some of the green pepper, onion and zucchini. Sprinkle lightly with mixed seasonings and cheeses. Repeat layers until casserole is filled, ending with cheese. Cover with greased foil and bake in a 400° oven for 20 minutes. Remove cover; reduce heat to 350° and continue baking for 45 additional minutes. Drain any excess liquid. Makes 6 to 8 servings.

GINGER PEAS

Canton special!

    2 pkg. frozen peas
    1 can mushrooms, drained
    1 can water chestnuts, sliced
    1 c. green onion, 1-inch slices
    ¾ t. ground ginger
    ¼ t. nutmeg
    1 c. chicken broth or consommé
    2 T. cornstarch
    1 t. salt
    ⅛ t. pepper
    ⅛ t. garlic powder

In saucepan separate peas; add mushrooms, water chestnuts, green onion, ginger, nutmeg and ¾ cup of the broth. Cover and simmer for 3 to 4 minutes. In cup blend cornstarch and remaining ¼ cup broth until smooth. Stir into peas; cook, stirring constantly, until liquid thickens and boils. Add salt, garlic powder and pepper. Serves 6 to 8.

KASHA

A wonderful grain with limitless variations. Use as a breakfast cereal, add to soup or serve with meat gravy. Sautéed onions, mushrooms and celery may be added and all reheated in a casserole.

    1 c. groats
    1 egg, slightly beaten
    1 t. salt
    2 c. boiling water
    1 t. instant bouillon crystals

Combine groats, egg and salt in a hot frying pan; stir constantly until each grain is separate and dry. Place in a heavy pot. Dissolve bouillon crystals in boiling water. Add water to groats; steam over low heat for 30 minutes until water is absorbed and grains are tender. Serves 4.

COUSCOUS

Serve instead of rice with meat or fowl, or sweetened with milk in the morning.

    2 T. sweet butter
    1 c. couscous or semolina
    1 c. boiling water
      Pinch salt

Heat butter in a saucepan. Add couscous and mix carefully so all grains are coated with butter. Add boiling water and salt and cover. Remove from heat; let stand 15 minutes. Before serving, stir with fork to separate grains. Serves 4.

BAKED COTTAGE POTATOES

This may very well become your favorite potato dish.

    6 medium potatoes
    1 t. salt
    ¼ t. pepper
    4 T. butter

Wash and peel potatoes and cut into ⅛-inch slices. Soak 20 minutes in cold water. Drain and dry well. Arrange a layer of the potatoes, with edges overlapping, in the bottom of an 8-inch cake pan or iron skillet. Sprinkle some of the salt and pepper over the potatoes and dot with 1 tablespoon butter. Repeat with layers including the seasoning and butter until the pan is filled. Cover tightly with foil. Bake in a preheated 425° oven for 30 minutes. Remove cover and bake for an additional 10 minutes. To serve, turn out on a heated plate. Makes 6 servings.

POTATOES SAVOYARD

Make a good dish a great dish!

    2½ lbs. potatoes, peeled, thinly sliced
      6 T. butter
      2 T. snipped parsley
      1 c. grated Swiss cheese (¼ lb.)
      1 t. salt
      ⅛ t. freshly ground pepper
    1¼ c. boiling beef broth

Preheat oven to 425°. With 2 tablespoons of butter, grease a shallow 2-quart baking dish. Dry potatoes well; use half of them to line the dish, overlapping them. Dot with 2 tablespoons butter, half the parsley, salt, pepper and cheese. Add second layer of potatoes, again overlapping them, and sprinkle with remaining parsley, salt, pepper, cheese; dot with 2 tablespoons butter. Pour boiling broth over and bake in a 425° oven, 55 to 60 minutes until potatoes are fork tender, tops are browned and broth has been absorbed. Serves 6 to 8.

Pictured opposite:
Ginger Peas

111

FARFEL

A delightful change from potato and rice doldrums.

2 c. toasted farfel or square egg noodles
2 T. butter
1 onion, chopped
¼ lb. sliced mushrooms
½ green pepper, chopped
¼ t. ginger
1 T. brown sugar
4 T. soy sauce
Salt and pepper to taste

Cook farfel or egg noodles as directed on package and drain. Sauté onion, mushrooms and green pepper in butter and add with remaining ingredients to farfel. Place all in greased casserole. Bake in a 350° oven for 20 to 30 minutes until hot through. Serves 6 to 8.

NOODLE PUDDING

This will enhance a modest or a splendid meal.
2½ c. milk
1 c. butter
1 8-oz. pkg. cream cheese
¾ lb. egg noodles
6 eggs
1½ t. salt
Raisins, 2 T. sugar, chopped apple, pineapple tidbits (optional)

Heat milk, butter and cheese. Boil noodles according to package directions; drain. Lightly mix eggs, salt, and optional ingredients into cooled milk mixture and combine with noodles. Pour into a greased 11 x 13-inch oven-proof baking dish and bake in a preheated 325° oven for 45 to 60 minutes until golden brown and done. Makes 12 servings.

YORKSHIRE PUDDING

A must with roast beef!

1 or 2 pieces suet
3 eggs
1 c. milk
1 c. flour
½ t. salt

In a hot frying pan, heat suet to yield ¼ to ½ cup liquid. Beat eggs and add milk, salt and flour, beating until smooth and frothy. Pour rendered fat into oven-proof baking dish and heat in a 400° oven. Pour egg mixture into hot dish and bake for 35 to 45 minutes, until high, puffy and brown. Serve immediately. Makes 4 servings.

BARLEY PILAF MOLD

An addition of merit to any dinner.

2 c. quick barley
4 c. water with 2 t. instant chicken bouillon
2 ribs celery, chopped
½ green pepper, chopped
½ c. chopped green onion
¼ to ½ lb. mushrooms, sliced
2 to 3 T. salad oil
3 eggs, slightly beaten
1 c. sour cream
1 t. salt
½ t. white pepper

Stir barley into 4 cups boiling bouillon. Cover and simmer 15 to 20 minutes until tender, stirring occasionally. Drain. Sauté onion, celery, green pepper and mushrooms in oil for a few minutes. Combine sour cream, eggs salt, pepper and barley. Stir in vegetables. Spoon into a heavily greased 4-cup mold. Chill. Set mold in pan filled with 1½ inches of boiling water. Bake in a 375° oven for 1 hour. Allow to cool 5 minutes. Turn out on platter. Serves 10 to 12.

TURKEY STUFFING

Serve with chicken, turkey, veal or pork.

¼ c. butter or margarine
1 large onion, chopped
1 clove garlic, crushed
2 stalks celery, chopped
1 c. chopped walnuts (optional)
½ c. chopped parsley
8 hot dog rolls broken into bite-size pieces
¾ to 1 c. chicken bouillon
1 egg, slightly beaten

Melt butter and sauté onion, garlic, celery, nuts and parsley for a few minutes. Add bread and cook, stirring, until lightly toasted. Remove from heat; stir in egg and chicken bouillon. Place in a greased casserole and bake in a 350° oven for 45 to 60 minutes until toasty and brown. Makes 6 to 8 servings.

ÉPINARDS A LA CREME

This delightfully different combination of vegetables and creamy sauce goes well with baked or broiled fish.

- 2 pkgs. frozen chopped spinach
- 1 small onion, finely chopped
- 1 T. butter or margarine
- 1 T. flour
- ½ c. milk (or half-and-half)
- 1 jar small whole onions (or ½ pkg. frozen)
- ½ c. beef bouillon
- 1 t. salt
  Pinch of pepper
  Pinch of nutmeg

Cook spinach lightly, drain well. Sauté onion in butter until soft. Blend in flour and then stir in milk, bouillon, salt, pepper and nutmeg. Stir until mixture is creamy. Add spinach and remove from heat. Place whole onions in a lightly greased baking dish, pour spinach mixture over the onions and bake in a preheated 325° oven for about 20 minutes. Serves 8.

BROCCOLI SOUFFLÉ

This is the soufflé of your dreams, with nothing to rise or fall. It will keep its shape very nicely until you are ready to serve it. (Turn the oven down to 300° while it waits.)

- 2 10-oz. pkgs. frozen chopped broccoli or spinach
- ½ c. chicken broth
- 2 c. well-drained cottage cheese
- ½ c. grated Parmesan cheese
- 2 eggs, beaten
- 1 t. minced onion
- 1 t. salt

Cook the broccoli or spinach in chicken broth and drain well. Combine cheeses, eggs, onion and salt. Gently mix in the broccoli or spinach. Bake in a greased 2½-quart casserole in a preheated 350° oven about 30 minutes, or until a knife inserted in the center comes out clean. Makes 8 servings.

GREEN RICE RING

A lovely container for shrimp Creole but delicious with beef or fowl, too. Fill the center with glazed carrots if desired.

- 3 c. cooked white rice
- 3 egg yolks, beaten
- 1 c. light cream
- 1 t. salt
- ¼ t. pepper
- 1 c. minced parsley
- 1 c. minced green pepper
- ¼ c. minced onion
- ¼ lb. grated American or Cheddar cheese
- 3 egg whites

Combine egg yolks, cream, salt, pepper, parsley, green pepper and onion. Stir in the cooked rice and cheese. Beat egg whites until stiff but not dry and fold into the rice mixture. Grease a 3-quart ring mold generously, pour in rice mixture and bake in a pan of hot water in a preheated 350° oven about 45 minutes, or until a knife inserted in the center comes out clean. Serves 10 to 12.

ZUCCHINI PARMESAN

This dish is ready to serve in the same amount of time it takes to prepare a package of frozen vegetables. Everyone will think you've cooked for hours.

- 1 onion, sliced
- ¼ c. butter, margarine or vegetable oil
- 4 to 6 zucchini
- ¼ t. salt
- ⅛ t. pepper
- ½ c. grated Parmesan cheese

Sauté onion in butter, margarine or oil until soft. Add zucchini (scrubbed and cut into ¼-inch rounds), salt and pepper and cook, tossing lightly, for about 5 minutes. Add cheese just before serving and toss lightly to coat well. Makes 4 servings.

SWEET POTATOES IN ORANGE CUPS

Sweet potatoes are a natural with fowl or pork. Heaped into orange cups, they add a festive touch to any dinner.

- **6 yams or sweet potatoes**
- **2 T. butter**
- **¼ c. brown sugar**
- **½ c. orange juice**
- **12 Orange Cups**

Scrub sweet potatoes and cook in a covered saucepan in a small amount of water until very tender. Remove skins and mash until smooth. Add butter, sugar and enough orange juice to give them the consistency of mashed potatoes. Heap into the prepared orange cups. Decorate tops with a marshmallow or maraschino cherry.

Sweet potatoes may be kept hot over simmering water and placed in orange cups just before serving. Or they may be filled and kept in a 300° oven 30 minutes. Makes 12 cups.

ORANGE CUPS

Trace a line around the center of 6 oranges. Insert a small-bladed, pointed knife into the center of the orange at an angle to make one side of a point. Remove knife; insert to make opposite side of point. Continue around the orange, following the line to make halves equal sizes. Pull apart and scoop the fruit out of each half. You will have two shells with a picot edge. These cups may also be filled with cranberry relish.

SPICED PEACHES

A little competition for Grandma's recipe.

- **1 large can peach halves**
- **½ c. sugar**
- **½ c. peach juice**
- **¼ c. vinegar**
- **8 to 10 whole cloves**
- **1 stick cinnamon**

Combine sugar, juice, vinegar and spices. Bring to a boil and simmer 10 minutes. Add the fruit and heat thoroughly. Remove to a flat refrigerator dish. Be sure all fruit is covered with the syrup. Allow to stand refrigerated overnight.

MARINATED CARROTS

A lively change from the usual carrot sticks, Marinated Carrots keep for weeks in the refrigerator.

- **8 to 10 medium carrots, cut into sticks**
- **¼ c. olive or vegetable oil**
- **1½ T. cider vinegar**
- **1 T. chopped green pepper**
- **½ t. dry mustard**
- **1 t. paprika**
- **1 small clove garlic, minced**
- **1 T. chopped green onion, chives or instant minced onion**
- **1 t. salt**
- **⅛ t. pepper**
- **½ t. basil**
- **1 T. lemon juice**

Cook carrot sticks in 1 inch of boiling, salted water for 5 minutes. Drain. Combine the remaining ingredients, mix well and pour over the carrots. Refrigerate for at least 1 hour and serve cold.

CURRIED YAMS AND FRUIT

A touch of curry powder turns ordinary canned fruit into a gourmet treat. The yams are optional.

- **⅓ c. butter**
- **⅓ c. brown sugar**
- **1 to 2 T. curry powder**
- **1 1-lb. can pear halves**
- **1 1-lb. can peach halves**
- **1 1-lb. can pineapple slices**
- **1 1-lb. can apricot halves**
- **2 1-lb. cans yams or sweet potatoes (optional)**

Melt butter, add brown sugar and curry powder and mix well. Drain fruits and yams and arrange in a 2½-quart casserole. Top with curry mixture. Bake 1 hour in a preheated 325° oven. Yield: 10 to 12 servings.

Pictured opposite: Spiced Peaches

SPINACH FLORENTINE

Everyone will eat spinach cooked in this unusual way.

- 1 8-oz. pkg. wide noodles
- 1 onion, chopped fine
- ½ c. butter
- 2 10-oz. pkgs. chopped spinach, thawed and drained
- 1 t. salt
- 3 eggs, slightly beaten
- 1 c. sour cream

Cook noodles in salted water until barely tender, then drain. Sauté onion in butter. Combine all ingredients and place in a well-greased 6-cup ring mold. Place mold in pan of hot water and bake in a 350° oven 45 minutes. Unmold and serve hot. Makes 6 to 8 servings.

ZUCCHINI AU GRATIN

Zucchini with a surprise. A touch of tomato, topped with bubbly melted cheese, makes this deliciously different.

- 4 T. vegetable oil
- 4 zucchini
- 1 clove garlic, minced
- 1 small onion, chopped
- ¼ t. freshly ground pepper
- ½ t. salt
- 2 T. grated Parmesan cheese
- ¼ c. tomato sauce
- 2 to 3 slices processed Swiss cheese

Heat oil in a skillet. Add zucchini (scrubbed and cut into ¼-inch rounds), garlic and onion and sauté for 5 minutes. Add pepper, salt and Parmesan cheese and toss lightly. Place in a greased 1-quart casserole and brush with tomato sauce. Cover with slices of Swiss cheese and bake in a preheated 350° oven about 15 to 20 minutes until the cheese melts and is bubbly. Makes 4 servings.

CHINESE VEGETABLES

The Chinese call this method of cooking vegetables "stir-frying." Cooked very quickly and with a minimum of liquid, the vegetables remain tender, crisp and colorful. The flavor is enhanced by the broth, soy sauce and a touch of sugar.

- 1 lb. fresh green beens, carrots, cauliflower, broccoli or Brussels sprouts
- 3 T. vegetable oil
- 1 T. soy sauce
- ½ t. sugar
- ¼ c. chicken broth

Wash and slice vegetables. Heat oil in large skillet. Add vegetables and toss until coated with oil. Add soy sauce, sugar and broth. Cover skillet, reduce heat, steam for 8 to 10 minutes, shaking the pan occasionally to "stir" the vegetables. Serve immediately. Serves 4 to 6.

> Cold cheese grates easily. It may be grated in advance, rewrapped and returned to the refrigerator until needed.

CHINESE FRIED RICE

"May your rice never burn" is a Chinese New Year's greeting that means "Good Luck." When frying rice, you will have good luck if you keep stirring to prevent sticking. Fried rice is very tasty and well worth the effort. It is also a good way to use leftovers.

- 3 c. cooked cold rice
- 3 T. vegetable oil
- 1 c. cooked chicken, shrimp or leftover meat
- 2 eggs, slightly beaten
- ¾ t. salt
- ½ t. pepper
- 2 T. soy sauce
- 2 green onions, snipped

Heat oil in deep frying pan. Add meat or fish and cook 1 minute. Add eggs, salt and pepper and cook, stirring constantly, until well mixed. Add rice and soy sauce and cook, stirring constantly, for about 5 minutes, until rice is thoroughly heated. Garnish with green onions. Yield: 4 to 6 servings.

VEGETABLES VINAIGRETTE

Everyone will enjoy these vegetables marinated with a touch of dill. Heaped on a lettuce-lined platter, they are a picture in shades of green and white.

⅔ c. vegetable oil
⅓ c. tarragon vinegar
1 t. sugar
1 t. salt
¼ t. Tabasco
1 T. dried dill
2 T. snipped parsley
1 T. snipped chives
½ lb. fresh mushrooms, sliced
2 c. raw cauliflower floweretts
1 can artichoke hearts, drained
1 1-lb. can whole green beans, drained

Combine oil, vinegar, sugar, salt, Tabasco, dill, parsley and chives and mix until thoroughly blended. Pour over vegetables and marinate in the refrigerator at least 3 hours before serving. This vegetable dish improves with age and will keep for several days in the refrigerator. Makes 12 servings.

HOT WINE SAUCE
FOR VEGETABLES

Dress up an ordinary package of frozen vegetables with this easy last-minute sauce and you will have something extraordinary.

1 T. minced onion
¼ c. dry Sauterne
2 T. chopped parsley
1 T. lemon juice
¾ c. mayonnaise
   Asparagus, broccoli, green beans or cauliflower, cooked

Combine onion, wine, parsley, lemon juice and mayonnaise in the top of a double boiler and heat over hot, not boiling, water. Serve over one of the above vegetables. Makes about 1 cup. Serves 4.

POTATO PANCAKES

Crisp, lacy potato pancakes go well with beef and fowl as well as with breakfast ham and eggs.

2 c. raw grated potatoes
2 whole eggs, beaten
1 onion, grated
1½ t. salt
2 T. flour

Peel large potatoes and soak in cold water several hours. Grate potatoes and drain. (Grate in an electric blender if desired.) Add grated onion and beaten eggs, stir in salt and flour. Drop batter by spoonsful onto a hot, well-greased frying pan or griddle. Turn to brown other side. Serve hot with applesauce or sour cream. Made in a miniature size they are delightful for appetizers. Keep hot on a warming tray, serve with cold sour cream. Makes 20 to 22 pancakes or 4 dozen miniatures.

Parsley will keep fresh and crisp if stored in a covered jar in the refrigerator.

CORN PUDDING

This is a favorite with youngsters. Omit the green pepper and pimiento if desired. However, they add to both the flavor and the appearance of this pudding.

1 1-lb. can creamed corn
3 eggs, slightly beaten
½ t. salt
¼ t. pepper
1 T. sugar
¼ t. dry mustard
2 T. minced onion
½ c. chopped green pepper
½ c. chopped pimiento
1 c. coarse cracker crumbs
1 c. milk
2 T. butter, cut into dots

Combine all ingredients except butter. Pour into a greased casserole and dot with butter. Bake in a preheated 350° oven for 45 minutes to 1 hour, until a knife inserted into the center comes out clean. Makes 4 to 6 servings.

BREADS

ZUCCHINI BREAD

Bake a holiday gift.

1¼ c. wheat germ
3 c. flour
3 t. baking powder
1 t. salt
2 t. cinnamon
⅛ t. nutmeg
⅛ t. cloves
1 c. chopped nuts
2 eggs
1¾ c. sugar
2 t. vanilla
⅔ c. salad oil
3 c. grated unpeeled zucchini (about 1½ lbs.)

Mix together wheat germ, flour, baking powder, salt, cinnamon, nutmeg, cloves and nuts. Beat eggs until light and fluffy. Add sugar, oil and vanilla. Stir in zucchini. Gradually stir in flour mixture. Pour into 2 greased and floured 8½ x 4½ x 2½-inch loaf pans and bake in a preheated 350° oven for 1 hour or until done. (Reduce heat to 325° if using glass pans.) Cool 5 to 10 minutes and remove from pan. To freeze, wrap in foil. Makes 2 loaves.

BLUEBERRY CORN MUFFINS

Compatible cornmeal dressed in blue.

1 8½-oz. pkg. corn muffin mix
1 T. brown sugar
1 egg
⅓ c. milk
½ c. blueberries (canned, drained, fresh or frozen and thawed)

Blend muffin mix, sugar, egg and milk. Batter should be slightly lumpy. Stir in blueberries. Fill greased muffin cups half full. Bake in a preheated 400° oven 15 to 20 minutes until golden brown. Makes 8 to 12 muffins, depending on size.

LEMON BREAD

Delicious with luncheon salads or at high tea.

4 T. margarine or butter
¾ c. sugar
2 eggs, slightly beaten
2 t. grated lemon rind
2 c. flour
2½ t. baking powder
½ t. salt
¾ c. milk
¼ to ½ c. chopped nuts
2 T. lemon juice
2 T. sugar

Cream together butter and sugar until light and fluffy. Add eggs and lemon rind. Combine flour, baking powder and salt and add to mixture alternately with milk, beating until smooth after each addition. Stir in nuts. Pour into a greased 8½ x 4½ x 2½-inch loaf pan. Bake in a preheated 350° oven for 55 to 60 minutes or until done. Place pan on rack and cool for 10 minutes. Combine sugar and lemon juice and pour over the top of loaf. Makes 1 loaf.

WHOLE WHEAT BREAD

A quickie!

2 c. whole wheat flour
1 t. baking powder
1 t. baking soda
1 t. salt
1 egg, beaten
1¾ c. buttermilk
¼ c. honey
¼ c. melted margarine
½ c. chopped walnuts
½ c. raisins (optional)

Combine dry ingredients, stirring to mix. Combine egg, buttermilk, honey and margarine. Add to dry ingredients, stirring just until moistened. Stir in nuts and raisins. Spoon into greased 9 x 5 x 3-inch loaf pan. Bake in a preheated 350° oven for 55 to 60 minutes or until done. Remove from pan and cool on rack. Makes 1 loaf.

Pictured opposite:
Lemon Bread

BANANA DATE BREAD

Make a date with bananas to make bread.

- 2 c. flour
- 1 t. baking powder
- ¾ t. salt
- ½ t. baking soda
- ¼ lb. margarine or butter
- 1 c. sugar
- 2 eggs
- 2 ripe bananas, mashed
- ½ c. snipped dates
- ½ c. chopped nuts
- 1 T. carob powder (optional)

Sift together flour, baking powder, salt and baking soda. Cream margarine; gradually add sugar, creaming well. Add eggs, 1 at a time. Beat well. Blend in banana. Combine dry ingredients with carob powder, if desired, and add. Fold in nuts and dates. Pour into a 9 x 5 x 3-inch well-greased pan, leaving center slightly hollow. Let pan stand for 20 minutes before baking. Bake in a 350° oven 60 minutes. Cool before slicing.

CRUSTY FRENCH ONION BREAD

Zesty and crunchy; superb with soups, salads or any time you want a taste of onion.

- 1 loaf French bread
- ¼ lb. softened butter or margarine
- 2 to 4 T. dry onion soup mix
- ¼ c. snipped parsley

Diagonally cut bread into thick slices. Combine remaining ingredients and spread on sliced bread. Reassemble bread, wrap in foil and bake in a preheated 400° oven for 15 minutes.

MELBA TOAST

Got a minute, save a penny.

Using thinly sliced bread, stack and trim crusts. Restack 6 slices high and cut to make small triangles, fingers or squares. Lay in a single layer on a foil-lined cookie sheet. Bake in a 250° oven 50 to 60 minutes until light brown. Cool and store in tins for 1 month.

CHOCOLATE DATE NUT LOAF

Slice and spread with cream cheese for a special coffee break.

- 1 c. boiling water
- 1 c. chopped dates
- 6 T. margarine or butter
- 1 c. sugar
- 1 egg
- 1 t. vanilla
- 6 T. cocoa
- 2 c. flour
- ½ t. salt
- 1 t. baking soda
- 1 t. cinnamon
- ½ c. chopped walnuts

Pour boiling water over dates; cool. Cream butter, sugar, egg and vanilla. Mix cocoa, flour, salt, soda and cinnamon and add alternately with date-water mixture. Beat well after each addition. Stir in nuts. Pour batter into greased 9 x 5-inch loaf pan. Bake in a 350° oven for 60 to 70 minutes. Makes 1 loaf.

CRANBERRY NUT BREAD

Nut breads are a happy holiday thought. They will taste even better and be easier to slice if they are tightly wrapped and set aside for a day.

    2 c. flour
    1 c. sugar
 1½ t. baking powder
    ½ t. baking soda
    1 t. salt
    ¾ c. orange juice
    1 T. grated orange rind
    1 egg, well beaten
    ¼ c. melted butter or margarine
    2 c. coarsely chopped cranberries
    ½ c. chopped nuts

Sift together flour, sugar, baking powder, soda and salt. Combine orange juice, rind, egg and melted butter or margarine. Add to dry ingredients and mix only until flour mixture is moistened. Carefully fold in cranberries and chopped nuts. Spoon into 2 greased loaf pans and bake in a 350° oven 1 hour.

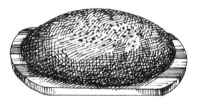

BATTER BREAD

Famous southern cooks say that good Batter Bread cannot possibly be made from a written recipe, but this is a very satisfactory try.

1½ c. water
  ⅛ lb. butter
  1 c. white cornmeal
  3 eggs
  2 t. baking powder
  ½ t. salt
  2 c. buttermilk
  2 to 3 T. vegetable oil

Bring water to a boil, add butter and melt. Remove from heat and add cornmeal. Stir well. Add eggs, one at a time, stirring well. Then add baking powder, salt and buttermilk. Stir until smooth and pour into a heated and well-greased (using the oil) 8- to 9-inch pan. Bake at 400° for 35 to 40 minutes. Makes 4 to 6 servings.

FRENCH OR ITALIAN BREAD

Everyone loves hot crusty French or Italian bread. Here are four different ways to serve it.

GARLIC BREAD

 ½ c. (¼ lb.) butter or margarine, softened
 1 large clove garlic, minced

Blend together.

HERB BREAD

 ¼ lb. butter or margarine, softened
   Parsley, chives, thyme, tarragon, dill

Use two of the spices and combine with butter to taste.

CHEESY-CHIVE BREAD

 ¼ lb. butter or margarine, softened
 4 ozs. Cheddar cheese, shredded
 ¼ c. snipped chives
 2 T. prepared mustard

Blend all ingredients together.

BOURBON STREET BREAD

 ½ c. snipped chives
 ½ c. grated Parmesan cheese
 ¾ c. mayonnaise

Mix all ingredients together.

Cut bread with a sharp knife into 1-inch-thick slices and butter each slice on both sides with the spread of your choice. Reassemble loaf and wrap in aluminum foil. Bake in a preheated 375° oven 15 minutes. To brown and crisp loaf, open foil and bake 5 minutes longer at 400°.

COLD OVEN POPOVERS

A quick version of the classic popover that dramatically shortens the usual preparation time of the original.

    3 eggs
    1 c. milk
    1 c. flour
    ½ t. salt

Butter 6 custard cups heavily. Beat eggs, milk, flour and salt until smooth. Pour batter into cups, place in a cold oven, turn oven to 450° and bake for 30 minutes. Pierce with a toothpick to hold for a while without collapsing.

HOT CHEESE BREAD

Your family will love the aroma of fresh bread baking, thanks to biscuit mix.

3¾ c. biscuit mix
1¼ c. shredded sharp Cheddar cheese
  2 T. poppy seed
  1 egg, slightly beaten
1¼ c. milk

Mix together the cheese, biscuit mix and poppy seed. Stir in the egg and milk until blended. Then beat by hand for a minute or two. Sprinkle with a teaspoon of poppy seed. Bake in a greased loaf pan at 350° for 55 to 60 minutes. Cool for a few minutes before slicing.

PUMPKIN BREAD

3½ c. sifted flour
  2 t. baking soda
1½ t. salt
  3 c. sugar
  1 t. nutmeg
  1 t. cinnamon
  4 eggs, beaten
  ⅔ c. water
  1 c. vegetable oil
  2 c. canned pumpkin
  ¾ c. chopped nuts

Sift together flour, soda, salt, sugar, nutmeg and cinnamon. Combine eggs, water, salad oil and pumpkin. Add to dry ingredients and mix only until well blended. Fold in nuts, pour batter into 2 well-greased loaf pans. Bake in a preheated 350° oven 1 hour or until a toothpick inserted into the center comes out clean.

FRENCH TOAST SANDWICH

Create a hearty brunch treat using your favorite sandwich combination of meats and cheese. Serve with a tossed salad or a fresh fruit bowl. A French Toast Sandwich makes a delicious luncheon.

- **4 slices white bread**
  Chicken, turkey, ham, luncheon meat, sliced
  American, Cheddar, Swiss, Gruyere cheese, sliced
- **1 egg**
- **¼ c. milk**

Beat egg lightly, add milk, stir. Dip the sandwiches, filled with meat and cheese, into the mixture, turning to coat both sides. Sauté in butter on both sides, using a skillet or electric frying pan, until golden brown. Serve with mustard or pancake syrup. Makes 2 sandwiches.

To soften butter or margarine for creaming, cut thin slices into bowl.

APPLE PANCAKE

A convenient, ever available standby for breakfast, brunch or a midnight supper.

- **1 apple**
- **4 T. butter**
- **2 T. sugar**
- **¼ t. cinnamon**
- **¼ t. nutmeg (optional)**
- **1 c. Bisquick**
- **⅔ c. milk**
- **1 egg**
- **1 T. sugar**

Core apple; do not peel. Cut into twelve slices. Melt butter in 9-inch iron skillet. Stir in cinnamon, 2 tablespoons sugar and apple slices; sauté until tender. Combine Bisquick, milk, egg and sugar until just moistened. Pour over apple slices. Turn heat to low and cook 10 minutes until surface of pancake looks dull. Place under broiler for a couple of minutes until lightly browned. To serve, turn upside down on plate and pass extra butter and syrup. Serves 2 to 4.

FRENCH BAKED PANCAKE

Happiness is Sunday morning brunch; this cheese-filled pancake will bake while you prepare the rest of your brunch.

- **¼ lb. butter or margarine**
- **4 t. sugar**
- **3 large eggs**
- **1¼ c. milk**
- **2 c. flour**
- **1½ t. baking powder**

Cream butter and sugar, add eggs. Add flour and baking powder alternately with milk and mix well. Place half of the batter (about 1½ cups) into a well-greased 13 x 9-inch baking dish.

FILLING

- **1½ lbs. creamed cottage cheese**
- **3 T. melted butter**
- **1 t. salt**
- **2 eggs**

Beat together cottage cheese, butter, salt and eggs. Spoon filling over batter and top with remaining batter. Bake in a 350° oven 45 minutes until golden brown. Cut into squares and serve hot with sour cream, preserves, honey or pancake syrup. Serves 6 to 8.

BUTTERMILK BISCUITS

Very southern and traditionally served with Virginia ham, these melt-in-the-mouth biscuits are good buttered and served with any meat or jam.

- **1¾ c. sifted flour**
- **1 t. salt**
- **2 t. baking powder**
- **1 t. sugar**
- **½ t. baking soda**
- **¼ c. shortening**
- **⅔ c. buttermilk**

Cut shortening into dry ingredients until the consistency of cornmeal. Make a well, add buttermilk. Stir until dough leaves side of bowl, about ½ minute. Turn dough onto floured board and knead lightly for ½ minute. Pat with floured hand to ¼- to ½-inch thick. Cut with floured biscuit cutter. Bake at 450° for 10 to 12 minutes. Makes 10 to 12 biscuits.

BLINTZES

Take the time, then take the credit for this versatile filled pancake, delicious as a brunch or luncheon entrée or as a dinner dessert.

PANCAKE

3 eggs
1⅓ c. water
1 c. flour
¼ t. salt

Beat eggs, add half of the water, the flour, the salt, and the remaining water. Beat until smooth in blender, with electric mixer or with whip. Let rest while mixing the filling.

FILLING

1 lb. dry cottage cheese
2 eggs
½ t. vanilla
1 t. sugar (optional)
½ t. cinnamon (optional)

Combine cheese, eggs and seasonings and beat until smooth. Lightly grease a 6-, 7-, or 8-inch skillet and heat on top of stove. Pour just enough batter in pan to coat thinly, tilting it from side to side and pouring out excess. Fry only on one side and turn out, brown side up, on a towel. Repeat until batter is used up, adding a little more water if it thickens. Place 1 heaping teaspoon of filling on each pancake and fold envelope-style. Refrigerate or freeze until ready to fry or bake. Sauté in butter or oil until brown on both sides or bake in a buttered pan in a 375° oven for 35 minutes or until brown. Serve with sour cream and hot blueberry, cherry or strawberry sauce or preserves. Or serve with sour cream and caviar and omit sugar and cinnamon.

Note: If frozen, thaw in refrigerator before browning. Makes 22 to 24 blintzes.

BLUEBERRY SAUCE

1 can blueberries, drained (save juice)
1 T. cornstarch
2 T. sugar
1 T. lemon juice

Blend cornstarch and sugar. Stir into blueberry juice and cook over low heat until clear. Add lemon juice and berries and heat.

ESTHER'S CHEESE DREAMS

To stretch the food budget and win acclaim, try Cheese Dreams for brunch, luncheon or a meatless supper.

¼ c. butter
¼ c. shortening
1¼ c. flour
¼ t. salt
¼ t. baking powder
½ c. sour cream

Mix pastry ingredients as for pie dough. Divide into 4 parts. Wrap in waxed paper and chill ½ to 1 hour. Roll out on floured waxed paper. Put cheese filling on dough and roll like a jelly roll. Cut into 2-inch slices, dot each with butter, and bake on a greased cookie sheet in a preheated 350° oven 40 minutes or until golden brown. Serve hot with sour cream and blueberry sauce or frozen strawberries.

FILLING

1¼ lbs. dry cottage cheese
2 eggs
2 t. melted butter
¼ t. salt

Mix all together until well blended.

Note: Cheese Dreams may be frozen unbaked.

GRANOLA

Close the nutrition gap with this delicious and nutritious toasty cereal. Serve with cold milk or use as an ice cream or pudding topping.

3 c. uncooked oats
½ c. wheat germ
1 c. flaked or shredded coconut
½ c. chopped nuts
½ c. sesame seeds
½ t. salt
¼ c. honey
¼ c. vegetable oil
½ t. vanilla
1 c. raisins

In a large bowl combine all ingredients except the raisins. Mix together thoroughly.

Bake mixture on a large baking sheet in a preheated 325° oven for about 20 minutes until golden brown. Shake pan occasionally. Add raisins. Cool and stir with fork until crumbly. Store in covered refrigerator jar.

CAESAR SALAD

Encourage a guest to show off his culinary skills by tossing this salad at the table. Of course you will have all the ingredients ready. Great Caesar!

1 large head romaine lettuce, washed, dried and crisped
1 clove garlic
½ c. vegetable oil
1 c. ½-inch French bread cubes
¾ t. salt
¼ t. dry mustard
¼ t. freshly ground pepper
1½ t. Worcestershire sauce
6 anchovy fillets, drained and chopped
1 egg
2 T. grated Parmesan cheese
2 T. lemon juice

Crush ½ clove of garlic and combine with oil in a covered jar. Let stand ½ hour. Heat 2 tablespoons of the oil-garlic mixture in a skillet. Trim crusts from bread and add bread cubes. Sauté until brown. Set aside. To remaining oil-garlic mixture, add lemon juice, salt, mustard, pepper, Worcestershire sauce and anchovies. Shake well. Bring 2 inches of water to a boil in a small pan. Turn off heat, place egg in water, let stand 1 minute, remove to cool. Whip into dressing.

Just before serving, rub inside of salad bowl with ½ clove of garlic; discard. Cut coarse ribs from romaine leaves and tear into bite-sized pieces in salad bowl. Shake dressing and pour over romaine. Sprinkle with cheese. Toss until well coated. Sprinkle bread cubes over salad, toss again and serve at once. Makes 4 to 6 servings.

WATER CHESTNUT SALAD

Water chestnuts have practically no calories, so indulge yourself with the dressing.

½ c. mayonnaise
¼ c. sour half-and-half
1 T. tarragon vinegar
2 t. anchovy paste
⅛ c. finely snipped chives
⅛ c. snipped parsley
½ clove garlic, minced
1 can water chestnuts, drained and sliced

Combine first 7 ingredients and pour over the water chestnuts. Chill several hours before serving. Makes 2 to 4 servings.

SALADE D'ÉPINARDS

This is the happiest way we know to eat spinach.

1 10-oz. bag fresh spinach
1 t. salt
½ t. pepper
2 t. Dijon mustard
2 T. red wine vinegar
½ c. olive oil
¼ t. lemon juice
5 radishes, sliced thin
1 small onion, sliced in rings

Wash spinach and dry completely. Break off stems and chill. Mix salt, pepper and mustard, then add vinegar. Beat in olive oil with fork until mixture has consistency of thin mayonnaise. Stir in lemon juice. Pour over chilled spinach, add sliced radishes and onions, toss. Yield: 4 to 6 servings.

Revive slightly wilted salad vegetables and greens in a bath of water and ice cubes.

CHICKEN SALAD SUPREME

Dress up chicken salad with cantaloupe balls and serve in hollowed-out scalloped cantaloupe shells. Hollowed-out pineapple shells with the pineapple cubes added to the salad make attractive servers, too.

4 c. diced cooked chicken
½ c. chopped celery
2 c. seedless grapes (optional)
½ t. salt
½ t. pepper
½ c. mayonnaise
½ c. sour cream
½ t. Dijon mustard
Salted pecan halves or toasted almonds

Sprinkle chicken with 1 teaspoon olive oil or 1 tablespoon French dressing. Combine chicken, celery, grapes, salt and pepper and toss lightly with mayonnaise, sour cream and mustard. Add nuts. Serves 6 to 8.

COOL AS A CUCUMBER SALAD

Prepare in the morning to enhance a warm summer night's dinner.

1 to 2 cucumbers, pared and thinly sliced
1½ T. vinegar
½ t. salt
1 T. sugar
1 c. sour cream or yogurt
1 green onion, snipped
1 t. dill weed, snipped
½ t. celery seed
¼ t. dry mustard

Combine all ingredients except cucumbers, mixing well. Pour over cucumbers. Refrigerate for several hours.

VARIATION ON CUCUMBER SALAD

3 unpeeled cucumbers, thinly sliced
1 red or Bermuda onion, thinly sliced
1 red or green pepper, thinly sliced
2 cloves of garlic on toothpicks
1 T. Kosher salt
½ c. vinegar
¾ c. sugar

Combine garlic, salt, vinegar and sugar. Mix well and pour over cucumbers, onion and pepper. Refrigerate for up to 3 weeks. Remove garlic before serving. Makes 4 to 6 servings.

TOMATOES VINAIGRETTE

Add a Mediterranean touch to summer or winter tomatoes.

4 to 6 tomatoes, sliced
1 clove garlic, minced
½ t. salt
¼ t. pepper
½ t. oregano
¼ t. thyme
2 T. wine vinegar
2 T. olive oil
1 T. minced onion

Combine all ingredients except tomatoes. Pour dressing over sliced tomatoes. Cover and chill for at least 6 hours or overnight. Serve as salad or relish. Serves 4.

DELI COLE SLAW

Make a big batch and have "crunch" on hand.

3 lbs. cabbage, shredded
2 onions, chopped
1 green pepper chopped or sliced
1 c. vinegar
1 c. safflower oil
1 T. celery seed
1 t. salt
1 c. sugar

In a saucepan, combine vinegar, oil, celery seed and salt; bring to a boil. Stir in sugar. Combine cabbage, onion and green pepper in a bowl. Pour dressing over and refrigerate up to 3 weeks if necessary. Serves 8 to 10.

GREEK SALAD

Fit for the gods; and the smart goddess makes the dressing the day before.

¼ c. wine vinegar
½ c. olive oil and anchovy oil
1 bay leaf
1 clove garlic
1 t. oregano
1 head romaine
½ head lettuce
4 endive leaves
2 red onions, thinly sliced
2 tomatoes, quartered
1 cucumber, scored and sliced
½ green pepper, cut in strips
6 radishes, sliced
8 to 10 Greek olives
1 can anchovy fillets, drained, save oil
¼ to ½ lb. feta cheese

Cut garlic in half and spear with toothpick. Combine vinegar, oils, bay leaf, garlic and oregano. Mix well and chill several hours or overnight. Wash and dry greens. Combine with remaining vegetables, anchovy fillets and cheese. Before serving, remove bay leaf and garlic from dressing; shake well and pour over salad. Makes 4 to 6 servings.

FRESH MUSHROOM SALAD

Do use a variety of salad greens.

  3 T. fresh lemon juice
  ⅔ c. olive oil
  3 T. wine vinegar
  1½ t. salt
  ¾ t. pepper
  3 cloves garlic, minced
  10 to 12 c. mixed greens
  1 lb. mushrooms, thinly sliced
  1 c. croutons

Place lemon juice, oil, vinegar, salt, pepper, and garlic in a jar; shake well and refrigerate. Prepare greens and mushrooms in salad bowl. Bring dressing to room temperature and shake well before pouring over greens and mushrooms. Sprinkle with croutons. Makes 6 to 8 servings.

WATERCRESS SALAD

  2 to 3 bunches watercress, leaves only
  16 cherry tomatoes
  3 T. olive oil
  1 T. lemon juice
  ½ t. Dijon mustard
  1 clove garlic, minced
    Salt and freshly ground pepper to taste

Wash and dry watercress leaves and tomatoes; place in a bowl. Combine remaining ingredients in a jar and shake well. Shake dressing again before adding to salad. Serves 4.

SUNNY CITRUS SALAD

  ½ lb. fresh spinach
  1 bunch romaine
  1 to 2 oranges
  1 sweet red onion, thinly sliced
  1 t. salt
  ½ t. dry mustard
  ½ t. paprika
  1 c. salad oil
  6 T. honey
  ¼ c. white vinegar
  2 T. lemon juice

Wash and dry greens; destem spinach. Tear greens into small pieces; and peel oranges and cut crosswise into about eight ⅛-inch slices. Combine greens, orange slices and onion in a bowl. Mix remaining ingredients; pour over salad and toss lightly. Serves 4 to 6.

SPINACH SALAD

This stupendous salad is a course by itself.

  1 lb. fresh spinach, washed, destemmed and dried
  ¼ c. salad oil
  ⅛ c. red wine vinegar
  ⅛ c. lemon juice
  1 clove garlic, minced
  ¼ t. salt
    Dash freshly ground pepper
  2 T. Parmesan cheese (optional)
  1 hard-boiled egg, chopped
    Bacon chips

Prepare spinach; refrigerate until ready to serve. Mix together oil, vinegar, lemon juice, garlic, salt and pepper and blend well. Just before serving, shake dressing well and pour over spinach, tossing well. Sprinkle eggs, bacon chips and cheese over all. Makes 4 to 6 servings.

ARTICHOKE-GRAPEFRUIT SALAD

Pastel and picture pretty.

  1 15-oz. can artichoke hearts
  ¼ c. salad oil
  2 T. vinegar
  1 t. Worcestershire sauce
  ½ t. salt
  ⅛ t. pepper
  1 T. chopped parsley
    Lettuce, romaine, endive
  2 pink grapefruits, sectioned

Drain artichoke hearts and cut in halves. Combine oil, vinegar, Worcestershire, salt, pepper and parsley; mixing well. Pour over artichokes in bowl and chill for several hours. Combine greens, add artichoke mixture and grapefruit. Toss and serve. Serves 4.

CREAMY GARLIC DRESSING

Dress-up mayonnaise.

  1 c. mayonnaise
  ½ c. buttermilk
  ¼ c. finely minced onion
  2 T. finely snipped parsley
  1 clove garlic, minced

Combine all ingredients and blend well. Makes 1½ cups.

LO-CAL DRESSING

½ c. cider vinegar
¼ c. water
3 T. salad oil
1 clove garlic, minced
½ t. dry mustard
½ Worcestershire sauce
¼ t. crushed oregano leaves
¼ t. salt

Shake all ingredients until well mixed. Keep refrigerated. Stir or shake before serving. Makes 1 cup.

COLE SLAW DRESSING

A cream-style dressing.

1 c. sour cream
½ c. mayonnaise
4 T. vinegar
2 t. sugar
½ t. salt
¼ t. pepper
1 t. minced onion

Combine all ingredients and chill. Pour over shredded cabbage, carrot and green pepper. Makes 1¾ cups.

FRENCH DRESSING

½ t. salt
¼ t. paprika
½ t. dry mustard
¼ t. white pepper
1 T. lemon juice
⅓ c. cider vinegar
1 clove garlic, minced
1 c. salad oil

Combine all ingredients in a covered jar and mix vigorously. Shake well before using. Makes 1⅓ cups.

ITALIAN DRESSING

½ c. olive oil
¼ c. wine vinegar
½ t. salt
1 clove garlic, minced
½ t. oregano, crushed
½ t. basil, crushed

Combine all ingredients in covered jar and shake well. Makes ¾ cup.

CREAMY ONION DRESSING

1 heaping T. onion soup mix
1 T. white vinegar
1 T. water
1 t. sugar
½ c. sour light cream

Mix together all ingredients. Makes ¾ cup.

HERB YOGURT DRESSING

1 c. plain yogurt
¼ c. parsley, minced
¼ c. mayonnaise
3 green onions, snipped
1 T. lemon juice or vinegar
  Salt and pepper to taste
2 t. sugar

Mix all ingredients until well blended. May be used for a green salad or as a sauce for cold meat or fish. Makes 1½ cups.

POPPY-SEED HONEY DRESSING

For fruit salads.

3 T. wine vinegar
3 T. lemon juice
3 T. honey
½ c. salad oil
1 t. poppy seed
½ t. dry mustard
½ t. paprika
¼ t. salt
⅛ t. pepper

Put all ingredients in a covered jar and shake vigorously until well blended. Makes 1 cup.

CREAMY CHEESE DRESSING

Add to 1 cup mayonnaise:
½ c. crumbled blue cheese
½ c. sour cream
1 t. Worcestershire sauce
1 clove garlic, minced (optional)
⅛ t. white pepper
¼ t. salt
2 T. milk

Combine all ingredients and blend well. Makes 1 cup.

Note: Calorie counters use ½ cup mayonnaise and ½ cup sour half and half.

SOUR CREAM DRESSING

1 c. sour cream
¼ t. salt
Celery salt to taste
1½ t. lemon juice
¼ c. honey
½ t. dry mustard

Combine all ingredients and chill.

MAYONNAISE DRESSING
(LOW-CAL)

½ c. cottage cheese
1 egg, beaten slightly
⅛ t. freshly ground pepper
⅛ t. dry mustard
1 T. tarragon vinegar

Place all ingredients in an electric blender and blend at low speed until creamy.

Note: Change ratio of 2 parts oil to 1 part vinegar. By reversing, you can reduce calories in a 2 tablespoon serving from 160 to 80 calories. Season wine vinegar with minced onion, crushed garlic, dry mustard, salt, pepper, thyme or basil.

THOUSAND ISLAND DRESSING

1 c. mayonnaise
1 t. Worcestershire sauce
1 t. instant minced onion
¼ c. sweet pickle relish
2 t. finely chopped green pepper
1 hard-boiled egg, finely chopped
1½ c. sour cream
½ c. chili sauce

Combine all ingredients, folding in sour cream last. Refrigerate.

FRENCH DRESSING NO. 2

⅓ c. sugar
1 t. celery salt
1 c. vegetable oil
4 T. vinegar
1 t. salt
1 t. paprika
½ t. minced onion (optional)
1 t. dry mustard

Combine all ingredients and blend until smooth. Chill.

CONDIMENTO DI ITALIANA

¼ c. olive oil
2 T. tarragon vinegar
½ t. sugar
½ t. dry mustard
Dash of freshly ground pepper

Mix all ingredients together, blend well. Chill.

VINAIGRETTE DRESSING

1 t. salt
½ t. pepper
2 t. Dijon mustard
2 T. red wine vinegar
½ c. olive oil
½ t. lemon juice

Mix all ingredients together, blend well. Chill.

OIL AND VINEGAR

1 t. salt
½ t. pepper
2 t. Dijon mustard
2 T. red wine vinegar
½ c. olive oil
¼ t. lemon juice

Mix all ingredients, blend well. Chill.

ITALIAN SALAD DRESSING

½ c. olive oil
¼ c. wine vinegar
1 t. salt
1 small clove garlic, cut into small pieces
1½ T. sugar

Combine ingredients in a jar and shake well until thoroughly blended. Keep refrigerated. Shake well before using.

GREEN GODDESS DRESSING

1 c. mayonnaise
½ c. sour cream
2 T. tarragon vinegar
1 clove garlic, minced
5 t. anchovy paste
¼ c. snipped chives
¼ c. snipped parsley

Combine all ingredients. Refrigerate several hours before serving.

Pictured opposite:
Artichoke-Grapefruit Salad, p. 128

MOLDS

CRANBERRY MOLD

A tradition at holiday dinners, here is one way to serve cranberries.

2 3-oz. pkgs. cherry gelatin
2 c. boiling water
1 c. pineapple juice (plus water)
1 lb. fresh cranberries
1 orange
1 c. sugar
1 7-oz. can crushed pineapple, drained
¼ c. chopped nuts (optional)

Dissolve gelatin in boiling water, add pineapple juice plus water. Stir and chill until of jelly-like consistency. Coarsely grind cranberries and orange. Drain and discard liquid. Add sugar and let stand for 10 minutes. Add crushed pineapple and nuts and stir into semiset gelatin. Spoon into lightly oiled 6-cup mold and refrigerate until firm. Serves 10 to 12.

Note: 1 16-oz. can whole cranberry sauce may be substituted for fresh berries. Omit sugar.

TOMATO ASPIC

Pretty and peppy with shrimp, crab meat, chicken or tuna salad.

4 c. tomato juice
1 bay leaf
⅛ t. pepper
1 small onion, sliced
1 T. parsley
1 T. celery leaves
1 t. salt
1 clove garlic
1 t. sugar
2 T. lemon juice
3 T. unflavored gelatin (dissolved in ½ c. cold water)

Simmer all ingredients except lemon juice and gelatin for 15 minutes. Strain and pour into lemon juice and gelatin mixture. Stir until dissolved. Cool, then pour into a lightly oiled 6-cup mold. Chill until firm. Yield: 10 to 12 servings.

EGG SALAD MOLD

A fix-ahead winner, serve as an hors d' oeuvre, appetizer or luncheon entrée.

12 hard-boiled eggs, chopped
½ c. chopped celery
½ c. chopped green pepper
2 t. grated onion
¼ t. white pepper
½ t. Worcestershire sauce
1 snipped green onion
1 c. mayonnaise
2 t. salt
1½ T. unflavored gelatin (dissolved in ¼ c. cold water)
¾ c. hot water

Combine all ingredients. Pour into a greased 6-cup mold. Chill until firm. Unmold and serve with bread rounds or crackers. Serve with shrimp sauce or decorate with black caviar if desired.

SHRIMP SAUCE

½ c. mayonnaise
1 t. chili sauce
1 can small shrimp, washed and drained

Stir together all ingredients and chill until needed. Makes 12 servings.

CUCUMBER RING

Put summer on your luncheon table— spring, fall or winter.

1 T. unflavored gelatin
½ c. cold water
½ t. salt
4 c. creamed cottage cheese
2 3-oz. pkgs. cream cheese, softened
½ c. mayonnaise
1 medium cucumber, pared, seeded and grated
1 green onion, snipped
⅔ c. finely chopped celery

Soften gelatin in cold water. Add salt. Heat and stir over low heat until gelatin is dissolved. Beat cheeses together; add mayonnaise and gelatin. Stir in cucumber, onion and celery. Pour into a lightly oiled 6-cup ring mold. Chill 6 to 8 hours or overnight. Garnish with cherry tomatoes and radishes.

SALMON MOUSSE

Use a slice of olive for an eye and the fish will look like a whole poached salmon, swimming on a sea of endive. Serve as an appetizer or luncheon entrée.

- 1 can tomato soup
- 1 8-oz. pkg. cream cheese, softened
- 2 T. unflavored gelatin
  (dissolved in ¼ c. cold water)
- 1 1-lb. can salmon, drained and flaked
- 1 c. mayonnaise
- 1 green pepper, finely chopped
- 1 c. chopped celery
- 1 small onion, grated
- 1 T. Worcestershire sauce
- ½ t. salt
- ¼ t. white pepper

Heat soup and cream cheese over low heat until cheese dissolves. Add softened gelatin and stir until well blended. Add remaining ingredients and mix well. Place in a well-greased fish mold and chill overnight in the refrigerator. Unmold on a bed of endive or leaf lettuce. Serve with Dill Sauce.

DILL SAUCE

- 2 c. sour cream (or sour half-and-half)
- ½ t. salt
- ¼ t. pepper
- 1 T. chopped fresh dill *or* 1½ t. dried dill
- 2 T. snipped chives or green onions
- ¾ c. coarsely chopped cucumber, drained well

Mix all ingredients and chill before serving. Serves 12.

ORANGE SHERBET MOLD

Tastes like summer sunshine!

- 2 3-oz. pkgs. orange gelatin
- 2 c. boiling water
- ⅓ c. lemon juice
- 1 pt. orange sherbet, softened
- 1 can mandarin oranges, drained
- 1 7-oz. can crushed pineapple, drained
  (save juice)

Dissolve gelatin in boiling water. Cool and add lemon and pineapple juices. Chill until of jelly-like consistency. Beat in softened sherbet, fold in oranges and pineapple. Place in a lightly oiled 6-cup mold and refrigerate until firm. Unmold and decorate with clusters of grapes. Yield: 10 to 12 servings.

BLUE CHEESE MOLD

This blend of cheeses is a perfect foil for fresh fruits or vegetables.

- 2 3-oz. pkgs. cream cheese, softened
- 1 4-oz. pkg. blue cheese
- 1 t. Worcestershire sauce
- 2 T. snipped parsley
- ½ t. salt
- ½ t. paprika
- 1 T. unflavored gelatin
- 2 T. water
- ½ c. hot water
- 1 c. heavy cream, whipped

Mix the two cheeses until well blended. Add Worcestershire sauce, parsley, salt and paprika. Soften gelatin in cold water. Add hot water and stir until gelatin dissolves. Blend in cheese mixture and chill until mixture is of jelly-like consistency. Fold in whipped cream and pour into a lightly oiled 6-cup mold. Chill until firm. Makes 10 to 12 servings.

RASPBERRY RING

A rhapsody in raspberry! Delicious with chicken or tuna salad.

- 2 10-oz. pkgs. frozen raspberries, thawed
  (save juice)
- 2 3-oz. pkgs. raspberry gelatin
- 3½ c. berry juice plus water
- 1 c. sour cream
- 2 ripe bananas, sliced

Drain berries. Add water to juice to make 3½ cups liquid. Heat 2 cups of liquid to boiling, add gelatin and dissolve. Add remaining liquid and chill until of jelly-like consistency. Fold in drained berries, sour cream and sliced bananas. Pour into a lightly greased 6-cup mold. Chill until firm. Makes 10 to 12 servings.

ACCOMPANIMENTS

REFRIGERATOR PICKLES

Keep a cool hand on a hot summer's day with no-cook pickles.

- 7 c. sliced cucumbers
- 1⅓ t. salt
- 1 c. chopped green pepper
- 1 c. sliced onion
- 1 c. vinegar
- 2 c. sugar
- 1 T. celery seed

Mix cucumber slices with salt. Let stand 2 hours. Drain and add pepper and onion. Combine vinegar, sugar and celery seed; pour over all and refrigerate.

BRANDIED APRICOTS

Just like Grandma's used to taste.

- 2 large cans apricots
- 2 c. apricot syrup
- ¾ c. brandy
- 2 cinnamon sticks, broken
- 6 whole cloves
- ½ c. sugar

Combine syrup, brandy, spices and sugar; bring to a boil and simmer for 15 minutes. Pour over apricots. Cover and chill 3 to 4 hours.

PEACH CHUTNEY

- 2 large cans sliced peaches, drained
- 1 large green pepper, chopped
- 1 large onion, chopped
- ¼ c. candied or preserved ginger, chopped
- 1 c. brown sugar, packed
- 1½ c. cider vinegar
- ½ c. white raisins
- ½ t. salt
- ¼ t. ground cloves
- ¼ t. nutmeg
- ½ t. cayenne pepper

Put all ingredients except peaches in a large saucepan; slowly bring to a boil and simmer, uncovered, for 30 minutes until sauce is reduced. Add peaches and simmer slowly for 1 hour, stirring occasionally. Spoon into jars and refrigerate.

CRANBERRY CHUTNEY

Back to the old-fashioned Thanksgiving.

- 1 lb. cranberries, washed and dried
- 1½ c. sugar
- 1½ c. water
- 1 orange, unpeeled, cut up
- ½ onion, diced
- 1 c. white raisins
- 1 apple, diced
- ½ c. chopped celery
- ½ c. chopped walnuts
- 1 t. ground ginger

In a 3-quart saucepan, bring cranberries, sugar, water and orange to a boil. Add onion and raisins and simmer 10 minutes. Add apple, celery, walnuts, and ginger and simmer another 5 minutes. Chill in a glass jar.

HOT CURRIED PEARS

Creative touch, serve with lamb or turkey.

- 1 large can pear halves, drained, save ¼ c. syrup
- ¼ c. pear syrup
- ¼ c. raisins
- 1 T. chopped nuts
- 2 T. melted butter
- ¼ t. curry powder
- 2 T. brown sugar

Place pears, cut side up, in greased baking dish. Fill centers with raisins and nuts. Combine butter, curry powder, brown sugar and pear syrup. Spoon over pears. Bake in a 300° oven for 15 minutes. Makes 6 to 8 servings.

CRANBERRY SHRUB

A twist of the wrist and you have a refreshing start for brunch, luncheon or dinner.

- 1 pt. chilled cranberry juice
- 1 6-oz. can frozen pineapple juice
- 5 7-oz. bottles carbonated lemon-lime beverage
- 1 pt. lemon ice

Combine juices. Slowly add the chilled lemon-lime beverage. Float a spoonful of lemon ice in each glass.

Pictured opposite:
Brandied Apricots
Baked Candied Cranberries, p. 136

BAKED CANDIED CRANBERRIES

Start with fresh cranberries.

    1 lb. cranberries, washed and dried
1¾ c. sugar
    2 T. water
    3 to 4 T. lemon juice
    1 8-oz. jar orange marmalade
       Grated lemon rind (optional)
    ½ c. brandy (optional)

Spread cranberries in a 9 x 13-inch pan. Sprinkle water and sugar evenly over the top of the berries. Cover with foil and place in a preheated 325° oven for 30 to 40 minutes, or until cranberries pop. Shake pan once or twice during baking. Remove from oven and stir in lemon juice, orange marmalade and rind and brandy if desired. Chill well before serving. Makes about 3½ cups.

MELANZA SICILIANA

Eggplant relish for an appetizer or serve along with any dinner. We like it cold, but may be served warm.

    1 1-lb. eggplant, unpeeled and sliced
    3 T. salad oil
    1 onion, sliced
    1 green pepper, seeded and sliced
    1 red pepper or pimiento, seeded and sliced (optional)
    1 clove garlic, minced
    1 t. salt
    1 c. tomato sauce with tomato bits

Sauté eggplant and onion in oil until golden brown. Add peppers, garlic, salt and tomato sauce. Cover and simmer until tender, about 10 minutes. Coarsely chop vegetables and refrigerate. Add more salt if desired. Serves 4.

TOMATO RELISH

Everyone will relish this spicy, crunchy accompaniment to any meal.

    5 medium tomatoes, peeled, seeded and diced
    1 medium green pepper, diced
    1 medium onion, diced
    1 stalk celery, diced
    1 small cucumber, diced
    1 T. prepared horseradish
    1 t. salt
    ½ c. wine vinegar
    ¼ c. sugar
    1 t. mustard seed
    ⅛ t. ground cloves
       Dash pepper

Combine vegetables, horseradish and salt. Cover and let stand at room temperature for 2 hours. Drain well. Pour vinegar, sugar, mustard seed, cloves and pepper over vegetables, mixing well. Chill for 6 hours or overnight. Keeps 4 to 6 days.

FRESH MELON CHUTNEY

For the discriminating palate.

    2 cantaloupes, peeled, seeded and cubed
    1 large onion, chopped
    1 green pepper, chopped
    ½ c. chopped candied ginger
    1 clove garlic, minced
    1 lime, seeded and chopped
    ½ lemon, seeded and chopped
    1 t. cinnamon
    ½ t. ground cloves
    ½ t. ground allspice
    ¾ t. salt
    2 c. packed brown sugar
    2 c. cider vinegar
    ¾ c. white raisins

Combine all ingredients in a large heavy pot and bring to a boil. Reduce heat and cook, stirring frequently, over moderate heat 1½ to 2 hours until syrup thickens. Ladle immediately into hot sterilized jars and seal, or cool and store in refrigerator jars. Fills four to six 8-ounce jars.

QUICK CHILI SAUCE

Beautiful, spicy red chili sauce to serve or give as a gift.

- 1 large can tomatoes, chopped
- 1 large onion, chopped
- 1 large green pepper, chopped
- ½ c. vinegar
- ¼ t. allspice
- ¼ t. cloves
- ½ c. sugar
  Few drops Tabasco
- 1 t. salt

Combine all ingredients in a large saucepan. Simmer slowly until thick, 1 to 1½ hours. Stir occasionally to prevent sticking.

CHINESE SAUCE

- 1 can bean sprouts, drained
- 4 to 6 green onions, chopped
- 1 stalk celery
- 1 c. cubed chicken or shrimp (cooked)
- ¼ t. ginger
  Dash sugar
- 2 T. soy sauce
  Salad oil

Stir fry vegetables and meat in a little oil. Add seasonings. Sauce may be thickened with 1 teaspoon cornstarch added to 1 tablespoon broth or water; stir in until clear.

MUSHROOM SAUCE

- ½ lb. fresh mushrooms
- 2 T. butter
- 3 T. flour
- ½ t. salt
  Dash pepper
- 1½ c. milk
- 2 t. lemon juice
- 1 T. dry sherry

Slice mushrooms and sauté in butter. Stir in flour, salt, pepper and milk. Cook, stirring, until smooth. Add lemon juice and sherry.

TOMATO SAUCE

- 1 1-lb. can tomatoes, chopped
- 1 onion, chopped
- ½ to 1 green pepper, chopped
- ⅛ t. ground cloves
- ⅛ t. allspice
  Tabasco
- ½ t. salt
- ¼ c. sugar
- 2 T. vinegar

Combine all ingredients in a saucepan. Simmer for about 1 hour.

SUPER SAUCE

This sauce has clout; keep it on hand to dress up ham or pork.

- 2 T. cream-style horseradish
- ½ t. dry mustard
- 1 10-oz. jar red currant jelly
- ½ c. raisins

Mix together all ingredients in a small saucepan. Heat over low heat, stirring, until melted and well-blended. Serve either hot or cold with baked or boiled ham, roast pork, or sautéed Canadian bacon.

MOCK BEARNAISE SAUCE

This sauce makes a steak very special.

- 2 T. tarragon vinegar
- ½ t. dried tarragon
- ½ c. mayonnaise
- 1 egg yolk
  Salt and pepper to taste

Combine vinegar, tarragon, mayonnaise and egg yolk in top of double boiler. Place over hot, not boiling, water. Beat with a whisk until mixture has thickened and is warm. Correct seasoning to taste with salt and pepper. Makes ¾ cup.

BEURRE MANIE

An uncooked thickening agent used to thicken sauces and gravies.

- ¼ c. butter
- 4 T. flour

Cream together and shape into tablespoon amounts (balls). Freeze in a plastic bag or box. When needed, add to hot liquid and stir until it is dissolved and the sauce is thickened to desired consistency. One tablespoon will thicken about ¾ cup liquid.

CHERRIES JUBILEE

Dim the lights and flame this delicious and dramatic dessert at the table.

1 1-lb. can pitted Bing cherries, drained
¾ c. currant jelly
½ c. Kirsch (or brandy)
Ice cream balls

In a chafing dish over direct heat, melt currant jelly, stirring gently. When jelly has melted, add cherries. Heat slowly until simmering. Pour Kirsch into center of fruit. Do not stir or it will not flame. Let it heat, then light carefully with a match. Immediately spoon flaming cherries over ice cream. Makes 4 to 6 servings.

CRANBERRY PUDDING

This very special recipe is unique to the Midwest, and has become a tradition in many households at holiday time. It is simple to prepare.

    1 egg, slightly beaten
    1 heaping T. sugar
    ½ c. light molasses
    ⅓ c. hot water
 1½ c. flour
    2 t. baking soda
    ½ t. salt
    2 c. fresh cranberries, washed and
        drained

Combine all ingredients in order listed. Pour into a greased mold and steam for 1 hour over simmering water, tightly covered. Make a steamer by punching holes in an aluminum pie pan and inverting it in the bottom of a saucepan with a tight-fitting cover. Serve warm with the following sauce. No other sauce will do!

SAUCE

    1 c. coffee cream
    ¼ lb. butter
    1 c. sugar
    ¼ t. salt
    1 t. vanilla

Heat cream, butter, sugar and salt to the boiling point. Remove from heat and add vanilla. Serve warm over warm pudding. Use the sauce liberally, as the pudding is tart.

CREME CAFÉ

A dessert spectacular; for a super spectacle, spoon into Chocolate Cups and top with whipped cream. Serve in champagne glasses if desired.

    1 c. coffee
    ½ lb. marshmallows
    2 T. brandy
    ½ pt. heavy cream, whipped
        (or whipped topping)

Melt marshmallows in coffee in a double boiler over hot water. Cool, add brandy. Fold in chilled whipped cream. Garnish with pecan or walnut half or a dollop of whipped cream if desired. Serves 6.

CHOCOLATE CUPS

One, two, three chocolate crinkle cups can be made days in advance and carefully stored in the refrigerator.

    8 1-oz. squares semisweet chocolate
    8 to 10 cupcake liners

Melt chocolate in the top of a double boiler over hot, not boiling, water. With a small spoon or pastry brush coat the insides of the paper cups with a thin layer of chocolate. Place cups in a muffin pan and refrigerate until firm.

Carefully peel paper from cups and refrigerate until ready to serve. Or fill cups with ice cream and place in the freezer.

Cups also may be filled with coffee ice cream or Crème Café and topped with whipped cream, chocolate curls or nuts. Makes 8 to 10 cups.

LEMON SURPRISE

A lemon sponge with custard sauce underneath is really a surprise.

    4 eggs, separated
 1½ c. milk
    1 c. sugar
    2 T. flour
    ¼ t. salt
    1 lemon, juice and grated rind

Beat egg yolks with milk. Mix together flour, sugar and salt and add to egg and milk mixture. Add lemon juice and rind. Beat egg whites until stiff and fold into custard. Pour into custard cups, then set in a shallow pan with water halfway up the cups. Bake in a preheated 350° oven 30 minutes. Refrigerate. Top with whipped cream and a cherry if desired. Serves 6.

CHOCOLATE MOUSSE

Sophisticated Chocolate Mousse in two versions. If you are cholesterol-conscious, try No. 2.

CHOCOLATE MOUSSE NO. 1

½ lb. German sweet cooking chocolate
5 eggs, separated
1 c. heavy cream, whipped
1 T. Grand Marnier (or Triple-Sec)
3 T. strong coffee

Melt chocolate in a double boiler over hot, not boiling, water. Cool. Beat egg yolks until thick and lemon-colored. Add liqueur and coffee. Combine with chocolate and blend until smooth. Beat egg whites until stiff. Fold carefully into chocolate mixture. Fold whipped cream into mixture and pour or spoon into glasses or greased mold. Makes 8 to 10 servings.

CHOCOLATE MOUSSE NO. 2

2 egg yolks
1 12-oz. pkg. semisweet chocolate pieces
1 c. scalded milk
½ t. instant coffee crystals.
3 ozs. brandy
4 egg whites
½ c. sugar
Whipped cream

Put egg yolks, chocolate, scalded milk, coffee and brandy in blender. Blend on high speed until chocolate chips liquefy. In a separate bowl, beat egg whites, slowly adding sugar and beating until very firm. Fold into chocolate mixture. Do not stir or beat. Refrigerate 2 hours. Serve with a dollop of whipped cream. Makes 12 4-oz. servings.

MACAROON MOUSSE

Cool, shimmering, amber elegance for a grand finale.

1 pkg. macaroon cookies
½ c. bourbon
½ c. water
1½ T. unflavored gelatin
4 eggs, separated
2 c. milk
1 c. sugar
½ pt. heavy cream, whipped

Soak macaroons in bourbon until most of liquid is absorbed. Line a lightly greased melon-shaped 4-cup mold with macaroons. Add gelatin to water and let stand 10 minutes. Beat egg yolks in a large saucepan. Add gelatin, milk, sugar and stir well. Cook over low heat until the mixture comes to a rolling boil, stirring constantly. Remove from heat. Beat egg whites until stiff. Fold them into the hot mixture, which will not be smooth. Pour into lined mold. Refrigerate overnight. Unmold and decorate with whipped cream around the white sides, leaving the amber gelatin top clear. Makes 12 servings.

FRAISES ET FRAMBOISES
(Strawberries and Raspberries)

Use your prettiest crystal sherbet, parfait, or champagne glasses so that the brilliant color of the two fruits will whet your appetite for the taste to follow.

1 to 1½ qts. strawberries, washed and hulled
½ c. sugar
1 10-oz. pkg. frozen raspberries, thawed
¼ c. Cointreau (or Triple-Sec)
2 T. confectioners' sugar
1 t. lemon juice

Refrigerate the strawberries, sprinkled with sugar, for 2 hours. Just before serving place raspberries, confectioners' sugar, lemon juice and Cointreau in blender and blend for about 1 minute or until smooth. Pour over individual servings of chilled strawberries. Garnish with a fresh mint leaf. Makes 6 to 8 servings.

FLAN

The simplicity of this recipe should not mislead you. It is a 1, 2, 3 way of preparing the classic dessert of Spain.

- 1 can sweetened condensed milk
- 2 c. whole milk
- 3 eggs
  Brown sugar

Beat eggs in a bowl, add sweetened condensed milk and whole milk and beat well. Pour mixture into individual custard cups. Place in a pan of water that comes up two-thirds of the way to sides of cup. Bake in a preheated 350° oven 1 hour or until a knife inserted in the center comes out clean. Remove from water bath and cool. Spread 1 tablespoon of brown sugar on top of each flan, spreading lightly to cover. Set under broiler for a couple of minutes until bubbly, watching carefully. Remove from oven and refrigerate. Makes 6 to 8 flans.

HOT FUDGE SAUCE

Fabulous! Pass it hot at the table.

- 3 1-oz. squares baking chocolate
- 1 T. butter
- 1 c. sugar
- 1 small can evaporated milk
- ½ t. vanilla

Melt chocolate and butter together in a heavy saucepan. Stir in sugar and milk. Continue stirring until sauce is thick. Add vanilla. Reheat over hot water if desired.

TORTONI

To complete an Italian dinner try this unusual dessert.

- 1 8-oz. pkg. cream cheese, softened
- 1 c. white corn syrup
- 1 c. milk
- 1 c. broken macaroons
- ½ c. chopped pecans
- 1 t. vanilla flavoring
- 1 t. almond extract
  Maraschino cherries

Mix cream cheese, syrup and milk until smooth. Stir in remaining ingredients. Spoon into paper baking cups set in muffin pan. Freeze until firm. Serve partially frozen and garnished with half a maraschino cherry. Makes 4 cups. Serves 16.

GEORGIAN TRIFLE

This dessert was originally created as a way to use stale cake. Our short cut to the custard sauce will send you hurrying to the market to buy fresh sponge cake.

- 1 sponge cake (or packaged shortcake shells)
- 1 jar raspberry jam
- ½ c. sherry
- 1 pkg. French vanilla instant pudding
- 2 c. milk
- ½ pt. heavy cream, whipped
  Strawberries, raspberries (optional)
  Slivered almonds (optional)

Split sponge cake into 1½-inch layers and spread each half with raspberry jam. Put cake together again and cut into cubes. Place in a crystal bowl and dampen with ¼ cup of the sherry, enough to flavor the cake but not to make it soggy.

Prepare pudding mix according to package directions and fold in remaining sherry. Whip cream and fold a quarter of it into the custard. Pour custard over cake cubes. Heap remaining whipped cream on top. Garnish with berries or slivered almonds. Refrigerate several hours before serving. Makes 8 to 10 servings.

CHOCOLATE MOUSSE PIE

Delicious chocolate! Served on a pretty plate, this chocolate pie is a heavenly treat.

- 1 9-inch baked pastry or crumb shell
- ⅔ c. sugar
- ¼ c. cocoa
- ⅛ t. salt
- 1 c. milk
- 1 T. unflavored gelatin
- ¼ c. cold water
- ½ t. vanilla
- 1 c. heavy cream, whipped

Combine sugar, cocoa and salt in a saucepan. Stir in milk and heat to boiling. Remove from heat. Dissolve gelatin in cold water and stir into hot mixture. Chill until mixture begins to thicken. Add vanilla. Fold in whipped cream and pour into pie shell. Chill until firm. Garnish with additional whipped cream if desired.

BOURBON POUND CAKE

Your husband will be glad to donate a little of his good bourbon to this cause.

- ½ lb. butter
- 1½ c. sugar
- 4 eggs, separated
- 1½ c. sifted flour
- 1 t. vanilla extract
- 1 t. almond extract
- ¼ c. (scant) bourbon
- ½ c. pecan halves

Cream butter and 1 cup of the sugar until light and fluffy. Add egg yolks one at a time, beating well after each addition. Add flour alternately with flavorings and bourbon, beating smooth after each addition. Beat egg whites until stiff but not dry. Beat remaining ½ cup of sugar gradually into egg whites. Fold batter gently into meringue. Sprinkle nuts into bottom of well-greased 9-inch tube or bundt pan and carefully turn batter into pan. Bake at 350° for 60 to 70 minutes or until a tester inserted in center comes out clean. Cool. Invert pan to turn out cake.

CHOCOLATE CAKE

Choc-o-holics will particularly enjoy this dessert. It is economical, both cost and time wise.

- 3 T. butter
- 1½ 1-oz. squares baking chocolate
- 1 c. sugar
- 1 c. flour
- 2 t. baking powder
- ¼ t. salt
- ½ c. milk
- 2 eggs
- 1 t. vanilla

Preheat oven to 350°. Put chocolate and butter in a baking dish and place in the oven to melt. In a large electric mixer bowl, measure and combine sugar, flour, baking powder and salt. Remove melted chocolate-butter mixture from oven and cool. Add cooled mixture to mixing bowl and beat at low speed of electric mixer for a couple of minutes. Add eggs, milk and vanilla and beat for 5 minutes at high speed. Turn into a greased 9 x 9-inch pan and bake 35 minutes at 350°. When cool either turn out of pan or frost in the pan with half of the recipe for Butter Cream Frosting Superb (see frostings).

FRUIT KUCHEN

An old-fashioned German dessert.

- 1¼ c. flour
- 1 t. baking powder
- 1 T. sugar
- ¼ lb. butter
- 1 egg, slightly beaten
- 1 T. milk

Mix first 3 ingredients together, then add butter and mix or cut in as for piecrust. Mix together egg and milk and add to above. Press in sides and bottom of 9 x 13-inch pan.

FILLING

- 4 to 6 peaches, peeled and halved
- 1 egg, slightly beaten
- 1 c. sour cream
- 1½ T. flour
- ¾ c. sugar

Place peaches on crust, cut side up. Mix egg, sour cream, flour and sugar. Pour over fruit.

STREUSEL

- ¾ c. sugar
- 2 T. butter
- 2 T. flour
- ½ t. cinnamon

Cream sugar and butter; cut in flour and cinnamon.

Cover fruit with streusel and bake at 350° for 45 minutes or until fruit is baked and streusel is a delicate brown.

Note: Use 1½ cups cherry or blueberry pie filling instead of peaches if desired. Pitted plums or peeled quartered apples are also good.

GREEK HONEY CAKE

Moist, rich and sweet, this is a traditional Greek dessert.

¾ c. butter
¾ c. sugar
3 eggs
1 c. sifted flour
1½ t. baking powder
½ t. salt
½ t. cinnamon
¼ c. milk
½ t. grated orange rind
1 c. chopped walnuts

Cream butter and sugar well. Add eggs, one at a time, beating well after each addition. Sift together flour, baking powder, salt and cinnamon and add to batter. Stir in milk and orange rind. Beat well and stir in nuts. Pour into a greased and floured 9 x 9-inch pan. Bake in a preheated 350° oven 30 minutes or until done. Remove from oven, cut into diamond shapes in pan while still hot. Pour cold syrup over the cake and refrigerate for at least 1 to 2 hours before serving.

SYRUP

½ c. sugar
1 c. honey
¾ c. water
1 t. lemon juice

Mix sugar, honey and water in a saucepan. Simmer 5 minutes. Skim, add lemon juice, boil 2 minutes and cool.

HOT MILK CAKE

This cake, with its down-home taste, needs no frosting.

5 eggs, beaten well
2 c. sugar
2½ c. flour
¼ c. butter
1 c. milk
1 t. baking powder
1 t. vanilla
1 t. lemon extract

Add sugar to the beaten eggs and beat. Add flour a little at a time. Add baking powder with the last of the flour. Heat milk and butter to boiling point and pour it over the first mixture. Stir in well. Add flavorings. Bake in a preheated 325° oven in an ungreased tube pan for 40 to 50 minutes.

DANISH PUFF

Come over for coffee. A special treat, Scandinavian-style.

BOTTOM LAYER

1 c. sifted flour
¼ lb. butter
2 T. water

Preheat oven to 350°. Measure flour into bowl. Cut in butter. Sprinkle with the water and mix with a fork. Round into a ball and divide in half. Pat dough with hands into two 12 x 3-inch strips. Place strips 3 inches apart on ungreased baking sheet.

TOP LAYER

¼ lb. butter
1 c. water
1 t. almond extract
1 c. sifted flour
3 eggs

Mix butter and water in a saucepan and bring to a rolling boil. Add almond extract and remove from heat. Stir in flour immediately, beating vigorously with a wooden spoon. When smooth and thick add one egg at a time, beating again after each addition until smooth. Divide in half and spread one half evenly over each strip of pastry. Bake about 60 minutes, until topping is crisp and nicely browned. Frost with a powdered sugar icing and sprinkle generously with chopped nuts.

CONFECTIONERS' SUGAR ICING

1½ c. confectioners' sugar
2 T. boiling water
1 t. lemon juice

Mix together and blend until smooth.

BLUEBERRY CAKE

Quick, easy, economical and freezes like a dream. A winner for a church or school bake sale!

¼ lb. butter or margarine
¾ c. sugar
1 egg
½ c. milk
1 t. vanilla
2 c. flour
2 t. baking powder
½ t. salt
1 pt. blueberries

Cream butter or margarine until soft. Beat in sugar and add egg. Beat until fluffy. Stir in milk and vanilla until blended. Stir in flour, salt and baking powder. Fold in blueberries. Spoon into a greased 9 x 9-inch cake pan.

TOPPING

½ c. sugar
⅛ stick butter or margarine
½ t. cinnamon

Mix all ingredients together lightly with a fork until crumbly. Spread on top of cake batter. Bake at 350° for 50 minutes.

SUMMER FRUITCAKE

The surprise ingredient in this cake is watermelon pickles, available year-round. And this cake takes only a few minutes to prepare.

1 c. sifted flour
¾ c. sugar
1 t. baking powder
½ t. salt
3 c. pecan halves
1 t. vanilla extract
1½ c. drained, cut-up watermelon pickles
1 c. maraschino cherries, drained and halved
3 eggs

Grease bottoms and sides of two 8½ x 4½ x 2½-inch loaf pans. Mix and sift flour, sugar, baking powder and salt; add nuts, pickles and cherries and mix. Beat eggs slightly; add extract. Add to flour mixture and mix until ingredients are well combined. Bake in a preheated 300° oven 1 hour. Makes two 1¼-pound cakes.

ORANGE BRUNCH CAKE

Cheerful and sunny for coffee time or Sunday brunch.

1 6-oz. can (¾ c.) frozen orange juice concentrate
2 c. sifted flour
1 c. sugar
1 t. baking soda
1 t. salt
¼ lb. butter or margarine
½ c. milk
2 eggs
1 c. raisins
⅓ c. chopped nuts

Grease and flour bottom of a 13 x 9-inch pan. In a large mixer bowl, combine ½ cup orange juice concentrate with flour, sugar, soda, salt, butter, milk and eggs. Blend at lowest speed of mixer 30 seconds. Beat 3 minutes at medium speed. Fold in raisins and nuts. Pour into pan. Bake in preheated 350° oven 30 to 40 minutes. Drizzle remaining orange juice concentrate over warm cake. Sprinkle with topping.

TOPPING

⅓ c. sugar
¼ c. chopped nuts
1 t. cinnamon

Combine all ingredients in a small bowl.

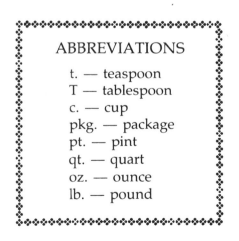

ABBREVIATIONS

t. — teaspoon
T — tablespoon
c. — cup
pkg. — package
pt. — pint
qt. — quart
oz. — ounce
lb. — pound

STRAWBERRY BAVARIAN SPONGE TORTE

2 pkgs. strawberry gelatin
1 c. boiling water
2 pkgs. frozen sliced strawberries, slightly thawed
½ pt. heavy cream, whipped (or whipped topping)
1 sponge cake, cut in cubes
Whipped cream to decorate
Fresh berries to decorate

Dissolve gelatin in boiling water. Add berries and allow to partially thicken. Fold in ½ pint whipped cream. Toss with cake cubes and place in a greased springform or large mixing bowl. Chill torte overnight. Turn out on platter and frost with whipped cream. Garnish with whole strawberries. Serves 10 to 12.

CARROT CAKE

Stays moist for days.

1 c. margarine
2 c. sugar
4 eggs
2 c. flour
2 t. baking soda
2 t. cinnamon
1 t. salt
1½ t. vanilla
3 c. grated carrots
¾ c. chopped nuts
½ c. raisins (optional)

Cream margarine with sugar until light and fluffy. Add eggs one at a time. Sift flour, soda, cinnamon and salt together and add to mixture. Add vanilla, carrots, nuts and raisins and mix well. Pour into a greased 13 x 9 x 2-inch pan and bake in a preheated 325° oven for 55 to 60 minutes or until done. Cool and frost with Cream Cheese Frosting.

Note: You may substitute 1¼ cup salad oil for margarine.

CREAM CHEESE FROSTING

1 3-oz. pkg. cream cheese
4 T. margarine
2 c. confectioners' sugar
1 t. vanilla

Cream cheese and margarine together. Add sugar gradually. Add vanilla and beat until smooth and creamy. Spread on cake. May be doubled for thicker frosting.

CHOCOLATE FUDGE SHEET CAKE

Short-cut to a long cake. Better than brownies because it tastes like fudge.

1 c. water
1 c. margarine or butter
¼ c. cocoa
2 c. flour
2 c. sugar
1 t. baking soda
½ t. salt
½ t. cinnamon
1 c. sour cream *or* ½ c. buttermilk
2 eggs
1 t. vanilla

Combine water, margarine and cocoa in a saucepan and bring to a boil. Remove from heat. Combine flour, sugar, soda, cinnamon and salt. Add hot cocoa mixture. Beat until smooth. Add sour cream or buttermilk, eggs and vanilla and beat well. Pour into a greased 15½ x 10½ x 1-inch pan. Bake in a preheated 350° oven for 20 to 30 minutes. Pour Frosting over hot cake.

FROSTING

½ c. butter
¼ c. cocoa
6 T. milk or buttermilk
1 t. coffee crystals
⅛ t. cinnamon
16 oz. confectioners' sugar
1 t. vanilla

In a saucepan, combine butter, cocoa, coffee crystals and milk. Bring to a boil; remove from heat. Beat in cinnamon, sugar, vanilla, beating until smooth and creamy. Pour over hot cake. Nuts may be sprinkled on top if desired. Freezes well.

Pictured opposite:
Strawberry Bavarian Sponge Torte

QUICK TORTES

Two desserts-for-a-crowd that must be made ahead and refrigerated overnight. One is lemon, one is chocolate; both are spectacular, with a checkerboard design visible when sliced.

LEMON TORTE

1 large or 1½ small angel food cakes
1 T. unflavored gelatin
¼ c. cold water
6 egg yolks
⅔ c. lemon juice
2 t. grated lemon rind
1½ c. sugar, divided
6 egg whites
1 pt. heavy cream, whipped
Shredded coconut (optional)

Trim brown crusts from cake and cut cake into cubes. Soften gelatin in the cold water. Combine egg yolks, ¾ cup sugar, lemon juice and rind. Cook over hot (not boiling) water. Stir until mixture coats spoon. Remove from heat and add gelatin, stirring until dissolved. Cook until partially thickened. Beat egg whites, gradually adding ¾ cup sugar. Beat until stiff. Fold into custard and mix with cake cubes. Pour into a lightly oiled torte pan or large bowl and refrigerate overnight. Remove from pan and frost with whipped cream. Sprinkle with coconut if desired. Serves 12.

CHOCOLATE TORTE

1 large angel food cake
1 c. sugar
1½ T. unflavored gelatin
¼ c. cold water
¾ c. boiling water
5 eggs, separated
2 1-oz. squares baking chocolate
1 pt. heavy cream, whipped

Trim brown crust from cake and cut cake into cubes. Melt chocolate and cool. Dissolve gelatin in the cold water. Add boiling water and let stand. Beat egg yolks, add chocolate and gelatin. In a separate bowl, beat egg whites until stiff but not dry and fold into chocolate mixture. Fold in cake cubes and pour into a lightly oiled springform or large bowl. Refrigerate at least 8 hours. Unmold and frost with whipped cream and shaved chocolate. Serves 12.

ELSIE'S SCHAUM TORTE

A gourmet dessert that's prepared in minutes and raved about for hours.

9 egg whites
2¾ c. sugar
1 T. vinegar
½ t. cream of tartar
1 t. almond extract
½ t. salt
½ pt. heavy cream, whipped
Strawberries

Preheat oven to 400°. Put first 6 ingredients into a large mixing bowl and beat until meringue holds its shape. Then beat some more, and still some more. Spoon into a 9-inch springform with an aluminum foil collar. Turn oven down to 275° and bake torte 1½ hours. Keep in oven until cool. Frost with whipped cream, refrigerate and garnish with fresh strawberries before serving. Serves 10 to 12.

Note: Do not bake on rainy or humid days.

APRICOT TORTE

A sweet show-off that's easy to make.

½ lb. vanilla wafers, crushed
1 c. butter
1⅓ c. confectioners' sugar
3 eggs
1 large can peeled apricots, drained
1 c. chopped pecans
1 pt. heavy cream, whipped

Line an 8 x 12-inch pan with waxed paper. Crush vanilla wafers into fine crumbs. Cream together butter, sugar and eggs until smooth. Cut up the apricots. Arrange in layers in the following order: crumbs (reserve 3 tablespoons crumbs for top), butter mixture, apricots, nuts, whipped cream, sprinkle of crumbs. Refrigerate for 12 hours. Makes 12 servings.

WHIPPED CREAM FROSTING

1 t. unflavored gelatin
4 T. cold water
1 c. heavy cream (or frozen whipped topping)
¼ c. confectioners' sugar
¼ t. vanilla

Combine gelatin and cold water. Dissolve over hot water and let stand. Beat whipping cream slightly. Pour cooled gelatin into cream. Add sugar gradually, then vanilla. Beat until stiff. Chill in refrigerator 10 minutes before frosting cake. Cake may be frosted hours before serving and returned to refrigerator. Add one of the variations if desired.

VARIATIONS

¼ c. chocolate syrup
½ c. crushed pineapple, drained
Sweetened cocoa mix to taste

Sprinkle top with one of the following:

Toasted coconut
Chopped nuts
Grated or shaved sweet or semisweet chocolate
Crushed toffee bars
Whole strawberries

Plain, sweetened or flavored whipped cream frosts a cake, too, but holds only a short time.

BROILED TOPPING

The finishing touch for a cake mix or a plain bakery cake.

⅓ c. melted butter
⅔ c. brown sugar
¼ c. cream or evaporated milk
½ c. coconut
½ c. chopped pecans

Mix all ingredients together and spread on a baked 8- or 9-inch cake. Broil carefully at low heat until bubbly and toasted. Watch it carefully to prevent burning.

CONFECTIONERS' ICING

6 T. butter, softened
1½ c. confectioners' sugar
1 T. milk
1 t. vanilla

Cream butter and sugar together. Add a little milk, cream well, add more milk if too stiff. Add vanilla and mix well.

VARIATIONS

Omit milk and add 1 tablespoon orange juice and ½ teaspoon grated orange rind, or 1 tablespoon lemon juice and ½ teaspoon grated lemon rind.

BUTTER CREAM FROSTING SUPERB

1 c. milk
4 T. flour
2 T. coffee or 2 1-oz. squares baking chocolate, melted (optional)
½ lb. butter or ¼ lb. butter and ¼ lb. margarine
1 c. sugar
1 t. vanilla

Mix milk, coffee or chocolate and flour together. Bring to a boil, lower heat and simmer until thick and smooth. Cool to room temperature, placing a small pat of butter on top. Beat butter and sugar together until light and fluffy. Add cooled flour mixture and beat at low speed of electric mixer 2 to 3 minutes. Add vanilla and blend. Sprinkle jimmies, nuts or coconut over the top if desired.

RICH GLAZE

An easy frosting for brownies or cake.

1 1-oz. square unsweetened chocolate
2 T. water
¼ c. butter
1 c. confectioners' sugar
1 t. vanilla

Combine chocolate, water and butter in a saucepan. Stir over low heat until chocolate and butter are melted. Remove from heat. Add sugar, blend well. Stir in vanilla.

PIES

FRUIT GLAZES FOR PIES, TORTES AND FLANS

PINEAPPLE GLAZE

1 16¼-oz. can crushed pineapple, drained (save juice)
1 T. cornstarch
1 T. sugar
½ t. vanilla
Yellow food coloring

Mix cornstarch and sugar together. Stir in pineapple juice and cook until thick and clear, about 5 minutes. Remove from heat and add vanilla, pineapple and 1 or 2 drops of yellow food coloring. Cool and spread over cake or pie.

BLUEBERRY GLAZE

1 c. water
2½ T. cornstarch
1 c. sugar
2 T. lemon juice
1 pt. blueberries, washed

Mix sugar and cornstarch together. Gradually add water and stir until smooth. Stir in ½ cup blueberries. Cook, stirring constantly, until thick and clear, about 5 minutes. When clear, add lemon juice. Cool. Arrange fruit on top of pie or cake. Add glaze. Chill until set.

STRAWBERRY OR RASPBERRY GLAZE

1 c. water
2½ T. cornstarch
1 c. sugar
2 T. lemon juice
1 pt. strawberries, washed and hulled (or 1 pint raspberries, washed)

Mix sugar and cornstarch together. Gradually add water and stir until smooth. Cook, stirring constantly, until thick and clear, about 5 minutes. When clear, add lemon juice and 1 or 2 drops of red food coloring. Cool. Arrange fruit on top of pie or cake. Add glaze. Chill until set.

BASIC CHEESE PIE

A dessert that always gets a smile; say, "cheese pie."

1 9-inch unbaked pie shell or graham cracker crust
1 8-oz. pkg. cream cheese, softened
½ c. sugar
3 eggs
2 T. flour
⅓ c. milk
1 t. vanilla

Put cream cheese in a bowl and beat until soft and smooth. Add sugar gradually and continue beating until smooth. Stir in flour and unbeaten eggs and beat. Add milk and vanilla and beat until cheese disappears. The filling will be liquid.

Pour filling into unbaked pie shell and bake at 350° for 40 minutes or until firm and delicately brown. To test doneness, insert tip of table knife into center of pie. If it comes out clean, pie is done.

TOPPING

1 c. sour cream
2 T. sugar
½ t. vanilla

Combine sour cream, sugar and vanilla. Spread on top of pie and return to oven for 10 minutes.

If preferred, omit topping and spread a fruit glaze on cool pie. Chill again before serving.

FRESH STRAWBERRY PIE

Pretty as a picture, this pie is fabulous.

1 9-inch graham cracker crust or baked pie shell
2 pts. strawberries, washed and hulled
1 c. sugar
3 T. cornstarch
2 T. lemon juice
Whipped cream

In a saucepan, crush 1 pint hulled fresh strawberries with a fork or a pastry blender. Stir in sugar combined with cornstarch and lemon juice. Cook over moderate heat, stirring until clear and thick. Cool. Halve another pint of berries; fold into cooled mixture. Pour into crust. Refrigerate until well chilled. Garnish with whipped cream.

Pictured opposite:
Pecan Pie, p. 152

CHOCOLATE SILK PIE

This smooth-as-silk pie is a classic man pleaser.

- 1 9-inch baked pie shell
- 1 c. butter, softened
- 1½ c. sugar
- 4 1-oz. squares baking chocolate, melted and cooled
- 4 eggs
- 1 t. vanilla
- Whipped cream

Cream butter and sugar. Add chocolate and vanilla. Beat with electric mixer at low speed until well blended. Add eggs and beat 10 minutes. Pour into baked pie shell. Chill for about 3 hours. Top with whipped cream if desired. May be frozen.

PECAN PIE

This southern treat is very rich, so why not compound your calories by serving each portion with a dollop of whipped cream. Tomorrow we diet.

- 1 9-inch unbaked pie shell
- 3 eggs, beaten
- ½ c. sugar
- 1 c. dark corn syrup
- ⅛ t. salt
- 1 t. vanilla
- ¼ c. melted butter or margarine
- 1 c. pecans

Add sugar and syrup to the beaten eggs. Then add salt, vanilla and melted butter. Place pecans in bottom of unbaked pie shell. Add filling and bake at 350° for 50 to 60 minutes. The nuts will rise to the top of the pie filling to form a brown crust.

FOOLPROOF CRUST

- ¼ lb. butter or margarine, softened
- 1 c. flour
- ¼ t. salt

Cut flour and salt into butter and mix until a ball forms. Pat dough with hands into a 9-inch pie plate, mending if necessary and fluting edge if desired. Add filling and bake as directed.

For pie shell, prick generously with a fork and bake at 400° for 12 to 15 minutes or until golden brown.

FRENCH APPLE PIE

Apple pie is the most popular pie in America, but this one is not like Grandma used to make.

BOTTOM CRUST

Crumble and pat in bottom and sides of 9- or 10-inch pie plate:

- 1½ c. flour
- 6 T. butter
- ¼ t. salt

Combine and put in lined pie plate:

- 5 c. chopped pared apples
- 1 T. lemon juice
- 3 T. flour
- ¾ c. sugar
- 1 t. cinnamon
- ¼ t. salt

TOP CRUST

- ½ c. butter
- ½ c. brown sugar
- ⅛ t. salt
- 1 c. flour

Cream butter, sugar and salt until fluffy. Cut in flour until lumps form, then sprinkle over top of pie. Bake at 375° for 55 minutes.

OLD-FASHIONED PUMPKIN PIE

- 1 9-inch unbaked pie shell
- 1 c. sugar
- 2 T. flour
- ½ t. salt
- ½ t. ground ginger
- ½ t. cinnamon
- ½ t. ground nutmeg
- ⅛ t. ground cloves
- 3 eggs
- 1½ c. pumpkin
- 2 c. milk (1 c. evaporated milk and 1 c. water)
- 1 T. brandy (optional)
- Whipped cream
- Pecans

Mix together sugar, flour, salt, ginger, cinnamon, nutmeg and cloves. Beat in eggs. Stir in pumpkin, milk and brandy. Pour into unbaked pie shell and bake in a preheated 400° oven 45 to 50 minutes or until a knife inserted in the center comes out clean. Cool and serve garnished with whipped cream and pecans.

NO-ROLL PASTRY FOR PIE SHELL

1 c. flour
½ t. salt
6 T. margarine
2 to 3 T. cold water

Cut margarine into flour and salt with pastry blender until coarse crumbs appear. Sprinkle 2 to 3 tablespoons cold water into mixture and mix until it holds together in a ball. With lightly floured hands press into bottom and sides of a 9-inch pie plate. Prick bottom and sides with a fork to release air bubbles. Bake in a preheated 425° oven for 12 to 15 minutes until golden brown. If bubbles appear during baking, prick with fork. Cool before adding filling.

CREOLE NUT PIE

Bake something to lure your love.

1 9-inch unbaked pie shell
4 T. butter or margarine
1 c. sugar
3 eggs, well beaten
½ c. white raisins
½ c. finely chopped nuts
1 T. flour
¼ t. salt
½ t. cinnamon
½ t. cloves
1 t. vinegar

Cream butter and sugar until fluffy. Add eggs and continue beating. Combine nuts and raisins with flour; add to creamed mixture with salt, cinnamon, cloves and vinegar. Spoon into unbaked pie shell and bake in a preheated 325° oven about 45 minutes. When done, a silver knife, inserted in center, should come out clean. Cool on rack and serve cool. Makes 6 to 8 servings.

CHOCOLATE WHIPPED CREAM PIE

A splendid pie for chocolate lovers.

1 9-inch baked pastry or crumb shell
⅔ c. sugar
¼ c. cocoa
⅛ t. salt
1 c. milk
1 envelope unflavored gelatin
¼ c. cold water
½ t. vanilla
1 c. heavy cream, whipped

Combine sugar, cocoa and salt in saucepan. Stir in milk and heat to boiling. Remove from heat. Dissolve gelatin in cold water and stir into the hot mixture. Chill until the mixture begins to thicken. Add vanilla. Fold in whipped cream and pour into pie shell. Chill until firm. Garnish with additional whipped cream, if desired.

DESSERT CREPES

3 eggs
1⅓ c. water
1 c. flour
¼ t. salt

Beat eggs with half of the water; stir in flour and salt. Add remaining water; beat until smooth in blender, with mixer or whip. Let batter rest while preparing filling.

To cook: Lightly oil a 7 or 8-inch skillet or crepe pan. When hot, pour in 2 to 3 tablespoons batter, enough to lightly coat the bottom of the pan; turn pan so batter spreads evenly. Cook over medium heat until edges pull away from side of pan. Turn out, brown side up, on tea towels to cool. Continue until all batter is used up. Fold in quarters and serve with Orange Sauce. Flame with an additional cup of warmed brandy. Serves 6 to 8.

APPLE FILLING FOR CREPES

4 to 6 tart apples, sliced
¼ c. butter
¼ to ½ c. sugar
1 t. cinnamon

Sauté apple slices in butter. Sprinkle with cinnamon and sugar. Place about 1 tablespoon on each crepe and roll up. Bake in a 350° oven for 20 minutes. Brush with butter or serve immediately with Orange Sauce.

Orange Sauce

½ c. butter
1 c. confectioners' sugar
1 6-oz. can frozen orange juice
¼ c. Triple Sec

Melt butter over low heat. Add sugar, orange juice and a sprinkle of salt. Stir until smooth and hot. Heat Triple Sec and flame over hot crepes. Makes 20 to 24 crepes.

POIRES AU CHOCOLAT

Special ending to any dinner.

1 c. sugar
4 c. water
Juice of 1 lemon
2 cinnamon sticks
4 whole cloves
2 T. creme de menthe
6 firm pears with stems
4 1-oz. squares semisweet chocolate
4 T. sweet butter
Fresh mint or ivy type leaves

Dissolve sugar in water. Add lemon juice, spices and creme de menthe; simmer, covered, for 20 to 25 minutes. Carefully peel pears, leaving stems intact. Cut off bottoms so they will stand upright. Poach pears in gently boiling syrup just until tender, about 30 minutes. While cooking, turn from side to side. Cool pears in syrup and chill thoroughly overnight. Melt chocolate with butter over very low heat. Remove pears from syrup and dry carefully with paper towel. Using spoon dip dried pears in melted chocolate to coat evenly. Place on waxed paper and refrigerate until serving time. Decorate with mint leaves. Makes 6 servings.

POTS DE CREME

Satin smooth French custard.

1 6-oz. pkg. semisweet chocolate chips
1¼ c. light cream
2 egg yolks, beaten until thick with a dash of salt

In a heavy dry saucepan, over very low heat, stir chocolate until nearly melted. Stir in light cream and stir until smooth. Gradually stir egg yolks into chocolate mixture. Spoon into pots de creme cups or small glasses, filling two-thirds full. Cover and chill at least 3 hours.

Variation: For Mocha Pots de Creme add: ¼ c. sugar, 1 T instant coffee and ¼ c. coffee-flavored liqueur to cream.

APRICOT RUSSE

Subtle, smooth and wonderful.

¾ lb. dried apricots
½ c. sugar
½ c. slivered almonds
2 T. kirsch
1 c. heavy cream, whipped
1 pkg. lady fingers, opened

In heavy saucepan, cover apricots with cold water and slowly bring to a boil. Reduce heat and simmer 25 minutes, stirring to prevent sticking. Stir in sugar and cook 5 minutes more. Put small amount at a time in the blender and puree. Add more sugar if desired. When cool, stir in kirsch, almonds and whipped cream. Spoon into individual glasses or a large crystal bowl lined with lady fingers. Serve with additional whipped cream if desired. Serves 6.

FRAISES BRULÉE
(Strawberries and Cream)

Simplicity is sophistication. Here is a festive dessert with a French accent.

1 qt. fresh strawberries, washed and hulled
1 pt. heavy cream, whipped
1 c. brown sugar
1 T. Kirsch
3 T. brandy

Cover the bottom of a 2-quart casserole or soufflé dish with berries. Add enough Kirsch and brandy to just cover the fruit. Add 2 inches of whipped cream and a 1-inch layer of brown sugar. Refrigerate 4 hours. To serve, place under broiler to brown lightly and quickly for 1 to 1½ minutes. Makes 8 servings.

Pictured opposite:
Pots de Creme

BANANAS FOSTER

Add a flaming finale to your candle-lit dinner.

- 4 bananas, peeled, cut in half lengthwise twice
- ½ c. firmly packed light brown sugar
- 4 T. butter or margarine
  Dash of cinnamon
- ½ c. light rum
- ¼ c. banana liqueur
  Ice cream

Combine brown sugar, cinnamon and butter in chafing dish or skillet; heat, stirring constantly. Add bananas and just heat through. Heat rum and liqueur in small saucepan. Pour over bananas (do not stir) and light carefully. Spoon sauce over bananas until flame dies; spoon bananas and sauce over ice cream balls and serve immediately. Serves 4.

CHERRIES A LA RUSSE

Simple sophistication in several minutes.

- 1 1-lb. can dark, sweet, pitted cherries, drained
- ½ of 10-oz. jar currant jelly
- 2 to 3 T. orange-flavored liqueur
- 1 c. sour cream

Melt jelly over low heat. Stir in liqueur. Pour over cherries and chill for 1½ to 2 hours. Spoon into serving dishes and top with a generous dollop of sour cream. Serves 4.

FRESH FRUIT FLAMBÉ

A light dessert for a flaming finish.

- ¼ c. butter
- ½ c. brown sugar
- ½ t. grated lemon rind
- ¾ c. orange juice
- 1 pineapple, cut in chunks
- 2 pears, unpeeled, cut into eighths
- 1 to 2 apples, unpeeled, cut into eighths
- 3 oranges, peeled and sectioned
- ½ c. apricot flavored brandy

Melt butter in chafing dish or skillet. Stir in brown sugar, lemon rind and orange juice. Simmer until sugar is dissolved, stirring constantly. Add pineapple, pears, apples, simmer 10 minutes. Add oranges and simmer 3 minutes. Gently heat brandy; pour over fruit and ignite. Spoon into dessert dishes.

PEACH CLAFOUTI

Like a cobbler, like a crepe—very quick and very good.

- 2 T. sugar
- 3 c. sliced peaches, plums or pears
- 2 c. milk
- 3 eggs
- ¼ c. flour
  Pinch salt
- 3 T. sugar
- 1 t. vanilla
  Confectioners' or brown sugar

Sprinkle a deep dish pie or quiche pan with 2 tablespoons sugar. Place peaches on top. In blender beat milk, eggs, flour, salt, 3 tablespoons sugar and vanilla. Blend for 2 minutes. Pour over fruit. Bake in a preheated 375° oven for 45 to 50 minutes until puffed and golden. Sprinkle with confectioners' or brown sugar and glaze under the broiler for a few seconds.

LEMON FROMAGE

It's a snap with lemons.

- 3 eggs
- 2 egg yolks
- ½ c. sugar
  Grated rind of 1 lemon
  Juice of 2 lemons
- 1 T. gelatin
- ½ pt. heavy cream, whipped stiff
  Strawberries (optional garnish)

Beat whole eggs and yolks until light and frothy. Gradually add sugar and beat until thick. Add rind. Soften gelatin in lemon juice and dissolve over hot water. When cool, add to egg mixture, beating well. Fold in whipped cream and pour into a 1-quart melon mold or bowl. Chill about 4 hours or until firm. Unmold and serve with garnish of berries and whipped cream if desired.

FRENCH CREAM SLICES

A Napoleonic confection with the American touch of ease.

FIRST LAYER

⅓ c. butter or margarine
¼ c. sugar
1 1-oz. square baking chocolate
1 t. vanilla
1 egg, beaten
1½ c. graham cracker crumbs
½ c. chopped nuts
1 c. flaked coconut

Combine butter, sugar, chocolate in a saucepan or double boiler. Stir over low heat. Add vanilla and egg and simmer 5 minutes. Add crumbs, nuts and coconut. Press into a 9-inch square pan and chill 15 minutes.

The egg may be omitted and butter or margarine increased to ½ cup.

SECOND LAYER

½ c. butter or margarine
2 T. instant French vanilla pudding mix
2 c. confectioners' sugar
3 T. milk

Cream butter, pudding mix, sugar and milk, beating until light and fluffy. Spread over chilled first layer. Chill again 15 minutes and prepare glaze.

GLAZE

1 T. butter or margarine
1 4-oz. squares semisweet chocolate

Melt butter with chocolate and spread over second layer. Chill and cut into 8 slices or small squares. Keep refrigerated or freeze.

SUGAR N' SPICE WALNUTS

. . . And everything nice because you don't use a candy thermometer for this treat.

1½ c. walnut halves
¼ c. sugar
1 T. cinnamon
⅛ t. ground cloves
⅛ t. nutmeg
1 egg white, beaten slightly

Coat nuts thoroughly in egg white, a few at a time. Mix sugar, cloves, cinnamon and nutmeg together. Drop nuts into mixture. Place on buttered cookie sheet or nonstick pan and bake in a preheated 300° oven for 30 minutes.

DIAMOND HEAD DREAMS

A new way of putting things together.

½ c. butter
½ c. brown sugar
½ t. salt
1 c. flour

Cream butter and sugar. Add flour and salt and mix until crumbly. Press into bottom of 9 x 13-inch pan. Bake in a preheated 350° oven for 12 to 15 minutes until golden brown.

FILLING

3 eggs, well beaten
1 c. brown sugar
2 T. flour
½ t. salt
1 t. vanilla
½ t. almond extract
1½ c. coconut
½ c. chopped nuts (optional)

Mix all together and spread on baked crust. Return to oven, bake 20 to 25 minutes until toothpick comes out clean. Cool for ½ hour and cut into bars or squares.

DATE TORTE BARS

A sweet thought to send to students away from home. The recipe is so simple you'll want to make it often, and there are no bowls or beaters to wash.

¼ lb. butter
1 c. brown sugar, packed
2 eggs, slightly beaten
¾ c. flour
½ c. chopped nuts
½ c. chopped dates
1 t. vanilla
½ t. baking soda
¼ t. salt

Melt butter in 8- or 9-inch pan. Remove from heat. Add remaining ingredients and beat with fork until mixture is smooth and creamy. Bake at 350° for 35 minutes. Cut in squares or bars. Sprinkle with powdered sugar if desired.

WALNUT SHORTBREAD

This crisp, nutty shortbread will keep in a tightly covered tin for several weeks.

- 1 c. butter
- 1 c. margarine
- 1 c. sugar
- 1 c. chopped walnuts
- 1 t. vanilla
- 4 c. sifted flour

Cream butter and margarine; add sugar and beat until light and fluffy. Beat nuts and vanilla into mixture. Add flour and mix well. Pat dough into a 15½ x 10½ x 1-inch jelly roll pan, smoothing out to fill the pan evenly and level. Bake in a preheated 325° oven for 40 to 45 minutes or until golden. Cool in pan and then cut into bars. Makes seventy-five 1 x 2-inch bars.

TEA CRISPS

End your dinner with a light touch: tea crisps and sherbet.

- 1 c. butter or margarine
- 1 c. sugar (white or brown)
- 1 egg yolk
- 1 t. vanilla
- ⅛ t. salt
- 2 c. sifted flour
- ¼ t. nutmeg (optional)
- 1 t. cinnamon (optional)
- 1 egg white, slightly beaten
- ¾ c. chopped walnuts

Cream butter or margarine and sugar until light. Beat in egg yolk, vanilla and salt. Mix flour, nutmeg and cinnamon and stir into creamed mixture. Press mixture into an ungreased 15½ x 10½ x 1-inch baking pan. Brush with egg white and sprinkle with nuts, pressing them lightly into the surface. Bake in a preheated 350° oven 18 to 20 minutes. Cut into diamonds, squares or fingers while warm. Makes about 4 dozen.

TURTLES

- 2 c. flour
- 1 c. light brown sugar
- ½ c. softened butter
- 1¼ c. whole pecan halves
- 1 c. butter
- ¾ c. brown sugar
- 1 c. chocolate chips (semisweet or milk chocolate)

Mix together flour, 1 cup brown sugar and ½ cup butter. Firmly pat into a 9 x 13-inch glass pan. Place pecans evenly over crust. In a heavy saucepan, heat remaining brown sugar and butter, stirring constantly, until it comes to a boil. Boil just under 1 minute, stirring constantly. Pour evenly over pecan crust and bake in a preheated 325° oven 20 minutes. Remove from oven and sprinkle with chocolate chips. Wait 2 minutes and swirl as they melt, leaving some whole. Do not spread. Cool and cut into 3 to 4 dozen bars.

PATISSERIES FRAMBOISES
RASPBERRY BARS

A nice addition to your sweet table.

- ½ c. butter or margarine
- ½ c. brown sugar, firmly packed
- 1 c. sifted flour
- ¼ t. baking soda
- ¼ t. salt
- 1½ c. rolled oats
- 1 c. raspberry jam (or apricot preserves)
- 1 t. grated lemon rind

Beat butter or margarine and brown sugar in a bowl until fluffy. Sift together flour, soda and salt and stir into butter-sugar mixture. Add oats and blend thoroughly. Press two-thirds of mixture over bottom of a greased 9 x 9-inch baking pan. Mix lemon rind into the jam and spread evenly over bottom crust. Sprinkle with remaining one-third crumb mixture, patting lightly onto filling. Bake 30 minutes in a preheated 350° oven or until lightly browned. Cut into bars while slightly warm. Makes 2 dozen.

LEMON BARS

These lemony little cakes are perfect for coffee time, tea time, party time, anytime.

    2 c. sifted flour
    ½ c. confectioners' sugar, sifted
    ½ lb. butter or margarine

Sift flour and sugar. Cut in butter until mixture clings together. Press evenly into a 9 x 13-inch baking pan. Bake in a preheated 350° oven for 20 to 25 minutes or until lightly browned.

FILLING

    4 eggs, beaten
    1 c. sugar
    ⅓ c. lemon juice
    1 t. grated lemon rind
    1 c. flaked coconut (optional in crust)
    ¼ c. flour
    ½ t. baking powder

To the beaten eggs add sugar combined with flour and baking powder, lemon juice and rind. Pour over baked crust and bake for 20 to 25 more minutes. Cut while warm. When cool sprinkle with confectioners' sugar or ice with the following glaze.

GLAZE

    ½ c. confectioners' sugar
    1 T. melted butter
    1 T. lemon juice

Combine sugar with butter and lemon juice and beat until smooth. Spread lightly on bars.

DATE BALLS

A nutritious nibble for health food enthusiasts. Wheat germ supplies the crunch.

    1 3-oz. pkg. cream cheese, softened
    2 c. confectioners' sugar
    1 c. snipped dates
    ½ t. salt
    ½ c. wheat germ
    ½ t. cinnamon

Mix sugar into softened cream cheese until smooth. Add dates and salt and mix well. Form into balls. Mix wheat germ and cinnamon together. Roll date balls in the mixture to coat. Chill. Makes 12 to 18 balls.

PECAN TARTS

These bit-sized tarts are a show-off treat for a tea or ladies' luncheon.

PASTRY

    1 3-oz. pkg. cream cheese
    ½ c. butter or margarine
    1 c. flour

Soften butter and cream cheese at room temperature. Blend and stir in flour. Chill slightly about 1 hour. Shape in 2 dozen 1-inch balls and place in ungreased tiny muffin cups. Press dough on bottom and sides of cups.

FILLING

    ¾ c. brown sugar
    1 egg
    1 T. butter, softened
    1 t. vanilla
      Dash of salt
    ½ c. chopped pecans
    24 pecan halves

Beat together egg, sugar, butter, vanilla and salt until smooth. Add chopped nuts to mixture and fill pastry-lined cups. Top with pecan half. Bake at 325° for 25 minutes. Cool and remove from pans. Makes 24 tarts. Recipe may be doubled.

SCOTCH SHORTBREAD

In Scotland, shortbread is eaten with a glass of Scotch. Tea-time favorites with us, they will become a cookie tin favorite with you. But don't expect them to stay there long. No one can eat just one.

    ½ lb. butter
    ½ c. sugar
    2 c. flour

Cream butter until very soft. Add sugar and beat until light and fluffy. Add flour ½ cup at a time, mixing well after each addition. Mix until all flour is blended and the bowl is clean. Press the mixture into an 8 x 12-inch ungreased cookie pan with hands to about ¼- to ½-inch thick. Bake at 350° for 30 minutes. It should be slightly brown when done and may be soft in the center. Score for cutting while warm, cut when cool. Makes 2 to 3 dozen shortbreads.

KANELLA

These traditional Greek cookies are easy to make and keep indefinitely in a tightly covered container.

½ c. butter
½ c. sugar
½ c. brown sugar, packed
1 egg
2 T. milk
1 t. vanilla
2¼ c. flour
1 t. baking powder
1 t. cinnamon
½ t. salt
1 c. ground walnuts

Cream butter and sugars. Add egg, milk, vanilla and beat well. Sift flour with baking powder, cinnamon and salt. Add to batter gradually, mixing well after each addition. Stir in nuts. Pinch off pieces about ½ teaspoonful, roll into a ball and flatten into ovals. Bake on a greased or nonstick cookie sheet in a preheated 350° oven 12 to 15 minutes. Makes 6 dozen. Roll in confectioners' sugar while hot.

LACE WAFERS

These cookies are light and lacy. Do not try them on humid days, as they require dry air to become crisp.

½ c. sifted flour
½ c. shredded coconut
¼ c. brown sugar, packed
¼ c. butter or margarine
¼ c. dark corn syrup
½ t. vanilla

Combine flour and coconut. In a heavy saucepan melt butter, brown sugar and syrup. Bring to a boil. Remove from heat, blend in flour-coconut mixture. Add vanilla. Drop by scant teaspoonful about 3 inches apart on an ungreased cookie sheet. Bake at 325° for 8 to 10 minutes.

Allow cookies to set for a few minutes before removing to rack covered with paper towels. If cookies are hard to remove, return to oven for a few seconds to soften. Makes about 2 dozen.

MUD HENS

These puffy nut squares, topped with a dollop of whipped cream, will make dessert for a crowd. You will also like them "as is."

1 c. sugar
¼ lb. butter or margarine
3 eggs
1½ c. flour
1 t. baking powder
¼ t. salt
1 t. vanilla
2 c. brown sugar
1 c. chopped nuts

Cream butter and sugar until fluffy. Add 3 egg yolks and 1 egg white. Blend well. Add flour, baking powder and salt. Mix well. Add vanilla. Pat into a 10½ x 15½-inch greased jelly roll pan, using flour for your hands (dough will be sticky).

Cream brown sugar and 2 egg whites together and spread on dough. Sprinkle with nuts. Bake in a preheated 375° oven 20 to 25 minutes. It will be puffy. Cool for a few minutes before cutting into squares. Makes 35 large squares.

PRALINES

Cookie type.

1 c. dark brown sugar
1 T. flour
¼ t. salt
1 egg white
1 t. vanilla
2 c. chopped pecans

Mix together sugar, flour and salt until smooth and free of lumps. Beat egg white until stiff. Fold sugar mixture into egg white. Add vanilla and nuts and stir gently. Drop by teaspoonfuls onto a heavily greased cookie sheet. Bake in a preheated 275° oven for 25 to 30 minutes until brown. Cool 5 minutes. With a spatula, remove to wire rack to cool completely. Makes about 32 cookies.

> Shelled nuts should be refrigerated and will keep indefinitely in the freezer.

Have a Gourmet Christmas

The recipes in this festive section were selected from *Have a Gourmet Christmas*, the extra-special holiday cookbook for busy gourmets. In addition to delicious and traditional recipes such as Holiday Roast Duckling, Merrie Roast Pork Loin, and elegant Beef en Croute, the authors have included scrumptious desserts and delicious sweet breads to serve your family or use as holiday gifts for friends. This section provides easy, attractive party recipes planned to help you have a gourmet holiday season that will last throughout the year.

Contents

HOLIDAY WASSAIL

Fill the bowl and lift the cup to toast the holiday season with steaming hot wassail.

- 1 gal. apple cider
- 1 c. light brown sugar
- 1 6-oz. can frozen lemonade
- 1 6-oz. can frozen orange juice
- 12 whole cloves
- 6 whole allspice
- 1 t. ground nutmeg
- 1 4-inch cinnamon stick
- 2 bottles of port (optional)

In a large kettle, combine cider, sugar, lemonade and orange juice. Tie cloves and allspice into a small piece of cloth and add to cider. Add nutmeg and cinnamon stick; simmer gently for 20 minutes. Add wine; heat to steaming. *Do not boil.* Remove spice bag, discard and serve hot. Makes 30 to 35 servings.

Beverages

"'Tis the season to be jolly . . ." and here's a jolly good collection of holiday drinks—both hot and cold.

CRANBERRY PUNCH

- 2 qts. cranberry juice cocktail
- 2 small cans frozen lemonade, thawed
- 2 qts. ginger ale

Pour juices and ginger ale over ice in punch bowl and serve. Makes 25 to 30 servings.

MILKSHAKE PUNCH

Punch for the peanut butter set. Candy canes make colorful stirrers.

- 1 qt. milk
- 1 pt. vanilla ice cream, softened
- 1 pt. chocolate ice cream, softened
- ½ t. vanilla
- 2 T. sugar
- ¼ t. cinnamon

Beat together all ingredients until frothy. Makes 8 to 10 servings.

EGGNOG

Eggnog, festive and wickedly rich, is a Christmas tradition for many families. Recipe may be doubled.

- 10 eggs, separated
- ¾ c. sugar
  Dash salt
- 2 to 4 c. rum, brandy, bourbon, or rye (a combination of two is best)
- 1 qt. heavy cream, whipped
  Nutmeg

Beat egg yolks until lemon-colored and thick. Beat in sugar and salt. Slowly add liquor, constantly beating with a wire whisk. When all liquor is whisked in, stir in cream. Beat egg whites until stiff and fold into eggnog. Chill for several hours before serving. Dust each serving with nutmeg. Makes 25 to 30 servings.

SERVE COFFEE WITH A FLAIR OR A FLOURISH

A wonderful way to start an afternoon or end an evening.
Before dinner offer a selection of spices and garnishes such as:
  cinnamon sticks
  nutmeg
  orange or lemon peel
  brown or white sugar
  grated chocolate
  stiffly whipped cream

After dinner, to accompany coffee, serve:
  Curacao
  creme de cacao
  creme de menthe
  anise flavored liqueur

Anytime additions from almost everywhere:
  As in the West Indies, use rum, brown sugar and whipped cream.
  When in Vienna, use a dash of brandy.
  Go Hungarian with cinnamon stick, grated chocolate and whipped cream.
  Think Persian with cardamom seeds.
  Be Irish: whipped cream, sugar and dash of Irish whisky.

MULLED CIDER

Rendezvous around the bowl of hot spicy cider.

- 1 qt. apple cider
- ¼ c. firmly packed brown sugar
- 6 whole cloves
- 2 2-inch cinnamon sticks

Combine all ingredients in a saucpan. Bring to a boil and simmer 5 minutes. Serve in mugs or in cups. Makes 6 servings.

ARTILLERY PUNCH

This punch is aptly named.

1 c. sugar
Juice of 6 lemons
1 T. Angostura bitters
1 qt. sherry
1 qt. Burgundy
1 qt. Scotch
1 qt. brandy
1 qt. sparkling water

Combine sugar, lemon juice, bitters and liquors. Chill to blend flavors. Pour punch over ice, then add sparkling water. Makes 50 servings.

CAFE BRULOT

1 c. brandy
Peel of 1 orange
6 whole cloves
4 whole allspice
4 cinnamon sticks
3 T. sugar
3 c. hot double-strength coffee

In chafing dish, over direct heat, combine all ingredients except coffee. Heat until hot. Carefully ignite brandy with a long match. Let it flame for 1 to 2 minutes. Slowly pour coffee into flaming brandy. Ladle into cafe brulot cups or demitasse cups. Makes 8 servings.

COCOA

¼ c. cocoa
4 T. sugar
Pinch salt
Pinch cinnamon
1 c. water
3 c. milk
Marshmallow
Whipped cream

Combine dry ingredients in a small saucepan and add water gradually, stirring well. Cook over low heat for 3 to 4 minutes. Slowly add milk and heat until steaming hot. Serve with marshmallow or a dollop of whipped cream. Serves 4.

FRENCH CHOCOLATE

A warm way to toast the season.

2½ 1-oz. squares unsweetened chocolate
½ c. water
⅔ c. sugar
1 t. vanilla
¼ t. salt
½ c. heavy cream, whipped
4 c. hot milk

Heat chocolate and water over low heat, stirring until chocolate is melted. Add sugar and salt and bring to a boil. Add vanilla. Cool to room temperature. Fold in whipped cream. To serve, place 1 generous tablespoon in each cup and fill with hot milk. Makes 8 to 10 cups.

COFFEE LIQUEUR

2 oz. instant coffee crystals
2 c. boiling water
4 c. sugar
1 vanilla bean, diced
2 c. brandy

Stir instant coffee into boiling water. Add sugar, stirring until dissolved. Cool. Place half of diced vanilla bean in each of two 4/5-quart bottles. Pour 1 cup brandy into each bottle. Pour in cooled coffee mixture. Add more brandy if necessary to fill bottles to top. Cap and store at least 30 days.

COFFEE ALEXANDER

2 c. strong hot coffee
⅓ c. brandy
¼ c. heavy cream
2 T. creme de cacao
Whipped cream
Chocolate curls

In a heat-proof pitcher, combine strong coffee, brandy, heavy cream and creme de cacao. Pour into 4 or 5 heat-proof cups or mugs. Garnish with a dollop of whipped cream and a chocolate curl. Makes 4 servings.

Appetizers

"Deck the halls with boughs of holly . . ." sprays of evergreen and candles, candles, candles; and what is a more glowingly beautiful decoration than a buffet table laden with delicious appetizers and hors d'oeuvres?

CHEESY SHRIMP

A delicious beginning.

  1 c. cooked shrimp, chopped
  ½ c. grated Cheddar cheese
  1 T. minced celery
  1 T. minced onion
  3 T. mayonnaise
  ¼ t. dry mustard
  ½ t. lemon juice
  ¼ t. Worcestershire sauce
  2½ dozen bread rounds, toasted on 1 side

Combine all ingredients and spread on bread rounds. Broil 3 to 5 minutes until bubbly. Serve immediately. Makes 30 rounds.

QUICK PARMESAN PUFFS

A simple snack.

  1 c. mayonnaise
  ½ c. grated Parmesan cheese
    Dash cayenne or Tabasco sauce
  2 t. instant minced onion
    Party rye rounds

Combine all ingredients and mound generously on rye. Broil about 4 inches from heat 3 to 4 minutes until puffed. Makes about 32 puffs.

CAVIAR STAR

This will be the star of your show.

  2 8-oz. pkgs. cream cheese, softened
  ¼ t. beef bouillon crystals
  ½ c. sour cream
  ¼ c. mayonnaise
  1 to 2 green onions, minced
  2 small jars red caviar

Combine cream cheese, bouillon crystals, sour cream, mayonnaise and green onions; mix until well blended. Form into a square on a serving plate. Place caviar on top, forming into the shape of a star. Garnish platter with parsley, lemon slices, deviled eggs, black olives or any combination. Serve with melba toast or party pumpernickel.

MUSHROOM TARTS FOR A CROWD

Make the shells at your leisure and freeze. Let thaw at room temperature, bake and fill.

PASTRY

  2 c. flour
  ½ lb. butter or margarine, softened
  1 8-oz. pkg. cream cheese, softened

Blend together all ingredients to form a dough. Chill about 1 hour. Shape into 4 dozen 1-inch balls. Place each ball in an ungreased 1¾-inch muffin cup. Press dough against the bottom and sides of the cup. Bake in a preheated 400° oven 12 to 15 minutes or until golden brown.

FILLING

  ¾ lb. finely chopped mushrooms
  2 T. minced green onion
  2 to 3 T. butter
  ¼ c. flour
  ½ t. salt
  1 c. sour cream
  1 T. mayonnaise

Sauté mushrooms and green onion in butter. Blend in flour and salt. Cook, stirring constantly, until thickened and smooth. Add sour cream and mayonnaise; heat through. Spoon mixture into baked shells. Makes 48 Tarts.

GREAT LAKES DIP

For a tasteful gathering.

  ½ lb. smoked fish, skin and bones removed
  1 c. sour cream
  2 T. lemon juice
  2 T. snipped green onion
    Freshly ground pepper to taste
  ½ t. salt
    Parsley to garnish

Flake the fish. Combine all ingredients and chill for at least 60 minutes. Garnish with parsley and serve with crackers or an assortment of raw vegetables. Makes 1¾ cups.

Pictured opposite:
Caviar Star

FOR THE HORS D'OEUVRES TABLE

Beautiful, bright cherry tomatoes make colorful containers for endless fillings. Scoop inside out with a grapefruit knife or spoon. Invert and drain on paper towels while you make the fillings. Fills about 2 to 3 dozen.

HAM SALAD

1 c. ground or minced ham
1 T. prepared mustard
1 t. horseradish
1 t. minced onion
3 T. mayonnaise

Combine all ingredients and mix well.

DEVILED EGGS

4 hard-boiled eggs, minced
1 t. vinegar
1 t. mustard
1 t. Worcestershire sauce
2 T. mayonnaise

Combine all ingredients and mix well.

CHEESE

1 c. cottage cheese
2 T. chopped chives
2 T. mayonnaise
1 t. dried dill weed

Combine all ingredients and mix well.

CREAM CHEESE AND ANCHOVIES

1 8-oz. pkg. cream cheese, softened
1 can anchovies with capers, chopped
1 T. mayonnaise

Combine all ingredients and mix well.

CHEESE AND BACON

1 c. grated Cheddar cheese
4 slices bacon, cooked and crumbled
3 T. mayonnaise
1 t. mustard

Combine all ingredients and mix well.

CHICKEN SALAD

1 c. cooked chicken, minced
2 T. celery, minced
2 T. mayonnaise
1 T. sour cream
½ t. sherry

Combine all ingredients and mix well.

MINI CLAM BAKE

Ready in a minute!

1 8-oz. pkg. cream cheese, softened
1 8-oz. can minced clams, drained
2 t. instant minced onion
½ t. Tabasco sauce
48 round crackers
   Paprika
   Sliced black olives for garnish

Combine first 4 ingredients and mix well to blend. May be stored in refrigerator. Just before serving, spread 1 teaspoonful on each cracker. Place on a cookie sheet and bake in a preheated 400° oven 5 minutes. Sprinkle with paprika or garnish each with a sliver of black olive. Makes 4 dozen.

SMOKY PUFF

3½ oz. dried smoked beef, chopped
4 oz. grated Cheddar cheese
1 t. instant minced onion
5 T. mayonnaise
32 melba toast rounds

Combine first 4 ingredients and spread on melba toast rounds. Broil until cheese melts. Serve piping hot. Makes 32 Puffs.

FROSTED PATÉ

2 T. butter
¼ lb. mushrooms, chopped
1 medium onion, minced
3 T. butter
1 lb. liverwurst
½ c. ripe olives, sliced
1 8-oz. pkg. cream cheese, softened
½ c. sour cream
1 t. chicken bouillon crystals

Sauté mushrooms and onion in 2 tablespoons butter. Blend remaining 3 tablespoons butter with liverwurst; stir in mushrooms and onion. Using half of the mixture, form bottom half of loaf and stud with olive slices. Form top half of loaf from remaining mixture. Combine cream cheese, sour cream and bouillon crystals, mixing well. Frost loaf with cheese mixture. May be garnished with parsley, green or black olives, and pimiento slices. Serve with melba toast, party rye or pumpernickel.

SHRIMP SPREAD

For easy hostessing!

- 1 8-oz. pkg. cream cheese, softened
- 2 T. mayonnaise
- 1 T. lemon juice
- 1 t. chopped chives
- 1 garlic clove, crushed
- ½ lb. tiny, cooked shrimp

Blend all ingredients except shrimp. Stir in shrimp and serve with crackers and celery chunks. Makes 1½ cups.

PARTY IDEAS
CHRISTMAS OPEN HOUSE

Stop in and see the tree—open house from 5 to 8! This kind of party can be for all ages and very informal; it can be just for children or just for adults. The theme also can be more formal. All these parties are fun to have and fun to attend.
ALL AGES
Cranberry Punch, p. 164
Eggnog, p. 164
Coffee, p. 164
With these hours, some people may be coming before dinner, and some after, so you can have a wide assortment of things to nibble: trays of cheese and crackers, raw vegetables and dips, nuts, a turkey with assorted breads, and . . .
Fruitcake, p. 214
Cookies, pp. 216 to 219
Candies, pp. 219 to 220

COCKTAIL NUTS

Spicy nibbles!

- 2 T. butter
- 2 T. Worcestershire sauce
- ½ t. hot pepper sauce
- ¼ t. garlic powder
- 2 c. walnut or pecan halves
  Salt

Melt butter in a 13 x 9 x 2-inch baking pan. Stir in Worcestershire sauce, pepper sauce and garlic. Add nuts, stirring to coat each nut. Spread nuts in a single layer in pan. Bake in a preheated 250° oven 45 to 60 minutes, stirring occasionally, until nuts are lightly browned. Cool completely on paper toweling. Sprinkle with salt to taste. Store in a tightly covered container. Makes 2 cups.

ORIENTAL BEEF CUBES

A delicious blend of East and West

- ½ c. soy sauce
- ¼ c. sesame oil
- ¼ c. dry sherry
- 1 T. finely chopped ginger
- 1 T. sugar
- 2 large cloves garlic, minced
- 1½ to 2 lbs. boneless sirloin or top round, cut into ½-inch cubes

Combine first 6 ingredients in a glass bowl; stir to blend. Add meat cubes and refrigerate for at least 4 hours or overnight. Turn meat several times. Remove meat from marinade, reserving liquid. Broil meat 3 to 4 inches from heat for about 10 minutes; place in a chafing dish. Heat marinade just to boiling and pour over meat. Serve with wooden picks. Makes about 40 "bites."

ANCHOVY DIP

Serve with assorted raw vegetables.

- 1 c. mayonnaise
- ½ c. snipped watercress
- 1 2-oz. can anchovy fillets, chopped
- 1 clove garlic, minced
- 2 T. lemon juice

Combine all ingredients and chill.

CHEDDAR IN PORT

Keep refrigerated for a quick start.

- 2 T. butter or margarine
- 1 t. dry mustard
  Dash cayenne
- ½ lb. Cheddar cheese, grated
- 5 T. port wine

Cream butter with mustard and cayenne. Stir in finely grated cheese and wine. Blend thoroughly. Makes 1¼ cups.

BROIL UNTIL BUBBLY

Slices of party rye, melba toast or crackers, when topped with one of the following and broiled are nice to pass as a hot appetizer.

MUSHROOM

1 8-oz. pkg. cream cheese, softened
2 T. butter, softened
1 clove garlic, minced
1 small can mushrooms, drained and chopped

Mix together all ingredients. Heap on party bread slices and broil. Makes about 48.

CHEESE

2 c. grated Cheddar cheese
¼ c. mayonnaise
2 T. chili sauce
1 t. Worcestershire sauce

Mix together all ingredients. Heap on party bread or crackers. Broil. Makes about 48.

TURKEY

1 4-oz. pkg. Roquefort or blue cheese
¼ c. mayonnaise
Slices of turkey, small and thin

Combine cheese and mayonnaise, mixing well. Place turkey on bread; top with cheese mixture. Broil. Makes about 24.

CORNED BEEF

Tomato paste
Corned beef slices
Swiss cheese slices

Spread rye or pumpernickel with 1 teaspoon tomato paste. Top with corned beef and then cheese. Broil until cheese melts.

CURRIED CHICKEN

2 c. minced chicken
½ c. mayonnaise
1 t. curry powder (or to taste)

Mix together all ingredients. Heap on melba toast and broil. Makes about 48.

CHEESE BALL

Surround with crackers or sliced party bread.

1 8-oz. pkg. cream cheese
1 4-oz. pkg. blue cheese
⅛ t. Tabasco sauce
¼ t. Worcestershire sauce
¾ c. chopped nuts

Cream together softened cheeses. Blend in seasonings and ¼ cup of the nuts. Shape into a ball and roll in the remaining nuts. Wrap in clear plastic and chill.

MOCK LIVER PATÉ

½ lb. fresh liver sausage
1 3-oz. pkg. cream cheese
2 to 4 T. mayonnaise
2 hard-boiled eggs, finely chopped
1 t. instant minced onion
Sieved egg yolk or minced parsley for garnish

Combine first 5 ingredients and shape into a ball. Garnish with additional sieved hard-boiled egg yolk or minced parsley. Serve with crackers.

SWISS APPETIZERS

Swiss, swift and super! Prepare ahead and slide under the broiler just before serving.

Party rye or rounds of any bread toasted on one side
2 T. mayonnaise
1 t. mustard
Sliced processed Swiss cheese, cut in quarters

Spread untoasted side of bread with mayonnaise mixed with mustard. Top with a slice of cheese. Place on a cookie sheet and broil until the cheese starts to melt. Serve immediately while still bubbly hot. Makes as many as you need, up to 32.

Pictured opposite:
Onion Supper Soup, p. 173

Soups

"Strike the harp and join the chorus..." you'll sing the praises of soups which are easy to cook in the oven or from quick combinations on the pantry shelf.

SHRIMP BISQUE

1 10-oz. can tomato soup
1 10-oz. can green pea soup
1 10-oz. can beef consommé
1 soup can light cream
½ lb. cooked shrimp
¼ c. sherry
1 hard-boiled egg, chopped

Combine all soups in a saucepan; bring to a boil. Add cream, shrimp and sherry. Heat to steaming and serve garnished with egg. Serves 4 to 6.

SHERRIED PEA SOUP

1 10-oz. can split pea soup
1 soup can milk
1 10-oz. can chicken broth
½ c. dry sherry
Sour cream (optional)
Garlic croutons (optional)

Combine soups and milk. Heat gently until steaming. Add sherry. Garnish with sour cream or croutons or both if desired. Makes 4 to 6 servings.

MINESTRONE SOUP

1 lb. beef chuck, cut in 1-inch cubes
1 T. vegetable oil
1 28-oz. can tomatoes
3 c. water
1 t. salt
1 t. Italian seasoning
1 10-oz. pkg. frozen mixed vegetables
1 onion, chopped
1 6-oz. pkg. spiral noodles, cooked and drained
Grated Romano cheese

Brown meat in 1 tablespoon oil. Add tomatoes, water and seasonings. Cover and simmer 1 hour. Add vegetables, onion and cooked noodles; continue cooking until vegetables are tender. Sprinkle with grated Romano cheese before serving. Makes about 6 servings.

MULLIGATAWNY SOUP

Spicy chicken soup with vegetables; you may also use turkey if you like. Serve over a small mound of cooked rice, if desired.

1 cut-up fryer
¼ c. flour
1 t. salt
1 T. curry powder
¼ t. nutmeg
¼ t. pepper
¼ c. butter or margarine
3 carrots, sliced
2 tart apples, cut in eighths
1 medium onion, chopped
½ green pepper, chopped
¼ c. chopped parsley
2 stalks celery, chopped
1 28-oz. can tomatoes
4 c. water

Dredge chicken in mixture of flour, salt, curry powder, nutmeg and pepper. Melt butter in heavy kettle or Dutch oven and brown chicken. Add remaining ingredients; bring to a boil and simmer, covered, for 45 minutes to 1 hour. Remove chicken, discard skin and bones, cut into chunks and return to soup. Makes 4 to 6 servings.

RED BEAN SOUP

A quick and hearty soup made from in-the-house ingredients.

2 1-lb. cans kidney beans, drained
3 10-oz. cans beef consommé
1 c. water
1 medium onion, finely chopped
1 carrot, finely chopped
¼ t. basil
1 T. tomato paste
¼ c. sherry (optional)
2 slices bacon, fried and crumbled

Combine all ingredients except sherry and bacon; simmer for 60 minutes. Blend in blender or strain, if you like. Just before serving, add sherry and garnish with bacon. Serves 4 to 6.

MUSHROOM SOUP

2 10-oz. cans cream of mushroom soup
2 soup cans milk
¼ lb. mushrooms
2 T. butter
¼ c. sherry

Combine soup and milk; heat. Sauté mushrooms in butter and add to steaming soup. Stir in sherry and serve. Serves 2 to 4.

OYSTER STEW

Traditional Christmas Eve supper in many families. Delicious any time you can get fresh oysters.

1 pt. oysters with liquor
4 c. milk
¼ c. butter
Salt and pepper to taste
Sprinkle celery salt

Place oysters and liquor in a saucepan and cover. Simmer until the edges curl slightly. Add remaining ingredients; heat to steaming and serve. Makes 4 to 6 servings.

BEAN SOUP

This soup cooks in the oven while you go about your holiday business.

3 qts. water
1 lb. dried navy beans
1 ham bone
1 lb. ham or ham steak, cubed
2 stalks celery, diced
2 carrots, diced
1 onion, diced
1 8-oz. can tomato sauce
Salt and pepper to taste

Combine all ingredients in a large pot or roaster. Cover and bake in a preheated 325° oven 3 to 4 hours.

ONION SUPPER SOUP

A tureen of soup is a welcome gift. Take along a loaf of French bread.

1 lb. ground chuck
2 1¼-oz. pkg. onion soup mix
5 c. water
1 c. Burgundy wine
1 c. grated Parmesan cheese

Brown meat in soup pot; drain fat. Sprinkle with soup mix and stir in water. Bring to a boil and simmer slowly for 12 to 15 minutes. Add wine and heat through. When ready to serve, ladle into soup bowls and sprinkle with Parmesan cheese. Makes 4 to 6 servings.

NEW YEAR'S EVE GALA
A midnight supper is a festive way with
which to start the new year. Serve a steaming
tureen or two of soup, such as,
Oyster Stew, p. 173
Shrimp Bisque, p. 172
sliced ham, turkey or beef with cheeses
and assorted breads.
If you prefer a little more formality, serve
Mushroom Tarts, p. 166
Turkey Tetrazzini, pp. 102, 184
Beef en Croute, p. 176
Lamb Navarin, p. 177
Tomatoes Florentine, p. 191
Cranberry Sour Cream Mold, p. 194
Fruitcake, p. 214
Spumoni Parfait, p. 206
Any combination of these will make a
beautiful supper table.

"See the blazing Yule before us…" you probably won't roast your dinner on an open spit, but here are some how-to tips which will make you a blazing success.

Entrées

STANDING BEEF RIB ROAST

1 8-lb. standing rib roast
Salt
Pepper
Garlic powder

Place roast, fat side up, on rack in an open, shallow roasting pan. Insert meat thermometer into the thickest part of meat, not touching bone or fat. Do not add water. Sprinkle with salt, pepper and garlic powder. Place in a preheated 325° oven 3 to 3¼ hours or until thermometer registers 140° for rare or 160° for medium. Allow roast to stand 15 to 20 minutes before carving. May be served with Horseradish Sauce (p. 16). Makes 8 servings.

CARBONNADES FLAMANDES

Cook once—eat twice.

4 lbs. lean beef, cut in large cubes
Flour
2 t. salt
½ t. pepper
Oil to brown meat
4 medium onions, thinly sliced
2 cloves garlic
¼ c. butter
2 12-oz. cans beer
½ c. bouillon
2 T. brown sugar
2 T. catsup
1 t. marjoram
1 t. thyme
¼ c. minced parsley
¼ c. vinegar (optional)

Dredge meat in flour mixed with salt and pepper and brown in oil. In another skillet, sauté onions and garlic in butter. Add to meat along with beer, bouillon, sugar, catsup, marjoram, thyme and parsley. Cover and cook over low heat until meat is tender, 1 to 1½ hours. Just before serving, stir in vinegar. Serves 6 to 8.

PEPPER STEAK

3 to 4 green peppers, seeded and cut in chunks
½ to 1 lb. fresh mushrooms
3 T. butter
2 to 3 T. oil
1 2½ to 3-lb. beef tenderloin, thinly sliced
2 t. salt
½ to 1 t. pepper
1 t. oregano
2 cloves garlic, minced
2 T. tomato paste
¼ c. dry sherry
2 tomatoes, cut in eighths

Sauté green peppers and mushrooms in 1 tablespoon butter and 2 tablespoons oil until tender crisp. Set aside. Brown meat quickly (a few slices at a time) in 2 tablespoons butter and 1 tablespoon oil. Remove meat slices from pan as soon as they are seared. Combine all ingredients except tomatoes and place in large pan. Cook, covered, 5 minutes. Uncover; stir in tomatoes and heat thoroughly. Serve immediately. Serves 8.

RUSSIAN STEW

2 lbs. stewing beef, cut into chunks
2 c. chicken broth
1 8-oz. can tomato sauce
4 carrots, cut into chunks
2 onions, quartered
2 stalks celery, cut into chunks
1 t. dill
1 t. thyme
1 t. salt
1 cabbage, cut into eighths
Sour cream

Set aside cabbage and sour cream. Combine remaining ingredients in a covered casserole. Bake in a preheated 325° oven for 2 hours. Add cabbage and bake an additional 30 minutes. Serve with sour cream. Serves 4 to 6.

Pictured opposite:
Pepper Steak

175

BEEF EN CROUTE

1 2½ to 3-lb. fillet of beef tenderloin, trimmed
Salt and pepper to taste
2 t. garlic powder
2 7-oz. pkgs. onion crescent rolls
1 egg white

Turn thin tail of beef under and tie securely with string. The fillet should be about 9 or 10 inches long after securing. Sprinkle salt, pepper and garlic powder on top and place on a rack in a shallow pan. Roast in a preheated 425° oven 40 minutes. Remove from oven and cool. Cover and chill in refrigerator 4 hours or overnight. Remove string. Open rolls and carefully unroll dough. Do not separate rolls. Arrange dough pieces to form a rectangle on a lightly floured board. Pinch perforations together to make 1 piece of dough. With lightly floured rolling pin, roll dough to a 13 x 10-inch rectangle. Place the chilled fillet on dough, top side down. Bring edges of dough together down the center of the fillet. Brush with lightly beaten egg white and pinch to close. Turn ends of dough under meat to form a smooth seam. Place fillet, seam side down, in a shallow baking pan. Lightly roll out any leftover pieces of dough and use to cut flowers or leaves. Moisten with egg white and arrange over top of dough. Brush entire surface with egg white. Bake in a preheated 400° oven about 25 minutes, or until crust is browned. With 2 broad spatulas, lift fillet to serving platter. To serve, cut into thin slices. Serve with Madiera Sauce. Serves 6 to 8.

MADIERA SAUCE

1 c. sliced mushrooms
4 T. butter
2 T. flour
1 10-oz. can consommé
2 T. tomato paste
1 envelope beef concentrate
½ c. Madiera wine (or dry sherry)

Brown mushrooms in 2 tablespoons of the butter. Set aside. Slightly brown remaining 2 tablespoons butter; add flour and stir to a paste. Gradually add consommé, stirring constantly. Add tomato paste and beef concentrate; simmer, uncovered, about 10 minutes or until mixture is reduced by one-quarter. Add mushrooms and wine. Check for saltiness and add water, if necessary.

POT ROAST

½ 6-oz. can tomato paste
1 T. sugar
½ pkg. onion soup mix
½ c. Burgundy
½ c. water
1½ lbs. chuck roast

Mix together the first 5 ingredients. Pour over meat in a casserole. Cover and bake in a preheated 325° oven for 3 hours. Serves 2 to 4.

HORSERADISH SAUCE

3 T. prepared horseradish
1 T. prepared mustard
3 T. lemon juice
½ t. salt
1 c. sour cream

Combine all ingredients and mix well. Refrigerate, covered, until serving time. Makes about 1½ cups.

MERRIE ROAST PORK LOIN

1 3-lb. rolled pork loin roast
1 10-oz. jar apple jelly
¼ c. soy sauce
2 T. salad oil
2 T. lemon juice
2 cloves garlic, minced
½ t. ginger

Place roast in a glass baking dish. Combine remaining ingredients in a saucepan and cook over low heat until the jelly is melted. Remove from heat. Pour sauce over and refrigerate 3 hours, turning meat several times. Remove from sauce and roast in a preheated 350° oven about 2 hours, or until meat thermometer inserted in the center of roast registers 170°. During roasting, brush meat a few times with sauce. Let stand 10 minutes before serving. Serves 6.

CROWN ROAST OF PORK

The prince of roasts for your royal occasion.

Crown Roast, 2 ribs per serving
12 to 15 c. stuffing

Place roast in shallow roasting pan, rib side up. Heap stuffing in center. Cover stuffing and rib ends with foil. Roast in a 325° oven for about 3 hours until internal temperature registers 180° on a meat thermometer. Remove foil and roast an additional 60 minutes until well done (185°). Let stand 10 to 20 minutes before carving. Rib ends may be garnished with cherry tomatoes or small crab apples.

Note: Optional additions to stuffing may include cooked sausage, walnuts, chopped apples or green grapes.

MAPLE GLAZED HAM

A tempting entrée.

1 7 to 8-lb. fully cooked smoked ham shank
1 c. maple syrup
2 T. cider vinegar
1 T. prepared mustard
Whole cloves

Combine syrup, vinegar and mustard. Place ham, fat side up, on rack in shallow roasting pan. Pour about ½ cup mixture over ham and bake, uncovered, in a preheated 325° oven for 1½ hours. Baste every 30 minutes with additional sauce. Remove ham from oven and score fat into diamond shapes. Insert a clove into each diamond. Bake ham an additional 30 minutes or until a meat thermometer inserted into the thickest part of meat registers 140°. Let ham rest 15 minutes before carving. Makes 10 to 12 servings.

CURRIED HAM STEAK

Economical ham steak with a tasty topping of curried fruit.

2 ham steaks, ¼ to ½ inch thick
¼ c. butter
¼ c. brown sugar
1 T. curry powder
¼ c. raisins
1 1-lb. can pineapple slices, drained
1 1-lb. can apricot halves, drained
1 1-lb. can pear halves, drained

Melt together butter and brown sugar. Stir in curry powder. Place ham steaks in a large shallow baking dish. Top with fruit. Pour brown sugar sauce over all and bake for 30 to 45 minutes in a 350° oven until it bubbles and sizzles. Serves 4 to 6.

CURRY SAUCE

Try a curried sauce to make holiday ham or turkey leftovers take on a new air.

1 10-oz. can cream of celery or chicken soup
½ c. milk
1 T. curry (more or less to taste)
½ c. raisins
Snipped green onions

Heat soup, milk and curry powder, stirring until smooth. Add onion and raisins; serve over meat with rice.

LAMB NAVARIN

A combination of lamb and vegetables simmered with wine and herbs in the oven.

3 lbs. lamb, cut into 1-inch cubes
1 large onion, chopped
1 clove garlic, minced
2 c. chicken broth
¼ c. tomato paste
1 c. dry white wine
1 bay leaf
1 t. thyme
1 t. salt
1 10-oz. pkg. frozen peas
1 20-oz. pkg. frozen onions
3 carrots, cut into chunks

Combine first 9 ingredients in a covered casserole. Bake in a preheated 350° oven 2 hours. Add peas, onions and carrots. Bake an additional 45 minutes. Serves 6.

ROAST GOOSE

For a festive entrée.

1 goose, thawed, cleaned and dried

Choose the largest available goose. Remove all loose fat from the body cavity. Prepare Stuffing. Lightly fill wishbone area and body cavity with stuffing. Fasten neck skin to the back with a skewer. Fold wing tips onto back. Tuck drumsticks under band of skin at tail or tie together with string. Place goose, breast side up, on a rack in a shallow pan. Prick skin (not meat) all over with a fork. Insert meat thermometer deep into thigh muscle away from bone. Roast goose at 400° for 60 minutes. Reduce heat to 325° and roast an additional 2 to 2½ hours until meat thermometer registers 185°. Check stuffing temperature also for 165°. During entire roasting period, spoon off accumulated fat. Do not baste. When cooked, allow goose to rest 10 minutes before carving.

STUFFING

- **1 11-oz. can mandarin oranges**
- **1 c. white raisins**
- **2 c. chopped, unpeeled apple**
- **4 to 6 c. seasoned stuffing mix**
- **1 c. water**
- **½ c. apple juice**
  Sautéed onion and celery (optional)

Combine all ingredients and toss lightly. May be served with Plum Sauce.

PLUM SAUCE FOR PORK OR GOOSE

- **¾ c. port wine**
- **⅓ c. goose or pork drippings**
- **1 1 lb. 14-oz. can purple plums, pitted and drained**
  Few grains cayenne pepper
- **1 T. cornstarch**
- **2 T. cold water**
- **2 T. lemon juice**

Simmer port wine over moderate heat until just ¼ cup remains. Add drippings and simmer 5 minutes. Crush plums with fork and add to pan with cayenne. Mix cornstarch with cold water and stir into plum mixture. Stir until boiling, then simmer over low heat 15 minutes. Add lemon juice. Makes 2 cups sauce.

HOLIDAY ROAST DUCKLINGS

- **1 to 2 ducklings, thawed cleaned and dried**
  Salt
  Garlic powder
- **1 can whole cranberry sauce**
- **½ c. orange marmalade**
- **1 t. prepared mustard**
- **2 T. brandy**

Cut ducklings lengthwise in half. Slash skin around bottom of duck to keep from curling while roasting. Remove all loose pieces of fat. Sprinkle inside with salt and garlic powder. Place cut side down on rack in shallow pan and roast at 350° for about 2 to 2½ hours. During baking time, pierce skin and spoon out all fat. Duck is done when skin is brown and meat is no longer pink when pierced between leg and body. Combine remaining ingredients in a saucepan and heat, stirring to blend. Pass at table. Allow ½ duck per person.

ROCK CORNISH HENS

- **6 to 8 Rock Cornish hens, thawed and cleaned**
  Salt and pepper to taste
  Butter or margarine
  Paprika
  Garlic, minced
- **1 10-oz. jar currant jelly**

Sprinkle insides of hens with salt and pepper. Tie legs together with string. Rub hens with softened butter mixed with garlic and paprika to taste. Refrigerate or cook immediately. Arrange hens in a shallow pan and place in a preheated 425° oven for 60 minutes or until tender and well browned. Baste occasionally with melted butter. Heat currant jelly in a saucepan. Remove hens to a platter, cut strings and spoon melted warm currant jelly over each hen. Pass remaining jelly at the table. Serves 6 to 8.

Pictured opposite:
Chicken Della Robbia, p. 180

CHICKEN DELLA ROBBIA

Golden chicken with a wreath of beautiful fruit.

- 2 to 3 fryers, cut up
- 4 T. butter
- 2 T. salad oil
- 2 onions, sliced
- 1¼ c. water
- ½ t. instant chicken bouillon
- ½ lb. mushrooms, sliced
- 1 c. white raisins
- 2 t. salt
- ¼ c. lemon juice
- 1 clove garlic, minced
- ½ t. ground cloves
- ½ t. allspice
- ½ t. ginger
- ¼ c. brown sugar
- 1 c. walnut halves
- ½ c. water
- 1 T. cornstarch
- 2 c. green seedless grapes
- 2 c. orange sections
- 12 cherries

In a large Dutch oven or fryer, sauté chicken pieces in butter and oil until golden brown. Add onions and sauté. Combine 1¼ cup water with ½ teaspoon instant chicken bouillon. Add with mushrooms, raisins, salt, lemon juice, garlic, spices and brown sugar. Simmer, covered, turning 1 or 2 times, for 35 minutes or until tender. Add walnut halves. Push chicken to side of pan. Blend cornstarch with ½ cup water and stir into pan liquid. Heat until smooth and thickened. Add grapes, oranges and cherries and heat through for 2 to 3 minutes. Serve at once on heated platter or in a chafing dish. Serves 8 to 12.

CHICKEN COGNAC

Tempt your family with the unexpected.

- 4 chicken breasts
- ½ c. milk
- ½ c. biscuit mix
- ½ t. salt
- ½ t. minced garlic
- ½ t. paprika
- ½ c. sliced green onion
- 2 T. butter or margarine
- 1 egg yolk
- ½ c. light cream or milk
- ½ c. cognac

Dip chicken breasts in milk and drain. Combine biscuit mix, salt, garlic and paprika. Coat chicken with mixture and place, skin side down, in a greased baking dish. Bake in a preheated 425° oven for 30 minutes or until tender. Keep warm. Sauté onion in butter or margarine until tender. Beat egg yolk with cream and stir into onion. Cook over low heat, stirring constantly, until thickened. Heat cognac in a small saucepan until just hot (do not boil). Pour over chicken and ignite. When flame dies, pour hot sauce over chicken and serve immediately. Serves 2 to 4.

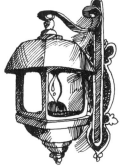

CHICKEN TARRAGON

- 2 fryers, cut up
- 2 T. salad oil
- 2 T. butter or margarine
- 6 shallots, chopped
- 2 carrots, sliced in rounds
- ¼ c. cognac
- 1 c. dry white wine
- ¼ c. water
- 1 T. dried tarragon
- 1 t. dried chervil
- 1 t. salt
- 1 t. pepper
- 1 c. light cream (optional)
- 1 egg yolk (optional)
- 1 T. flour (optional)

Wash chicken; dry well. In a 6-quart Dutch oven, heat oil and butter. Sauté a few pieces of chicken at a time until golden brown. Remove the chicken as it browns. Add shallots and carrots, stirring about 5 minutes. Return chicken to pan; sprinkle with warmed cognac and ignite. Add wine, water, crushed tarragon, chervil, salt and pepper. Bring to boil; reduce heat and let simmer gently 30 minutes. Remove chicken to a heated platter; keep warm. Optional: Strain drippings in pot. In a small bowl combine cream, egg yolk and flour; mix well. Stir into drippings; bring to a boil, reduce sauce by half. Pour over chicken. Makes 8 servings.

CHICKEN WITH POLYNESIAN VEGETABLES

2 frying chickens, cut up
2 T. butter or salad oil
Flour, seasoned with salt and pepper

Coat chicken lightly with seasoned flour. Melt butter or oil in a shallow baking dish. Arrange chicken pieces in pan. Bake, uncovered, in a 400° oven 20 minutes. Turn chicken, reduce heat to 350° and bake for 30 to 35 additional minutes, or until chicken is tender. Serves 6.

POLYNESIAN VEGETABLES

1 c. water
1 t. instant beef bouillon
1 T. soy sauce
½ t. ginger
2 c. diagonally sliced celery
2 c. diagonally sliced carrot
2 c. green pepper, cut into 1-inch pieces
1 c. sliced green onion
1 5-oz. can water chestnuts, thinly sliced
½ c. unsweetened pineapple juice
2 to 3 t. cornstarch

Combine first 4 ingredients in a saucepan. Bring to a boil; add celery, carrot and green pepper. Return to boiling; cover and simmer 5 minutes. Add green onion and water chestnuts. Cook 2 additional minutes. With slotted spoon, remove vegetables to heated dish and keep warm. Combine cornstarch and pineapple juice. Stir into broth and cook, stirring, until thickened. Pour over vegetables. Toss and serve. Serves 6.

SCALLOPED OYSTERS

A simple and delicious way to treat the delicate oyster.

1 qt. oysters with liquor
3 c. cracker crumbs
½ c. butter
1 to 2 c. milk
Dash pepper

In a greased casserole, make layers of oysters and crackers, ending with crackers. Dot each layer with butter. Pour enough milk over to bring liquid to the top layer of oysters. Sprinkle with pepper and dot with remaining butter. Bake in a preheated 350° oven for 50 to 60 minutes. Makes 6 to 8 servings.

BAKED FISH WITH OYSTER STUFFING

Whole baked fish with succulent oyster stuffing. This stuffing is also delicious with turkey.

1 4 to 5-lb. fish, dressed
Salt and pepper
1 T. lemon juice
¼ c. unsalted butter, melted

Wash and dry fish. Sprinkle cavity with salt, pepper and lemon juice. Place in a shallow, foil-lined baking dish. Stuff fish; secure opening and baste with butter. Bake in a preheated 350° oven for 45 to 60 minutes. Baste frequently. Allow ½ pound fish per person.

OYSTER STUFFING

2 stalks celery, diced
1 medium onion, chopped
½ c. butter
1 t. salt
1 t. poultry seasoning
½ t. sage
1 pt. oysters with liquor
4 slices bread, cubed and toasted

Sauté celery and onion in butter until golden. Add seasonings and oysters with liquor; simmer until edges of oysters curl. Remove from heat. Stir in bread cubes.

CLAMS AND SHELLS

Hear the good tidings!

1 large clove garlic, halved
⅛ c. salad oil
2 T. lemon juice
2 T. butter or margarine
2 cans clams (crushed or whole) and juice
½ t. salt
½ t. basil, crushed
¼ t. pepper
2 t. minced parsley, fresh or dried
1 7-oz. pkg. seashell pasta, cooked
¼ c. melted unsalted butter
1 c. grated Parmesan cheese

Brown garlic in oil; discard garlic. Stir in next 7 ingredients. Simmer 10 minutes, stirring occasionally. Cook and drain pasta; toss with butter. Mix with sauce and garnish with Parmesan cheese. Serves 2 to 4.

SOLE AND SHRIMP AU GRATIN

Pastel elegance.

  2 lbs. fillet of sole
  ½ t. salt
  ¼ c. dry sherry
  2 T. lemon juice
  2 T. butter or margarine
  2 T. flour
    Dash Tabasco sauce
  1 t. instant chicken bouillon
  ½ c. light cream
  ½ c. grated Parmesan cheese
  12 to 16-oz. shrimp, cooked and cleaned
    Snipped parsley

Arrange fillets in baking dish and sprinkle with salt. Combine sherry and lemon juice and pour over fish. Bake in a preheated 350° oven for 15 minutes. Drain juices and reserve. Return fish to oven and bake for another 10 minutes or until it flakes easily with fork. While it bakes, add enough water to the reserved broth to make 1 cup. Melt butter in saucepan over low heat. Stir in flour, Tabasco, broth and bouillon. Cook over low heat, stirring, until sauce is smooth and bubbly. Remove from heat; stir in cream. Heat just to boiling, stirring constantly. Add cheese and shrimp and stir until cheese is melted. Alternate layers of fish and sauce in a chafing dish, ending with sauce. Garnish with parsley. Serves 6.

STUFFED FLOUNDER

An elegant entrée with the Florentine touch.

  2 whole dressed flounder (1½ lbs. each)
  1 pkg. frozen spinach soufflé, thawed
  1 T. lemon juice
  ¼ c. melted butter

Have fish cut along the backbone and split from center to the outside edges, forming pockets. Spoon spinach soufflé into fish. Fasten opening with poultry skewers. Place flounder in a 9 x 13 x 2-inch buttered baking dish. Bake in a preheated 375° oven for 45 minutes, basting fish with butter and lemon juice every 15 minutes. Serves 2 to 4.

NEW YEAR'S DAY
All over America, New Year's Day is devoted to football. Since the games last from sunup to past sunset, why don't you have a football party? Serve lots of crunchy things to munch, hot and cold drinks and, as the main event, serve a casserole, such as:
Jambalaya or Russian Stew, p. 175
Crusty French Bread
Fruit and cheese for dessert

JAMBALAYA

  2 to 3 strips bacon
  1 onion, chopped
  1 clove garlic, minced
  1 stalk celery, chopped
  1 green pepper, chopped
  1 28-oz. can tomatoes
  ½ 6-oz. can tomato paste
  1 c. water
  ½ t. thyme
  1 bay leaf
  1 t. sugar
  1 t. salt
    Dash red pepper
  2 to 3 cooked pork sausages, diced
  1 c. cooked chicken, diced
  ½ lb. cooked ham, cut in strips
  1 lb. cooked shrimp
  3 c. cooked rice
  ¼ c. minced parsley

Fry bacon; drain and set aside. Sauté onion, garlic, celery and pepper in bacon fat for a few minutes. Add tomatoes, tomato paste, water, thyme, bay leaf, sugar, salt and red pepper. Simmer for 25 to 30 minutes. Add meats, shrimp and rice and simmer for 10 to 15 minutes until piping hot. Add a little water if necessary. Sprinkle with parsley and serve. Serves 6 to 8.

*Pictured opposite:
Curried Ham Steak, p. 177*

Yuletide treasures are recipes which cook themselves and leave time to enjoy family and friends.

TURKEY TETRAZZINI, 2

A rest-of-the-bird casserole.

- ¾ c. butter or margarine
- ¾ c. flour
- 3 t. salt
- ⅛ t. nutmeg
- 4 c. milk
- 2 c. turkey or chicken stock
- 4 egg yolks
- 1 c. milk
- ½ c. dry sherry
- 1 lb. thin spaghetti
- 6 c. leftover turkey or chicken (cut in 1½-inch pieces)
- ½ lb. mushrooms, sliced
- 1 T. butter
- 2 c. grated Swiss cheese
- ¼ c. grated Parmesan cheese

Melt ¾ cup butter in a large saucepan. Remove from heat and stir in flour, salt and nutmeg. Gradually add 4 cups milk and stock and bring to a boil, stirring constantly. Boil 2 minutes or until slightly thickened. In a small bowl, beat egg yolks with remaining milk. Pour 2 tablespoons hot mixture into yolks and then pour yolk mixture into saucepan, beating constantly until sauce is hot. Do not boil. Remove from heat and stir in sherry. Cook spaghetti as directed on package and drain. Return spaghetti to kettle and toss lightly with 2 cups sauce. Divide spaghetti in half and place in two 12 x 8 x 2-inch baking dishes. Sauté mushrooms in remaining butter. Add mushrooms and turkey to 2 cups of the sauce. Reserve remaining sauce. Spoon half of turkey mixture to center of each dish; sprinkle with Swiss cheese. Cover with foil and refrigerate 1 hour or overnight. One hour before serving, place in a preheated 350° oven for 45 minutes. Uncover and sprinkle with Parmesan cheese, broil 2 minutes. Heat reserved sauce and serve with casserole.
Note: Casserole can be frozen. Let thaw 1 hour and bake, covered, in a preheated 350° oven 60 minutes until bubbly. Serves 12.

TURKEY CASSEROLE

Can't be dismissed as casual leftovers.

- 6 eggs, beaten
- 2 c. milk *or* 1 c. milk and 1 c. cream of celery soup
- ½ t. salt
- 1 t. dry mustard
- 1 t. Worcestershire sauce
- 10 slices slightly stale bread, crusts trimmed
- 2 c. grated sharp Cheddar cheese
- 1 lb. cooked turkey slices or cubes

Combine eggs, milk, salt, mustard and Worcestershire sauce. Grease a 13 x 9 x 11-inch casserole. Alternate layers of bread, turkey and cheese, ending with bread. Cover with the liquid mixture and refrigerate for 4 hours or overnight. Bring to room temperature and bake in a preheated 350° oven for 45 to 60 minutes. Let stand 15 minutes before serving. Makes 8 servings.

SKILLET STEAK 'N' EGGS

One skillet makes a dinner. Also a great breakfast or lunch. Serve it directly from the skillet with buttered toast and catsup, if desired. For more helpings, increase beef and eggs.

- ½ lb. ground beef
- 1 small onion, chopped
- 2 eggs
  Salt and pepper to taste
- 1 pkg. frozen chopped spinach, thawed and drained (optional)

In frying pan, stir beef over medium heat until just browned. Add onion and cook until tender. Add spinach, if desired. Beat eggs with a fork or wire whisk; stir into meat and scramble. Season with salt and pepper. Serves 2.

EGG CASSEROLE

Have a brunch during the holidays. This casserole can be put together the day before needed. Served with sausage, sweet rolls, nut bread and fruit, it is an elegant and easy party.

- ¼ c. butter
- ¼ c. flour
- 2½ c. milk
- ¼ t. thyme
- ¼ t. marjoram
- 1 lb. grated Cheddar cheese
- 2 dozen hard-boiled eggs, sliced
- 1 lb. bacon, fried and crumbled
- ½ c. snipped parsley

Melt butter; stir in flour. Gradually stir in milk, stirring constantly. Add thyme, marjoram and cheese, stirring constantly, until cheese melts. In a large greased casserole, make layers of boiled egg, bacon, cheese sauce and parsley. Bake in a preheated 350° oven 30 minutes. Serves 8 to 10.

SCRAMBLED EGGS AU GRATIN

Assemble this casserole the day before needed and enjoy Christmas morning while breakfast cooks itself.

- 6 T. butter or margarine
- 6 T. flour
- 3 c. milk
- ½ t. salt
- ½ t. pepper
- ½ lb. mushrooms
- ¼ c. vermouth or lemon juice
- 12 eggs
- ½ c. milk
- 2 T. butter
- ½ lb. bacon, cooked and crumbled
- ½ lb. Cheddar cheese, grated

Melt 6 tablespoons butter; blend in flour until smooth. Slowly add 3 cups milk. Simmer and stir constantly until thickened and smooth. Season with salt and pepper. Sauté mushrooms in vermouth or lemon juice. Beat eggs with milk. Melt remaining butter and pour in eggs, stirring over medium heat until tender. In a greased, large and shallow casserole, combine cheese, mushrooms, bacon, eggs and sauce, stirring to blend. Refrigerate. Bring to room temperature and bake in a preheated 325° oven 30 minutes. Serves 10 to 12.

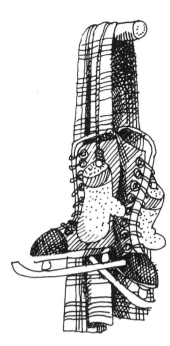

SPEEDY SPINACH LASAGNE

Great 1-dish meal.

- 1 pkg. spaghetti sauce mix
- 1 6-oz. can tomato paste
- 1 8-oz. can tomato sauce
- 1¾ c. cold water
- 2 eggs
- 1 15-oz. container Ricotta *or* 1 lb. creamed cottage cheese
- ½ t. salt
- 1 10-oz. pkg. frozen chopped spinach, thawed and drained
- ½ c. grated Parmesan cheese
- ½ lb. sliced mozzarella cheese
- ½ lb. uncooked lasagne noodles, broken in half

Empty spaghetti sauce mix into saucepan; add tomato paste, tomato sauce and water. Heat, stirring, until well blended. Remove from heat. Beat eggs in a large bowl and add Ricotta or cottage cheese, spinach, salt and ¼ cup Parmesan cheese. Lightly grease bottom of a 13 x 9 x 2-inch baking dish; cover with a little sauce. Layer noodles, half of the cheese-spinach mixture, half the mozzarella cheese and half the tomato sauce. Repeat layers, ending with tomato sauce. Sprinkle with ¼ cup Parmesan cheese. Cover dish with a lightly greased sheet of aluminum foil and bake in a preheated 350° oven for 60 minutes or until noodles are tender. Let stand 10 minutes before cutting in squares and serving. Serves 8.

BARLEY CASSEROLE

¾ c. barley
1 onion, thinly sliced
3 t. instant beef bouillon
2 c. boiling water
½ c. sliced canned mushrooms

Mix all ingredients together in a 1½-quart casserole. Cover and bake in a 400° oven for 60 minutes, or until liquid is absorbed and barley is tender. Makes 4 to 6 servings.

BAKED RICE

¼ c. chopped onion
¼ c. butter or margarine
1 c. rice
2 c. chicken broth
¼ c. chopped parsley
Salt to taste

Sauté onion in butter until translucent. Add rice and stir until coated. Bring chicken broth to a boil; add with parsley and salt. Pour into a 1-quart casserole; cover and bake in a 375° oven for about 20 minutes or until liquid is absorbed. Serves 6.

BROWN RICE PILAF

4 slices bacon
¼ lb. mushrooms, sliced
½ c. chopped onion
1 c. brown rice
3 c. beef broth
½ c. dry white wine
¼ c. slivered toasted almonds

Sauté bacon until crisp. Drain and save 2 tablespoons drippings. Crumble bacon. Cook mushrooms and onion in drippings until tender. Add rice; stir and sauté 1 minute. Stir in broth, wine, almonds and bacon; bring to a boil. Pour into a 1½-quart casserole and bake, covered, in a 325° oven 60 minutes. Serves 6 to 8.

NOODLES ALFREDO

A delicious difference if your entrée is roast beef or pork.

1 lb. broad noodles, cooked and drained
½ c. butter
¾ c. light cream, warmed
1½ c. grated Parmesan cheese
Chopped parsley
Chives

Place cooked noodles in a large serving dish. Melt butter. Pour butter, cream and grated cheese over noodles; mix well. Toss to coat and sprinkle with parsley and chives. Serves 6 to 8.

TREE PARTY
Some trees are so beautiful, they deserve to have a party just to admire them. With that in mind, we offer the following serving suggestions:
bowl of cold shrimp with Curry Sauce, p. 17
thinly sliced ham, turkey or beef with assorted breads
Caviar Star, p. 166
Cheese Ball, p. 171
nuts
mixed drinks
soft drinks
wine or eggnog

TOMATO PILAU

This festive rice dish is traditional in many Southern homes.

2 slices bacon, fried and crumbled
1 medium onion, diced
1 green pepper, diced
1 6-oz. can tomato paste
1 can water
1 t. sugar
1 t. salt
½ t. pepper
2½ to 3 c. rice
6 c. boiling water

Drain bacon and set aside. Sauté onion and pepper in bacon fat for 2 to 3 minutes. Add tomato paste, water, seasonings and rice. Sauté for about 5 minutes. Pour into boiling water and cook according to time on rice box. Serve garnished with bacon. Serves 8 to 10.

Pictured opposite:
Speedy Spinach Lasagne, p. 185

Vegetables

GREEN BEANS AND BACON

The meaty flavor makes this a hearty vegetable.

¼ to ½ c. diced salt pork or bacon
1½ lbs. green beans *or* 2 9-oz. pkgs. frozen whole green beans
1 c. water
½ t. salt
1 t. instant minced onion
1 T. sugar

Sauté salt pork until crisp and brown; save pork and fat. Cook beans in water to which salt has been added. Heat to boiling and simmer, uncovered, 5 minutes. Cover and cook until tender, about 10 minutes. Drain. (If using frozen beans, cook as directed on package.) Toss beans with pork fat, minced onion and sugar. Makes 6 to 8 servings.

TURKISH GREEN BEANS

For a flavorful surprise.

2 T. olive oil
1 T. tomato paste
1 t. instant minced onion
¼ c. chopped green pepper
½ t. salt
1 9-oz. pkg. frozen whole green beans

Combine oil, tomato paste, onion, green pepper and salt. Pour over beans in a saucepan. Cook 10 minutes or until tender. Makes 4 servings.

CAULIFLOWER MOIRÉ

A new topping with tang.

1 head cauliflower
½ c. sour cream
1 T. prepared mustard
¼ t. salt
¼ t. pepper
2 to 3 green onions, snipped

Steam or cook cauliflower for about 20 minutes until just tender. Combine remaining ingredients. Heat but do not boil. Pour over hot cauliflower and sprinkle with paprika. Serves 6 to 8.

GREEN PEPPERS WITH STUFFING

Green pepper shells can be stuffed and frozen days ahead; then thawed and baked with the turkey.

6 to 8 green peppers, halved and seeded
2 medium onions, chopped
3 stalks celery, chopped
½ c. butter or margarine
2 8-oz. pkgs. herbed bread stuffing
1 to 1½ c. chicken broth

Sauté onions and celery in butter until tender crisp. Add stuffing. Moisten with broth and spoon lightly, but firmly, into peppers. Freeze at this point or place on a cookie sheet. Bake in a preheated 325° oven 20 to 30 minutes.

FRENCH PEAS

1 10-oz. pkg. peas
¼ c. chicken bouillon
¼ head lettuce, shredded
½ c. light cream
Pepper

Cook peas in chicken bouillon. When tender, place lettuce on top, stir with a fork until lettuce wilts. Add cream and sprinkle with pepper. Serves 4.

GREEN PEAS AND ONIONS

Instant glamour.

1 10-oz. pkg. green peas
½ 20-oz. pkg. small pearl onions
1 pkg. sherry wine sauce mix *or* 1 pkg. white sauce mix
2 T. butter
½ c. bread crumbs
¼ c. grated Romano cheese

Place peas and onions in a casserole. Stir in sauce. Sprinkle crumbs and cheese on top and dot with butter. Bake in a 350° oven for 20 to 30 minutes. Serves 4 to 6.

WHIPPED RUTABAGAS AU GRATIN

Not to be neglected for the holidays.

    3 lbs. rutabagas, cooked and mashed
    ¼ c. butter
    1 T. sugar
    3 eggs
    1 c. bread crumbs
    2 T. melted butter

Beat rutabagas, butter, sugar and eggs together. Turn into greased casserole. Top with crumbs and melted butter. Bake in a 350° oven 50 to 60 minutes until lightly browned. Serves 8 to 10.

STUFFED YAMS

To complement a roast.

    6 medium yams, washed and dried
    4 T. butter or margarine, softened
    2 T. brown sugar
    1 t. salt
      Orange juice
      Walnut or pecan halves

Bake yams in a 425° oven 40 minutes or until done. Remove from oven. Cut slice from top of each yam and scoop out inside, taking care not to break the shell. Add butter, brown sugar, salt and enough orange juice to moisten; beat until fluffy. Spoon mixture into shells. Return to oven and bake 15 to 20 minutes until heated through. Garnish each with a nut half. Makes 6 servings.

SPINACH, ARTICHOKE AND MUSHROOM CASSEROLE

    ½ lb. mushrooms, sliced
    2 onions, chopped
    2 jars artichoke hearts (drain and save marinade)
    1 pkg. frozen chopped spinach, thawed and drained
    5 eggs, lightly beaten
    1½ c. grated Cheddar cheese
      Salt and pepper to taste

Sauté mushrooms and onion in 2 to 3 tablespoons of the marinade. Combine with remaining ingredients in a lightly greased shallow casserole and bake in a 350° oven 30 to 45 minutes. Serves 4.

SPINACH RICE CHEESE BAKE

A combination of simple leaf and grain.

    2 pkgs. frozen spinach, cooked and drained
    1 c. cooked rice
    1 c. cream of mushroom soup
    1 t. instant minced onion
    ¼ lb. Cheddar cheese, shredded

Combine all ingredients and place in a greased casserole. Bake in a 350° oven for 30 minutes. Serves 6.

DILLED BRUSSELS SPROUTS

This is a dilly!

    2 pkgs. Brussels sprouts, cooked and drained
    ¼ c. salad oil
    2 T. lemon juice
    ½ small onion, minced
    1 t. dill weed
      Salt and pepper to taste

Combine oil, lemon juice, onion, dill and salt and pepper. Pour over Brussels sprouts. Cover and chill overnight. Serve cold. Serves 4 to 6.

PILAF AND BRUSSELS SPROUTS

A bowl of rice pilaf ringed with Brussels sprouts rounds out a feast.

    2½ c. chicken or turkey broth or instant bouillon
    1 T. lemon juice
    1 T. butter
    ½ t. salt
    ½ t. cinnamon
    ½ c. raisins
    1 c. uncooked, long grain rice
    1 can mushrooms, drained
    1 or 2 pkgs. frozen Brussels sprouts, cooked according to package directions
      Pimiento strips

Heat broth, lemon juice, butter, salt, cinnamon and raisins to a boil in a large saucepan. Stir in rice. Cover and simmer over low heat until all liquid is absorbed. Stir in mushrooms; place on serving platter. Garnish with pimiento strips and Brussels sprouts. Makes 4 to 6 servings.

TOMATOES FLORENTINE

This beautiful vegetable casserole can be put together in the morning for easy baking at dinner time.

    2 pkgs. frozen chopped spinach
    ½ t. garlic salt
    ¼ c. mayonnaise
    4 to 6 tomatoes, sliced ½ inch thick
       Cheddar cheese slices
       Butter

In a shallow baking dish, combine spinach, garlic salt and mayonnaise. Arrange tomato slices over spinach and top with cheese. Dot with butter and bake in a 325° oven 20 to 30 minutes. Serves 4 to 6.

TOMATOES A LA PROVENCALE

A handsome garnish for a roast or fowl. Prepare in the morning and refrigerate until you are ready to bake it.

    12 tomatoes
    ½ c. butter or margarine
    1 c. chopped onion
    1 clove garlic, minced
    1½ c. fine dry bread crumbs
    ½ c. snipped fresh parsley
    2 t. basil
    1 t. thyme
    ½ t. salt
    ¼ t. freshly ground pepper

Cut a thin slice off the stem end of the tomatoes and cut out a wedge-shaped piece halfway down. Gently squeeze out the juice and remove seeds, not breaking skin. Melt butter in a skillet; sauté onion and garlic until soft. Remove pan from heat and stir in crumbs, parsley, basil, thyme, salt and pepper. Spoon this mixture into the tomatoes, then place tomatoes in a shallow baking dish. Bake in a preheated 350° oven about 20 minutes until the filling is lightly browned and the tomatoes are tender. Makes 12 servings.

Pictured opposite:
Savory Vegetable Platter

BAKED TOMATOES

A colorful brunch or breakfast dish when served with grilled bacon and toasted English muffins.

    8 tomatoes, sliced ½ inch thick
    ½ c. flour
    ½ t. salt
    ½ t. pepper
    1 T. sugar
    2 to 3 T. butter
    1 c. light cream
    1 T. sugar
    ⅛ t. baking soda

Dust tomato slices with flour seasoned with salt, pepper, and sugar. Brown lightly in butter and transfer to a baking dish. Stir cream, sugar and soda into pan drippings, blending well. Pour over tomatoes and bake at 325° for 15 to 20 minutes. Serves 4 to 6.

CHEESY ONIONS

Easy does it.

    2 1-lb. cans onions, drained
    1 10-oz. can condensed cream of celery soup
    ½ c. shredded Cheddar cheese
    ¼ c. slivered almonds

Place onions in a 1-quart casserole. Pour soup over. Sprinkle with cheese and nuts. Bake in a preheated 375° oven 20 to 25 minutes until heated thoroughly. Serves 6.

SAVORY VEGETABLE PLATTER

    3 c. beef bouillon
    ½ t. savory
    ½ t. tarragon
    4 to 5 carrots, cut in 2-inch chunks
    1 head cauliflower, trimmed
    ½ lb. green beans, whole (trimmed)
    4 to 5 stalks celery, cut into 2-inch chunks
    2 T. butter
    2 T. sesame seeds
    2 T. lemon juice

Heat bouillon, savory and tarragon to a boil. Add cauliflower; cover and simmer 10 minutes. Add remaining vegetables. Cover and simmer for 20 minutes. Make sauce of butter, seeds and juice. Serve vegetables in clusters on a large platter. Drizzle sauce over all. Serves 8 to 10.

JULIENNED CARROTS

10 to 12 carrots, cut into julienne strips
2 green onions, sliced
½ c. butter
½ c. chopped walnuts
Sprinkle of nutmeg

Steam carrots until tender crisp. Melt butter. Add carrots, onions and nuts and sizzle for a few minutes. Dust with a sprinkle of nutmeg. Serves 6 to 8.

SESAME CARROTS

4 c. thinly sliced carrots
2 T. butter
1 T. salad oil
1 T. orange juice
½ t. ground ginger
½ t. salt
Dash pepper
2 T. sesame seeds

Stir fry carrots in butter and oil over moderate heat until tender crisp, about 5 minutes. Stir in orange juice, ginger, salt, pepper and sesame seeds. Toss, heat well and serve. Serves 8 to 10.

BAKED-AHEAD POTATOES

Bake, stuff and refrigerate or freeze potatoes. Double or triple recipe as needed.

6 large baking potatoes
¼ c. butter
1 t. salt
½ t. pepper
½ c. sour cream
Grated Swiss or Parmesan cheese

Scrub, pierce and bake potatoes in a 425° oven for 1 hour or until tender. Cool slightly. Break in half lengthwise and scoop potato into a large bowl. Beat in butter, salt, pepper and sour cream; refill shells. Sprinkle Parmesan or grated Swiss cheese on top. Bake in a 350° oven for 30 to 40 minutes. Freeze or refrigerate as desired.

POTATOES ANNA

6 large potatoes, pared and thinly sliced
½ c. melted butter
Salt, pepper, paprika

Dip each potato into melted butter and layer in circles in a greased 9-inch iron skillet. Season each layer with salt, pepper and paprika. Cover and bake in a 450° oven 15 to 20 minutes. Loosen and invert onto a platter. Makes 6 servings.

JUST FOR CHILDREN
Present each child with two ornaments made of decorated cookies or popcorn balls. They can hang one on your tree and take one home. After the tree has been trimmed, serve:
Cranberry Punch, p. 164
Milkshake Punch, p. 164
Plates of cookies, nuts and candies
If you have a good storyteller, a Christmas story near the tree or in front of the fireplace is a nice finale. Also, singing carols is fun for all ages.

BROCCOLI OR ASPARAGUS

1 lb. fresh broccoli or asparagus *or*
1 10-oz. pkg. frozen broccoli or asparagus
1 t. chicken boullion crystals
Water

Place broccoli or asparagus in a steamer with a small amount of water (about ¼ cup). Sprinkle with chicken boullion crystals. Steam until tender-crisp, 10 to 15 minutes. (Time will vary according to the density of vegetables.) Serve with Hollandaise Sauce. Serves 2.

INSTANT HOLLANDAISE SAUCE

1 c. sour cream
1 c. mayonnaise
¼ c. lemon juice

Combine all ingredients and blend together. Heat slowly and serve hot over asparagus or broccoli.

"Sing we joyous all together . . ." we've composed this medley of salads and dressings to echo the zestiness of the season.

Salads and Dressings

fa la la la la

GALA FRUIT MOLD

An all-American combination.

2¼ c. boiling water
 1 3-oz. pkg. lemon gelatin
 ¾ c. blueberry juice
 1 3-oz. pkg. lime gelatin
 ¾ c. pineapple juice
 1 3-oz. pkg. strawberry gelatin
 ¾ c. strawberry juice and water
 1 pt. heavy cream
 1 can blueberries
1½ c. crushed pineapple
 1 10-oz. pkg. frozen strawberries, thawed

In 3 separate bowls, dissolve lemon gelatin in ¾ cup boiling water and blueberry juice. Dissolve lime gelatin in ¾ cup boiling water and pineapple juice. Dissolve strawberry gelatin in ¾ cup boiling water and strawberry juice and water. Refrigerate until slightly thickened. Whip cream and divide in thirds. Fold whipped cream into each bowl of partially set gelatin. Fold in corresponding fruits. Refrigerate each 10 minutes. Grease a very large mold or bowl. Spoon in gelatin, making 3 layers. Chill until completely set. Serves 8 to 10.

CARAWAY COLESLAW

Caraway studded cabbage slaw.

 3 to 4 c. shredded cabbage
 ½ c. chopped green pepper
 ½ small onion, minced
 ½ carrot, grated
 ⅓ c. mayonnaise
 2 T. lemon juice
 ½ t. sugar
 ½ t. caraway seed
 ¼ t. celery salt

Prepare cabbage, green pepper, onion and carrot. Combine remaining ingredients, mixing well. Pour over vegetables and toss well.

SEAFOAM MOLD

1½ c. boiling water
 2 3-oz. pkgs. lime gelatin
1½ c. cold water
 1 8-oz. can crushed pineapple with juice
 1 c. sour cream
 1 16-oz. can sliced pears, drained

Dissolve gelatin in boiling water. Add cold water, pineapple with juice and sour cream. Mix gently. Line a lightly oiled 5-cup mold with pear slices and pour gelatin fruit mixture in. Chill until set. Makes 6 to 8 servings.

CRANBERRY SALAD MOLD

 1 3-oz. pkg. lemon gelatin
 1 c. boiling water
 1 c. cranberry juice
 1 10½-oz. pkg. cranberry orange relish, partially thawed
 ½ c. chopped celery
 ½ c. chopped walnuts

Dissolve gelatin in boiling water. Stir in juice and relish. Chill until partially thickened; stir in celery and nuts. Pour into small mold. Chill until firm.

CHERRY JUBILEE MOLD

 1 16-oz. can pitted dark sweet cherries
 2 3-oz. pkgs. cherry gelatin
 ½ c. cream sherry
 1 can pear halves
 1 3-oz. pkg. cream cheese
 Chopped nuts

Drain cherries and reserve syrup. Add enough water to make 3 cups liquid. In a saucepan, combine gelatin and liquid. Heat and stir until gelatin dissolves. Remove from heat and stir in sherry. Chill until partially set. Fold in cherries and pour into a lightly oiled mold. Chill until firm. Drain pears. Form cream cheese into small balls and roll in nuts. Place on pear halves. Turn out mold on lettuce leaves and surround with pear halves. Serves 8 to 10.

CRANBERRY SOUR CREAM MOLD

2 3-oz. pkg. red gelatin
1¾ c. boiling water
1 can jellied cranberry sauce
1 c. sour cream

Dissolve gelatin in boiling water. Chill until slightly thickened. Beat cranberry sauce and sour cream until smooth. Fold into gelatin; pour into mold and chill until firm. Serves 4 to 6.

PINEAPPLE CRANBERRY MOLD

Ring in the season.

2 6-oz. pkgs. raspberry gelatin
3 c. boiling water
2 c. cold water
½ c. pineapple juice
1 T. lemon juice
¼ t. salt
18 pecan halves (optional)
1 20-oz. can crushed pineapple, drained
1 16-oz. can whole cranberry sauce

Dissolve gelatin in boiling water. Stir in 2 cups cold water, pineapple juice, lemon juice and salt. Pour ½ cup gelatin into an 8-cup ring mold. Arrange pecan halves in mold and refrigerate until set. Refrigerate remaining gelatin until slightly thickened, about 1½ hours. Spoon 1¾ cups gelatin into mold. Stir pineapple and cranberry sauce into remaining gelatin and spoon over gelatin in mold. Refrigerate until set. Makes 16 servings.

FRESH VEGETABLES VINAIGRETTE

Crudities are very stylish.

6 to 8 c. assorted fresh vegetables
1 c. olive or safflower oil
¼ c. white wine vinegar
2 T. lemon juice
1 t. dry mustard
½ t. salt
  Freshly ground pepper
2 T. snipped parsley
1 T. snipped green onion

Wash and prepare vegetables such as carrots, red and green pepper slices, cauliflowerets, cucumber slices, celery, cherry tomatoes, kohlrabi slices, zucchini slices, mushrooms and any other vegetable you like. Combine remaining ingredients, mixing thoroughly. Pour over vegetables and chill for 6 hours. Drain vegetables and arrange on a platter.

SPINACH SALAD DELUXE

1 lb. fresh spinach, washed, dried and shredded
4 to 6 green onions, chopped
4 slices bacon, fried and crumbled
½ c. mayonnaise
½ c. sour cream
3 T. grated Parmesan cheese
  Bacon to garnish

Toss spinach, onions and bacon. Mix mayonnaise, sour cream and cheese together. Toss with salad. Garnish with bacon and serve. Serves 2 to 4.

WALDORF SALAD AU VIN

An apple a day in this special way.

4 Winesap or Jonathan apples
1 rib celery, diced
1 c. seedless green grapes
½ c. walnut pieces
½ c. mayonnaise
¼ c. dry white wine

Core apples but do not peel; chop into cubes. In a salad bowl, combine apples, celery, grapes and walnuts. Mix mayonnaise with wine and pour over fruit. Toss lightly. Makes 8 servings.

Pictured opposite:
Gala Fruit Mold, p. 193

MIMOSA SALAD

Add a spring-like touch of color to any season!

1 head romaine lettuce
2 heads of bibb lettuce
1 bunch of watercress
1 T. prepared mustard
6 T. salad oil
1 clove garlic, minced
2 T. wine vinegar
Juice of 1 lemon
Salt and pepper
1 can sliced beets, drained
2 hard-boiled eggs, sieved

Wash and dry greens; toss lightly. Combine mustard, oil, garlic, vinegar, juice of lemon, salt and freshly ground pepper. Toss with greens. Add sliced beets and sieved whites and yolks as garnish to justify its name. Serves 6 to 8.

SPRING SALAD

A touch of spring all year long.

1 1-lb. can whole tomatoes, chopped and drained (save juice for soup or sauces)
3 to 4 green onions, chopped
½ green pepper, chopped
1 stalk celery, chopped
1 cucumber, thinly sliced
1 carrot, thinly sliced
2 to 3 T. olive or salad oil
2 to 3 T. wine vinegar
½ t. salt
¼ t. pepper
½ t. sugar
Mixed greens

Combine first 6 ingredients. Add oil, vinegar, salt, pepper and sugar. Stir gently to blend. Chill for 1 hour or more and serve over mixed greens. Serves 4 to 6.

GARDEN MOLD

For the beauty of a molded salad.

1 16-oz. can diced beets
1 3-oz. pkg. lemon gelatin
1 c. Burgundy wine
1 t. horseradish
¼ t. salt
1 c. boiling water
1 3-oz. pkg. lemon gelatin
1 c. cold water
1 c. sour cream
1 pkg. frozen tiny peas
3 hard-boiled eggs, chopped
2 T. snipped green onion
½ t. Worcestershire sauce
2 drops Tabasco sauce
1 t. salt
Salad greens
Hard-boiled egg wedges

Drain beets, saving liquid. Add enough water to beet liquid to make 1 cup; bring to a boil. Add 1 package gelatin, stirring to dissolve. Stir in wine, horseradish and salt. Chill until slightly thickened. Dissolve remaining package gelatin in 1 cup boiling water. Stir in cold water and chill until slightly thickened. Fold beets into thickened beet gelatin. Pour into an 8-cup mold and chill until just set. Mix sour cream with next 6 ingredients and fold into lemon gelatin. Spoon mixture over beet layer. Chill at least 4 hours. Unmold onto salad greens. Garnish with hard-boiled egg slices, if desired. Serves 8 to 12.

RASPBERRY MOLD

A colorful complement.

    2 10-oz. pkgs. frozen raspberries, thaw
      and reserve juice
    ½ pt. sour cream
    2 c. boiling water
    2 3-oz. pkgs. raspberry gelatin

Dissolve gelatin in boiling water. Add enough water to raspberry juice to make 1¾ cups liquid. Add to gelatin and chill until partially thickened. Fold in sour cream and berries. Chill until firm. Serves 8.

GRAPEFRUIT RING

For winter sunshine.

    2 3-oz. pkgs. lemon gelatin
    1½ c. boiling water
    1¾ c. cold water
    ½ c. frozen lemonade concentrate
    2 grapefruits, pared and sectioned (2 c.
      segments)
    1 c. red grapes, halved and seeded
    ½ c. slivered almonds (optional)

Dissolve gelatin in boiling water. Stir in cold water and lemonade. Chill until mixture is partially set. Fold in grapefruit segments, grapes and almonds. Spoon into a 6-cup mold. Chill until firm. Serves 8.

THOUSAND ISLAND SALAD

A toss for winners!

    ½ large head lettuce, shredded
      Handful spinach, washed and torn up
    1 sweet red onion, cut in rings
    3 hard-boiled eggs, sliced
    4 to 6 water chestnuts, sliced
    1 c. mayonnaise
    ¼ c. chili sauce
    1 T. Worcestershire sauce

Toss first 5 ingredients together. Combine remaining ingredients and add, tossing to blend. Serves 4.

SALAD DRESSING

    ½ c. olive oil
    ¼ c. tarragon vinegar
    1 clove garlic
    1 t. brown sugar
    ¼ t. dry mustard
    ½ t. salt

Combine all ingredients and blend. Makes about ¾ cup.

CHEF'S SALAD DRESSING

Serve with greens topped with julienne strips of turkey, ham and cheese. Garnish with hard-boiled egg and tomato.

    ½ pt. sour cream
    1 c. mayonnaise
    1½ T. vinegar
    1 t. salt
      Dash pepper
    1 t. sugar
    ¼ t. dry mustard
    1 T. minced onion
    1 clove garlic, minced

Combine all ingredients and chill overnight. Makes about 2 cups.

HONEY-CELERY SEED DRESSING

May be used over a grapefruit ring.

    ⅓ c. sugar
    3 T. honey
    1 t. salt
    1 t. dry mustard
    1 t. celery seed
    1 t. paprika
    1 c. safflower oil
    ¼ c. vinegar

Combine all ingredients in a blender until well mixed. Makes 1⅔ cups.

197

"Hail the new, ye lads and lasses . . ." here's a delightful assortment of condiments and relishes to accompany the most discriminating palate into the new year.

Condiments

END-OF-SUMMER RELISH

Vary this vegetable combination to suit your taste and the contents of your vegetable crisper.

- 2 c. sliced cauliflower flowerets (about ½ small head)
- 2 carrots, julienne strips
- 1 green pepper, cut in strips
- 10 to 12 green beans
- 1 zucchini, cut in disks
- 1 small jar stuffed olives
- ¾ c. wine vinegar
- ¼ c. olive oil
- 1 T. sugar
- 1 t. salt
- ½ t. oregano
- ¼ t. pepper
- ¼ c. water
- Cherry tomatoes (optional)

Combine all ingredients in a large pan. Bring to a boil and simmer, covered, 5 minutes. Cool and let marinate at least 24 hours. Cherry tomatoes may be added just before serving. Makes 2½ quarts.

APPLE CHUTNEY

To accompany a curry or just to sweeten up a meal.

- 3 lbs. green apples, cubed
- 1 lime, cut up
- 1 orange, cut up
- 2 c. packed light brown sugar
- 1½ c. golden raisins
- ¼ c. cider vinegar
- ½ t. salt
- 1 t. cinnamon
- ½ t. ground cloves
- ¼ t. ground ginger
- ¼ t. nutmeg

Combine all ingredients in a heavy saucepan. Bring to a boil over medium heat. Lower heat to a simmer and cook for about 30 minutes, or until tender. Makes about 4 cups.

BRANDY BERRIES

Cranberries with new sophistication and flavor.

- 1 lb. fresh cranberries, washed and dried
- 2 c. sugar
- 1 T. grated orange rind
- ½ c. Triple Sec, Cointreau or Grand Marnier

Combine all ingredients in a large flat ovenproof dish. Set aside for 20 to 30 minutes. Cover dish with foil and bake in a preheated 325° oven for 40 minutes. Cool slightly and pour into glass containers. Refrigerate.

NUTS AND FRUITS

A delicious snack, full of vitamins and proteins.

- ½ lb. raw cashews
- ½ lb. pecans
- ½ lb. almonds
- 1 c. sunflower seeds
- 1 c. pepitas
- 1 c. raisins
- 1 c. dried apricots, chopped

Mix together all ingredients. Store covered. Makes about 5½ cups.

CANDIED ORANGE PEEL

- 2 large navel oranges, sliced crosswise
- ½ c. sugar
- ¼ c. hot water
- ¼ c. sugar (for coating)

Remove peel from orange slices and cut circles in half. Place peel in saucepan, cover with cold water and bring to boil; drain. Repeat this 4 or 5 times. Drain and put on plate. In same saucepan, heat ½ cup sugar and water, stirring constantly until sugar is dissolved. Add orange peel and cook slowly until syrup is reduced to half. Remove peel, and roll in ¼ cup sugar on a sheet of waxed paper. Cool.

Pictured opposite:
End-of-Summer Relish
Nuts and Fruits

CURRIED PEARS

A winter fruit with flavor.

4 firm, fresh pears
¼ c. butter
¾ c. packed brown sugar
2 t. curry powder

Peel and core pears and cut in half. Arrange in shallow baking dish. Melt butter and stir in brown sugar and curry powder. Pour over pears. Cover and bake in a preheated 350° oven about 20 minutes. Serve slightly warm or cool with turkey, chicken or ham. Makes 8 servings.

MUSTARD BEANS

A "snappy" relish.

2 lbs. green beans
½ red pepper, sliced
1 onion, sliced into thin rings
½ c. cider vinegar
½ c. water
½ c. sugar
1 T. flour
2 T. prepared mustard

Cook beans until tender crisp and drain. Combine with pepper and onion slices. In a saucepan, heat vinegar, water, sugar, flour and mustard to boiling. Pour hot mixture over vegetables. Refrigerate at least 24 hours in a glass container.

DRIED FRUIT AND NUT CHUTNEY

A "perker-upper" for any meal.

½ lb. dried apples
½ lb. dried peaches
½ lb. dried apricots
½ lb. pitted dates
½ lb. golden raisins
1¼ c. sugar
1 c. brown sugar
3 cloves garlic, minced
1 t. salt
1 t. dry mustard
½ t. ground ginger
½ t. pepper
½ t. ground allspice
½ t. cinnamon
1 c. chopped nuts
3 c. cider vinegar

Cut fruits in ½-inch pieces; cover with water and set aside for 4 to 6 hours. Drain fruit, reserving 1½ cups liquid. Bring liquid to a boil; add fruit and remaining ingredients. Bring again to a boil, simmer, stirring often, until tender and thick, about 30 minutes. Cool and store in glass containers in the refrigerator. May be processed in a hot water bath, if desired. Makes 6 pints.

FROSTED CRANBERRIES

For a holiday touch around a mold or an entrée.

1 lb. washed and dried cranberries
1 egg white
Sugar

Beat egg white until frothy. Dip cranberries into egg white and then roll in sugar. Place on waxed paper to dry.

ORANGE SLICES, GLACÉS

Delicious with chicken, beef or lamb.

2 large navel oranges
2 T. butter or margarine
⅓ c. light brown sugar, firmly packed
¼ t. ground allspice
1 T. light corn syrup

Cut ends off oranges and cut crosswise into ½-inch slices. In large skillet, heat butter, brown sugar, allspice and corn syrup, stirring constantly until mixture is smooth. Add orange slices. Cook 10 minutes on each side or until oranges are shiny and glazed.

DILLYS

Keep on hand for munching. Also makes a pretty gift. Alternate bunches of beans or carrots in a tall jar.

Green beans (about ½ lb.)
Carrots (about 4 to 6 medium)
2 c. water
2 c. vinegar
¼ c. salt
½ t. red pepper
2 cloves garlic
2 T. dried dill weed
1 to 2 small dried red peppers (seeds removed)

Wash and trim beans. Scrape carrots and cut into sticks. Place beans and carrots in jars. Combine remaining ingredients in a saucepan and bring to a boil. Pour over vegetables. Chill for 8 to 10 days for maximum flavor.

"Heedless of the wind and weather . . . "the aroma of these quick breads and coffee cakes would warm Jack Frost himself!

Breads

CRANBERRY MUFFINS

1 c. coarsely chopped cranberries
2 T. sugar
2 c. flour
½ c. sugar
3 t. baking powder
¼ t. salt
1 c. milk
1 t. vanilla
¼ c. butter, melted
2 eggs

Add 2 tablespoons sugar to cranberries; set aside. Mix flour, remaining sugar, baking powder and salt in a large bowl. Set aside. Beat together eggs, milk, vanilla and butter. Make a well in the center of the flour. Pour in liquid all at once, stirring quickly with a fork just until mixed. Do not beat; batter will be lumpy. Fold in cranberries. Fill greased 2½-inch muffin tins two-thirds full and bake in a 400° oven 25 to 30 minutes. Makes 12 muffins.

FRUIT AND CHEESE BREAD

1 c. butter or margarine
1 8-oz. pkg. cream cheese
1½ c. sugar
4 eggs
1 t. vanilla
2¼ c. flour
2 t. baking powder
¼ t. salt
1 c. candied cut up cherries
1 c. candied cut up pineapple
1 c. chopped nuts
¼ c. flour for dredging fruit and nuts

Cream butter and cream cheese together. Beat in sugar until light and fluffy. Add eggs, one at a time, beating well. Add vanilla. Combine 2¼ cups flour, baking powder and salt and add to mixture. Dredge fruit in remaining flour. Stir floured fruits and nuts into batter. Bake in 2 small greased loaf pans in a 325° oven 60 to 70 minutes. Cool on rack for 10 minutes. Remove from pans and cool thoroughly. Makes 2 loaves.

COFFEE DATE LOAF

Good for all seasons.

2 c. flour
3 t. baking powder
1 t. baking soda
1 t. salt
1 t. instant coffee
⅔ c. sugar
¼ c. chopped nuts
1 c. snipped dates
1 egg
1 c. buttermilk
4 T. vegetable oil

Combine flour, baking powder, baking soda, salt, instant coffee and sugar. Add nuts and dates. In a separate bowl, beat egg, buttermilk and oil. Pour into dry ingredients and blend lightly. Pour into a greased 10½ x 3⅝ x 2⅝-inch pan and allow to rest 20 minutes. Bake in a preheated 375° oven about 45 minutes. Makes 1 loaf.

DATE AND NUT BREAD

Some breads take their place with the dinner—others entertain with coffee.

1¾ c. packed brown sugar
3 T. butter or margarine, softened
2 eggs
3 c. flour
1½ t. baking soda
¼ t. salt
1 c. sour milk *or* 1 T. vinegar plus milk to equal 1 c.
½ c. chopped nuts, lightly floured
1½ c. dates, cut in small pieces

Cream butter and brown sugar; add eggs, beating well. Combine flour, soda, salt and add alternately with milk. Stir in nuts and dates, mixing thoroughly. Spoon into 2 well-greased 9 x 5 x 3-inch loaf pans or five 16-ounce cans. Bake loaves in a preheated 350° oven for 60 minutes and cans in a 325° oven for 60 to 70 minutes, or until toothpick inserted in center comes out clean. Cool on rack for 10 minutes. Turn out of pans and continue cooling on rack. Makes 2 loaves.

APPLESAUCE BREAD

Spicy, moist and delicious. Keeps for weeks in refrigerator and months in the freezer.

4 eggs
1½ c. sugar
1 c. salad oil
2 c. applesauce
⅔ c. milk
3½ c. flour
2 t. baking soda
1 t. cinnamon
1 t. nutmeg
1 c. chopped nuts

Beat eggs. Add sugar, oil, applesauce and milk. Combine remaining ingredients, stirring well. Add to applesauce mixture, mixing well. Pour into three 8 x 4-inch loaf pans. Bake in a 350° oven for 1 hour or until done. Makes 3 loaves.

HONEY WHOLE WHEAT BREAD

The aroma from the oven is a joy.

2 c. flour
1¼ c. whole wheat flour
1 pkg. dry yeast
1 t. salt
½ c. milk
½ c. water
¼ c. honey
1 T. butter or margarine
1 small egg

In a large mixing bowl, combine ½ cup of the flour, whole wheat flour, yeast and salt, mixing well. In a saucepan, combine milk, water, honey and butter; heat until warm. Add to flour mixture. Add egg. Blend at low speed until moistened; beat 3 minutes at medium speed. By hand, stir in remaining flour to make a firm dough. Knead on floured surface until smooth and elastic, about 5 minutes. Place in a greased bowl, turning to grease top. Cover and let rise in a warm place until light and doubled in bulk, about 1 hour. Punch dough down. On a lightly floured surface, roll or pat dough to a 14 x 7-inch rectangle. Starting with the shorter side, roll up tightly, pressing dough into the roll with each turn. Pinch edges and ends to seal. Place in a greased 9 x 5-inch loaf pan. Cover and let rise in a warm place until doubled in bulk, about 30 minutes. Bake in a 375° oven 35 to 40 minutes until golden brown. Remove from pan and cool. Makes 1 loaf.

Pictured opposite:
Almond Coffee Cake

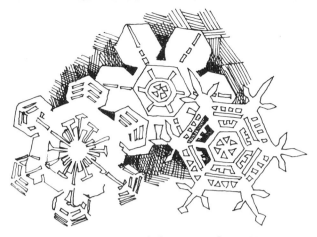

ALMOND COFFEE CAKE

For breakfast, brunch or for gifts.

1 c. milk
½ c. butter
1 pkg. dry yeast
½ c. sugar
½ t. salt
3 eggs, beaten
4½ c. flour
½ c. butter, softened
1 can almond paste filling for cakes
Slivered almonds

Scald milk and pour over ½ cup butter in a large mixing bowl. Cool to lukewarm; add yeast and stir until dissolved. Add sugar and salt to beaten eggs; add to milk mixture. Stir in flour to make a stiff dough. Place in a greased bowl, cover and let rise in a warm place until doubled in bulk, about 1½ hours. Divide dough in half and knead until smooth and elastic. On a lightly floured board, roll out each piece to a 12 x 8-inch rectangle. Spread with half the remaining butter and half a can of almond paste. Roll up as for a jelly roll. Curve in a ring, overlapping ends to seal. Place in greased round cake pans. With scissors, make cuts at 1-inch intervals, cutting two-thirds through the ring. (Start at the outside and cut toward the center.) Turn each section on its side. Cover and let rise again until doubled in bulk, 30 to 45 minutes. Bake in a 350° oven 45 minutes. When slightly cooled, ice and sprinkle with almonds. Makes 2 cakes.

ICING

1 T. butter or margarine, softened
1 c. confectioners' sugar
1½ T. milk
¼ t. almond extract

Combine all ingredients. Beat until smooth and of spreading consistency.

MINIATURE COFFEE CAKES

Easier than you think.

- 1 c. flour
- ¾ t. baking powder
- ½ t. baking soda
- ¼ t. salt
- ¼ c. butter
- ½ c. sugar
- 1 egg
- ½ t. vanilla
- ½ c. sour cream
- ½ c. golden raisins

Mix together dry ingredients. Cream butter and add sugar gradually. Beat until fluffy. Add egg and vanilla and beat well. Add sour cream and flour mixture alternately. Stir in raisins. Grease bottom only of 1½-inch muffin tins and fill two-thirds full. Sprinkle with Topping and bake at 425° for 12 minutes. Makes 24 miniature cakes.

TOPPING

- 3 T. brown sugar
- 2 T. granulated sugar
- ½ c. chopped nuts

Combine all ingredients.

CHOCOLATE NUT APPLESAUCE LOAF

A loaf with "pizzazz!"

- ½ c. butter or margarine
- 1 c. sugar
- 2 eggs
- 2 t. vanilla
- 2 1-oz. squares unsweetened chocolate, melted and cooled
- 1¾ c. flour
- 1½ t. baking powder
- ½ t. baking soda
- ½ t. salt
- ½ c. chopped nuts
- 1 c. canned applesauce

Cream butter and sugar until very light and fluffy. Add eggs, one at a time, beating well. Beat in chocolate and vanilla. Combine dry ingredients, mixing well. Add dry ingredients alternately with applesauce. Stir in nuts. Spoon into a greased and floured 9 x 5-inch loaf pan and bake in a preheated 325° oven for 75 minutes or until done. Cool on rack for 10 minutes. Remove from pan and cool thoroughly. May be frosted or sprinkled with confectioners' sugar. Makes 1 loaf.

OLIVE-NUT BREAD

Olives make a nice difference. Slice bread thin and serve with scrambled eggs or spread with cream cheese for party sandwiches.

- 2½ c. flour
- ¼ c. sugar
- 4 t. baking powder
- 1 egg, beaten
- 1 c. milk
- ½ c. salad oil
- 1 c. chopped olives
- 1 c. chopped walnuts

In a large bowl, combine flour, sugar, and baking powder. Stir in egg, milk and oil, mix until blended. Add olives and nuts. Turn into a 9 x 5-inch loaf pan. Bake in a 350° oven for 45 minutes or until done. Cool on rack. Makes 1 loaf.

CARAWAY RYE BREAD

- 2½ to 3 c. flour
- 1½ c. rye flour
- 2 pkgs. dry yeast
- 2 T. sugar
- 2 t. salt
- 1 T. caraway seed
- 1 c. milk
- ¾ c. water
- 2 T. butter or margarine

In a large mixing bowl, combine 1 cup of the flour, rye flour, yeast, sugar, salt and caraway seed, mixing well. In a saucepan, heat milk, water and butter until warm. Add to flour mixture. Blend at low speed until moistened; beat 3 minutes at medium speed. By hand, gradually stir in remaining flour to make a firm dough. Knead on floured surface until smooth and elastic, about 5 minutes. Place in a greased bowl, turning to grease top. Cover and let rise in a warm place until light and doubled, about 1 hour. Punch dough down and divide into 2 parts. On a lightly floured surface, roll or pat each half to a 7 x 14-inch rectangle. Starting with the shorter side, roll up tightly, pressing dough into the roll with each turn. Pinch edges and ends to seal. Place in 2 greased 9 x 5-inch or 8 x 4-inch loaf pans. Cover and let rise in a warm place until doubled in bulk, about 30 minutes. Bake in a 375° oven 35 to 40 minutes or until golden brown. Remove from pans to cool. Makes 2 loaves.

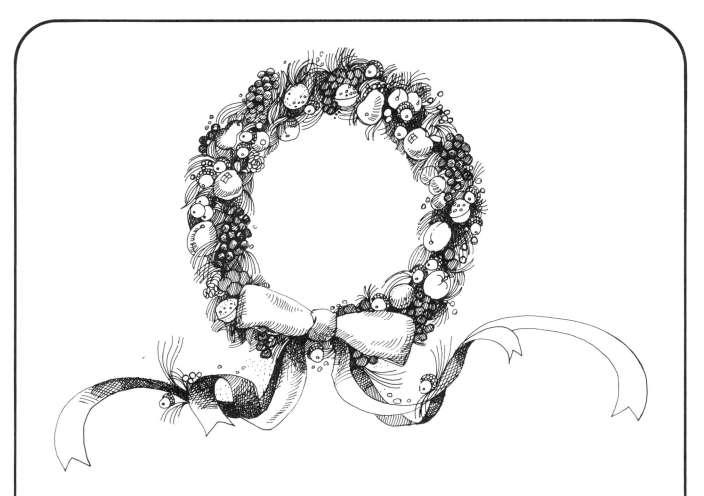

COFFEE RING
For late evening coffee and cake.

1 pkg. dry yeast
¼ c. warm water
¼ c. lukewarm milk
¼ c. sugar
½ t. salt
1 egg
¼ c. butter or margarine
2¼ to 2½ c. flour
2 T. butter or margarine, softened
½ c. packed brown sugar
1 t. cinnamon
½ c. raisins
½ c. nuts

Dissolve yeast in warm water in a large bowl. Stir in milk, sugar, salt, egg, butter and half of the flour. Beat until smooth. Mix in enough remaining flour to make dough easy to handle. Turn dough onto a lightly floured board and knead until smooth and elastic, about 5 minutes. Place in a greased bowl; turn greased side up and cover. Let rise in a warm place until doubled in bulk, about 1½ hours. Punch dough down; roll into a 15 x 9-inch rectangle. Spread with butter; sprinkle with brown sugar, cinnamon, raisins and nuts. Roll up tightly, beginning at the wide side. Pinch edges to seal. Place sealed side down in ring on lightly greased baking sheet. Join ends of ring and seal. Make cuts two-thirds through the ring at 1-inch intervals. Turn each section on its side. Let rise until doubled in bulk, about 45 minutes. Bake in a 375° oven about 25 to 30 minutes until golden. While warm, frost with confectioners' sugar icing. Decorate with almonds and cherries if desired.

CONFECTIONERS' ICING

½ c. confectioners' sugar
1 T. milk

Beat sugar and milk until smooth and of spreading consistency.

"Follow me in merry measure . . . " to ensure that you will turn out beautiful cakes, pies, cookies and candies.

Desserts

STRAWBERRY BAKED ALASKA

For a jolly holiday!

  2 egg whites
 ¼ t. cream of tartar
 ⅓ c. sugar
  1 pkg. frozen sliced strawberries, thawed and drained
  6 individual sponge cake shells
    Ice cream (butter pecan, strawberry, vanilla)

Beat egg whites with cream of tartar until foamy. Gradually beat in sugar until egg whites hold a stiff peak. Place 1 spoonful berries in shell and an ice cream ball on top; freeze. Cover ice cream and shell with meringue, sealing edges. Bake on a cookie sheet in a preheated 450° oven 3 minutes until golden brown. Garnish with a whole strawberry, if desired. Makes 6 servings.

VANILLA CREAM TRIFLE

For a yummy Yuletide.

 ½ c. sherry or rum
  1 angel food or sponge cake
  1 3-oz. pkg. French vanilla instant pudding mix
  2 c. milk
 ½ pt. heavy cream, whipped
 ½ c. slivered almonds
 ½ c. golden raisins

Cut cake into cubes and sprinkle with ¼ cup sherry or rum. Prepare pudding mix as directed on the package, using 2 cups milk and folding in remaining ¼ cup sherry and half of the whipped cream. Fold in raisins and nuts. In a glass serving bowl or 8 parfait glasses, make 3 layers of cake and pudding mixture, beginning with cake cubes and ending with pudding. Top with whipped cream. Chill at least 3 hours, but no longer than 24 hours. Makes 8 servings.

Pictured opposite:
Peaches Flambées

PEACHES FLAMBÉES

  1 2½-lb. can cling peach halves
 ⅔ c. brandy
 ½ c. syrup from peaches
  1 orange rind, coarsely shredded
 ⅓ c. currant jelly
  1 qt. vanilla ice cream

Drain peaches; pour one-third cup brandy over and set aside for about 1 hour. Heat syrup from peaches with orange rind in chafing dish (or saucepan on stove) and boil until volume is reduced by about half. Add currant jelly and stir until melted. Add peaches and heat thoroughly. Heat remaining one-third cup brandy and pour over hot peaches; carefully ignite with a match. Do not stir or it will not flame. When flames die, spoon over ice cream. Serves 4 to 6.

SPUMONI PARFAIT

Elegant dessert for the busy hostess. Can be made one or two days ahead. For the grand occasion, fix it in your crystal ice-tea or parfait glasses or in a mold.

  3 pts. chocolate ice cream, softened
  1 pt. pistachio ice cream, softened
  2 pts. strawberry ice cream, softened
 1½ c. heavy cream, whipped
  1 t. rum flavoring
    Almond slices, maraschino cherries or other garnish (optional)

Layer ice creams (chocolate, strawberry, pistachio, strawberry, chocolate) in glasses. Stir rum flavoring into whipped cream and top parfait with a dollop of cream.

For mold: Line mold or bowl with a 1-inch layer of chocolate; freeze. Next, line chocolate with a layer of pistachio and freeze. Fill with strawberry ice cream; freeze. To serve, unmold and frost with whipped cream to which flavoring has been added. Garnish with cherries and almond slices. Serves 14.

CRANBERRY MOUSSE

Pale pink and picture pretty.

    1 can whole-berry cranberry sauce
    ½ pt. heavy cream
    1 T. orange-flavored liqueur

Chill cranberry sauce for an hour or so. Place in blender with liqueur and whirl until smooth. Whip cream until stiff. Fold cranberry mixture into cream until well blended. Chill and serve. Makes 4 to 6 servings.

SHERRIED APPLE CRISP

    5 tart apples, cored and thinly sliced
    ½ t. cinnamon
    ¼ c. sweet sherry
    1 c. flour
    ½ c. sugar
    ½ c. butter
    1 egg

Arrange apple slices in a shallow baking dish. Sprinkle with cinnamon and sherry. Mix flour, sugar, butter and egg until crumbly. Sprinkle over apples. Bake in a 350° oven for 45 minutes. Serve warm with cream or ice cream. Serves 6 to 8.

GRAHAM CRACKER TORTE

Not lavish—just good.

    3 T. butter or margarine
    1¾ c. sugar
    2 eggs
    1½ t. baking soda
    2 c. buttermilk
    1 1-lb. box graham crackers, crushed
    1 c. chopped nuts
      Confectioners' sugar

Cream butter with sugar until light. Add eggs and beat well. Stir baking soda into buttermilk and stir until it bubbles. Alternately add graham cracker crumbs and buttermilk to creamed mixture. Mix well. Stir in nuts. Pour into a greased springform pan and bake in a preheated 350° oven for 1 hour or until toothpick inserted in center comes out clean. Cool on rack. Top with confectioners' sugar. Serves 10 to 12.

STRAWBERRY CREAM TORTE

For a final holiday party effect.

    4 egg whites, room temperature
    ½ c. sugar
    4 egg yolks
    ½ c. sugar
    1¼ c. flour
    ¼ t. salt
    2 T. lemon juice
    2 t. grated lemon peel
    2 T. water
    ¼ c. confectioners' sugar
    2 c. heavy cream, whipped
    1 12-oz. jar strawberry preserves
    6 fresh whole strawberries

In a large bowl, beat egg whites at high speed until frothy. Gradually beat in ½ cup sugar. Continue beating until soft peaks appear when beater is slowly raised. In small bowl at high speed with the same beater, beat egg yolks until thick and lemon colored. Gradually beat in ½ cup sugar and continue beating until mixture is well blended. At low speed, add flour and salt. Blend well and add lemon juice, lemon peel and water, beating about 1 minute. Gently fold yolk mixture into egg white mixture just until blended. Pour the batter into 2 round ungreased 8 x 1½-inch layer cake pans. Bake in a preheated 350° oven for 25 minutes or until surface springs back when gently touched. Invert cake pans by hanging pans between 2 other pans. Cool completely about 1 hour. Carefully loosen cake from pans and remove. Beat cream with confectioners' sugar until stiff. Refrigerate. Slice cake to make 4 layers. Place a layer, cut-side up on a plate. Spread with one-third cup preserves and ½ cup whipped cream. Repeat with remaining layers, ending with top layer down. Frost top and side of torte with whipped cream. Refrigerate 1 hour before cutting. Top with whole strawberries before serving. Makes 8 to 10 servings.

HEAVENLY TORTE

Forget about calories and enjoy!

½ c. margarine
½ c. butter
½ c. sugar
3 egg yolks
1 t. lemon juice
½ t. grated lemon peel
2 c. flour
1 t. baking powder
¼ t. salt
4 egg whites
¾ c. sugar
1 t. cinnamon
1 c. finely ground almonds
1 12-oz. jar raspberry jelly
1 12-oz. jar currant jelly

Cream butter, margarine, and sugar until fluffy. Add egg yolks, lemon juice and peel, flour, baking powder and salt. Pat into 3 springform pans, using thumbs to make dough into ridges around the edges of the pans. Beat 4 egg whites until frothy; gradually add ¾ cup sugar and cinnamon and beat until thick and glossy. Add almonds. Spread over 3 dough layers to the edge and bake in a preheated 400° oven until meringue is caramel color, about 25 minutes. Let cool. Mix jellies together; set aside 1 tablespoon. Spread jelly on 2 layers and stack. Place on top layer and put reserved jelly in the middle. Do not wrap cake—it will keep nicely uncovered for 1 week. Serves 12 to 14.

CAROB CARROT CAKE

Kids will never know they're eating carrots.

½ lb. butter or margarine, softened
2 c. sugar
3 eggs
2 t. vanilla
2½ c. flour
2 T. carob powder
1 t. baking powder
1 t. cinnamon
¼ t. salt
3 c. shredded carrot (about 1 lb.)
1 c. chopped nuts
½ c. semisweet chocolate chips

Cream butter and sugar; add eggs, one at a time. Add vanilla. Combine flour, carob, baking powder, salt, cinnamon and add to mixture. Remove beaters and, stirring by hand, add carrot, nuts and chocolate chips.

Pour into a greased and floured 9 x 13 x 2-inch pan and bake in a preheated 350° oven for 40 to 45 minutes or until toothpick inserted in center comes out clean. May be frosted or sprinkled with confectioners' sugar. Serves 12 to 16.

CHOCOLATE GLAZE

1 1-oz. square unsweetened chocolate
2 T. butter or margarine
½ c. confectioners' sugar
½ t. vanilla
1 T. hot water

Melt chocolate and butter over low heat. Remove from heat and stir in sugar and vanilla. Stir in water, 1 teaspoon at a time, until glaze is of proper spreading consistency.

BUTTERCREAM FROSTING

½ c. butter or margarine
⅛ t. salt
1 t. vanilla or almond flavoring
1 lb. confectioners' sugar
5 to 6 T. evaporated milk or cream

Cream butter until light and fluffy. Add salt, flavoring and half of the sugar. Beat until smooth. Add a few tablespoons milk. Beat in remaining sugar, beating until smooth. Slowly add remaining milk, adding just enough to make frosting of spreading consistency.

VARIATIONS

Orange Buttercream: Add 2 teaspoons grated orange rind and ½ cup orange juice instead of the milk.
Mocha Buttercream: Add ½ teaspoon vanilla and ¼ cup strong coffee instead of milk.
Chocolate Buttercream: Add ¼ teaspoon vanilla and 2 1-oz. squares unsweetened chocolate, melted.

CHEESE-MINCE PIE

A taste surprise.

- 1 9 or 10-inch baked pie shell
- 1½ 8-oz. pkgs. cream cheese, softened
- 2 eggs
- ½ c. sugar
- 1 T. orange liqueur
- 2 c. mincemeat
- ½ c. chopped nuts
- 1 c. sour cream
- ½ t. vanilla
- 2 T. sugar
- 1 can mandarin oranges (optional)

Beat cream cheese, eggs, ½ cup sugar and liqueur until smooth. Combine mincemeat and nuts and spread on bottom of pie shell. Pour cheese mixture over mincemeat. Bake in a preheated 375° oven 20 minutes. While pie is baking, combine sour cream, vanilla and sugar. Spread evenly on hot pie and return to oven for another 10 minutes. Chill at least 6 hours. May be decorated with drained mandarin orange segments. Serves 8 to 10.

RUM CREAM PIE

A dream of a dessert!

- 1 9-inch baked pie shell or graham cracker crust
- 6 egg yolks
- ¾ c. sugar
- 1 envelope unflavored gelatin
- ½ c. cold water
- ½ c. dark rum
- 1 c. heavy cream, whipped
  Whipped cream (optional)
  Chocolate curls or chopped nuts (optional)

In a large mixing bowl, beat egg yolks until light. Add sugar gradually, beating until thick and lemon colored (about 5 minutes). In a small saucepan, soak gelatin in cold water and then stir over low heat until gelatin is dissolved and just comes to a boil. Remove from heat. Add hot mixture in a slow stream to egg yolks, beating constantly. Beat in rum. Chill until mixture mounds when dropped from a spoon. Fold whipped cream into mixture and pile into pie shell. Chill until firm. Garnish with additional whipped cream and shaved semisweet chocolate or chopped nuts. Serves 8 to 10.

CREME CARAMEL PIE

This delicious pie has a surprise of crunchy caramel down under the smooth custard.

- 1 9-inch pie shell
- ¼ c. brown sugar
- ¼ c. butter

Heat brown sugar and butter in a saucepan until bubbly. Pour into pie shell, smoothing to cover bottom. Bake in a 425° oven for 10 minutes. Remove and pour on Custard. Reduce heat to 325° and bake an additional 30 minutes until a knife inserted in the middle comes out clean. Serves 8 to 10.

CUSTARD

- 6 eggs, slightly beaten
- ½ c. sugar
- ¼ t. salt
- 2 c. light cream
- 1 t. vanilla

Combine all ingredients and blend well.

PUMPKIN CHEESE PIE

- 1 8-oz. pkg. cream cheese, softened
- ¾ c. sugar
- 1 t. cinnamon
- ½ t. cloves
- ½ t. ginger
- ½ t. nutmeg
- ½ t. salt
- 3 eggs
- 1 16-oz. can pumpkin
- 1 t. vanilla
  Pecan halves (optional)
- 1 9-inch pie crust, unbaked

Beat cream cheese until fluffy, gradually adding sugar combined with spices. Add eggs one at a time, beating well after each. Beat in pumpkin and vanilla. Pour into prepared shell. Bake in a preheated 350° oven for 40 minutes or until knife inserted in center comes out clean. During last 15 minutes of baking, pecan halves may be placed on top as decoration. Chill before serving. Serves 8 to 10.

Pictured opposite:
Pumpkin Cheese Pie

COFFEE-CLOUD PIE

Beautiful, rich and different.

- ½ lb. marshmallows
- 1 c. strong coffee
- 1 T. butter
- 1 T. brandy
- 1 c. heavy cream, whipped
- 1 9-inch baked pie shell

In top of double boiler, combine marshmallows, coffee and butter; heat until marshmallows dissolve. Add brandy. Remove from heat and cool until stiff. Fold in whipped cream and heap into pie shell. Refrigerate. Serves 8 to 10.

CHOCOLATE PECAN PIE

Chocolate lovers, rejoice!

- 1 9-inch unbaked pastry shell
- ½ c. sugar
- 1 c. dark corn syrup
- 3 eggs
- ¼ t. salt
- 1 T. flour
- 2 T. butter
- 2 1-oz. squares bitter chocolate
- 1 t. vanilla
- 1½ c. pecan halves
- ½ c. heavy cream, whipped (optional)

Beat together sugar, syrup, eggs, salt and flour. Melt butter and chocolate. Beat into egg mixture with vanilla. Put pecans into a pastry shell, pour egg mixture over. Bake in a 300° oven 50 to 60 minutes, until custard is set. Garnish with unsweetened whipped cream. Serves 8 to 10.

LEMON CHESS PIE

A dessert with a "twist."

- ¼ c. butter or margarine, softened
- 2 c. sugar
- 4 eggs
- ¼ c. lemon juice
- 1 T. grated lemon peel
- ¼ c. milk
- 1½ T. flour
- 1 9-inch unbaked pie shell
- 1 t. cornmeal
  Whipped cream (optional)

Beat together butter, sugar, eggs, lemon juice and peel, milk and flour. Pour into pie shell. Sprinkle with cornmeal. Bake in a preheated 375° oven 45 minutes or until set. Serve with whipped cream. Serves 8 to 10.

EGGNOG BAVARIAN

Shimmering, ivory elegance.

- 3 T. unflavored gelatin
- ½ c. cold water
- ¼ c. sugar
- ½ t. nutmeg
- ½ c. boiling water
- 1 c. warmed eggnog
- 1½ c. cold eggnog
- ½ c. rum
  Yellow food coloring
- 2 egg whites
- ⅛ t. cream of tartar
- 2 T. sugar
- ¾ c. chopped walnuts
- ¾ c. heavy cream, whipped
  Walnut halves

In a large bowl, soften gelatin in cold water. Let set for 5 minutes. Add ¼ cup sugar, nutmeg and boiling water. Stir until gelatin is dissolved. Add warmed eggnog, stirring well. Chill until slightly thickened and then beat until fluffy. Add cold eggnog, rum and a couple of drops of yellow food coloring, if desired. Continue beating until mixture mounds and is smooth. Beat egg whites with cream of tartar until foamy; add 2 tablespoons sugar and beat until stiff. Fold into eggnog mixture. Fold in nuts and whipped cream. Pour into a lightly oiled 2-quart mold and chill until set (4 to 6 hours). Unmold and garnish with walnut halves. Serves 8.

CRANBERRY BREAD PUDDING

Delightful for the cook!

- 1¾ c. milk
- ½ t. salt
- ½ t. vanilla
- 2 c. soft, stale bread cubes
- ¼ c. honey
- 2 eggs, beaten
- 1 c. cranberries
  Whipped cream or light cream

Combine all ingredients except whipped cream. Pour into a shallow greased 1½-quart baking dish. Bake in a preheated 350° oven 25 minutes, or until firm. Serve warm with cream or a dollop of whipped cream. Makes 6 servings.

STEAMED CARROT PUDDING

This delicious pudding is a nice change from the traditional plum pudding. Serve with a choice of sauces.

- 2 eggs
- 1 c. molasses
- 2 T. butter or margarine, softened
- 2 c. carrots, cooked and mashed
- 1 c. flour
- 1 t. baking soda
- 1 t. cloves
- 1 t. cinnamon
- ½ t. allspice
- 1 t. nutmeg
- 1 c. raisins
- 1 c. chopped walnuts

Beat eggs slightly. Add molasses, butter and carrots, mixing well. Stir in flour, soda and spices; then stir in raisins and nuts. Turn into a heavily greased 1½-quart mold. Place a rack in any deep container which can be covered. (To make a rack, pierce an aluminum pie plate with a fork.) Cover container with foil and steam for 1½ to 2 hours, until done. Pudding will have a firm, solid feeling. Serves 8.

SAUCES FOR CARROT PUDDING

HARD SAUCE

- 1 c. confectioners' sugar
- ¼ c. butter
- 1 T. rum, brandy, sherry or 1 t. vanilla
- 1 to 3 T. cream

Cream butter and sugar. Add rum or vanilla and cream. Blend until smooth. Serve cold.

HOT WINE SAUCE

- ¼ c. butter
- 1 c. sugar
- 2 eggs
- ¾ c. dry sherry

Cream butter and sugar. Beat in eggs; stir in the sherry. Just before serving, heat in double boiler, beating or whisking constantly until steaming hot.

LEMON SAUCE

- ½ c. sugar
- 1 T. cornstarch
- 1 c. water
- 3 T. butter
- Grated rind of one lemon
- 2 T. lemon juice

Combine sugar, cornstarch and water. Cook over low heat until clear and thickened. Remove from heat and add butter, rind and juice.

WHITE FRUITCAKE, NOEL

Chill fruitcake before slicing. Makes thinner and prettier slices.

- 1 lb. butter
- 2 c. sugar
- 6 eggs
- 1 T. lemon flavoring
- 4 c. flour
- ½ t. salt
- 2 t. baking powder
- 1 lb. shelled pecans
- 1 lb. golden raisins
- 4 slices candied pineapple, cut up
- 1 lb. cut-up red and green candied cherries

Cover raisins with hot water; set aside.

Cream butter and sugar. Add eggs, one at a time, and lemon flavoring; beat well. Drain raisins. Flour nuts and fruits with ½ cup of the flour and stir into batter. Combine flour, baking powder and salt and add to egg mixture. Mix well. Line five 7½ x 3½-inch loaf pans with waxed paper; grease paper. Pour batter into pans and bake in a preheated 350° oven 1½ hours or until done. Place a pan of water in bottom of the oven to keep cakes from drying out. Wrap cakes in foil or plastic wrapping and store in a cool place.

MINIATURE FRUITCAKES (LITTLE JEWELS)

3 c. flour
1⅓ c. sugar
1 t. salt
1 t. baking powder
2 t. cinnamon
1 t. nutmeg
½ c. orange juice
½ c. brandy
1 c. salad oil
4 eggs
¼ c. light corn syrup
1 c. golden raisins
2 c. dried apricots, cut into small pieces
1 c. dried dates, cut up
2 c. blanched almonds
⅓ c. light corn syrup for glaze
Brandy

In a large mixing bowl, combine all ingredients except fruits, nuts, syrup and brandy. Blend with electric mixer 30 seconds at low speed, scraping bowl constantly, and 3 minutes at high speed, scraping bowl occasionally. Stir in fruit and nuts. Spoon batter into 36 paper-lined 2½-inch muffin cups. Bake in a preheated 275° oven 65 to 70 minutes. Remove to rack and cool thoroughly. Heat corn syrup in a small pan and brush over tops of cakes. Place cakes in a container and cover with a cheesecloth soaked in brandy. Cover tightly and store up to 2 weeks. May also be frozen. Makes 36 cakes.

Note: Two cups (1 lb.) mixed candied fruit may be substituted for apricots and dates.

PENUCHE GLAZE

Good on fruitcakes or coffee bread.

¼ c. butter or margarine
½ c. brown sugar, packed
2 T. milk
1 c. confectioners' sugar
¼ t. ground mace (optional)
1 to 2 T. milk

Melt butter in pan. Stir in brown sugar. Heat to boiling, stirring constantly. Boil and stir over medium heat for 2 minutes. Remove from heat. Stir in 2 tablespoons milk, sugar and mace. Beat until smooth. Add an additional 1 to 2 tablespoons milk, stirring until glaze is of spreading consistency.

MARZIPAN FROSTING FOR FRUITCAKE

2 c. almond paste
2 egg whites
3 c. confectioners' sugar
Few drops of rose water or lemon juice

Beat egg whites until fluffy. Gradually work in almond paste. Add sugar and blend until smooth. Add a few drops of rose water or lemon juice until frosting is of spreading consistency.

FRUITCAKE

Make several weeks ahead for a Christmas favorite.

1 c. golden raisins
1 c. dark raisins
1 c. *each* of candied citron, lemon peel and orange peel
½ c. *each* of candied pineapple and cherries, halved
1½ c. snipped figs
1 c. chopped dates
½ c. currants
1 c. almonds, pecan or walnut halves
4 c. flour
½ t. salt
2 t. baking powder
½ lb. butter or margarine
2 c. sugar
6 eggs
1 t. lemon extract
1 c. sherry

In a large bowl, combine all fruits and nuts. Combine flour, salt and baking powder and sprinkle over the fruit and nuts. Toss lightly until fruit and nuts are well coated. In a large bowl with electric mixer at medium speed, cream butter and sugar. Add eggs and lemon extract and beat until light and fluffy (about 4 minutes). Add to flour and fruit mixture along with sherry; stir until just mixed. Turn into a greased 10-inch tube pan or a 12-cup bundt cake pan and bake in a preheated 300° oven for 3 hours or until toothpick inserted in the center comes out clean. Cool in pan on cake rack for 1 hour. Loosen cake all around with a spatula and turn out of pan onto rack to cool completely. Wrap in foil and freeze. Thaw cake at room temperature, unwrapped. Serve frosted with a confectioners' sugar icing or just sprinkle with confectioners' sugar. Makes 16 servings.

Pictured opposite: Fruitcake

SWISS MERINGUE DROPS WITH FUDGE FILLING

2 egg whites
⅛ t. cream of tartar
⅛ t. salt
¼ c. sugar
¼ t. almond extract
2 T. chopped pistachio nuts (optional)

Beat egg whites until foamy. Add cream of tartar and salt; beat until stiff peaks form. Add sugar, a tablespoonful at a time, and beat until smooth and satiny. Fold in almond extract. Cover ungreased cookie sheets with brown paper. Drop meringue by teaspoonfuls and shape into mounds the size of a small walnut. Make a depression in the center of each cookie with a spoon. Bake in a preheated 250° oven for about 30 to 45 minutes. Fill Meringues with a teaspoonful of cooled Fudge Filling. Sprinkle with nuts. Makes 5 dozen.

FUDGE FILLING

¼ c. butter
⅓ c. chocolate chips
2 T. confectioners' sugar
2 egg yolks

Melt butter and chocolate in a saucepan. Beat egg yolks slightly; stir in sugar; blend into chocolate. Cook at a very low heat 1 minute, stirring constantly. Remove from heat and stir until cool.

FILBERT DROPS

½ c. butter or margarine
1 c. sugar
1 egg yolk
1 T. water
½ t. grated lemon peel
1 t. grated orange peel
1 c. flour
¼ t. salt
1 egg white
⅔ c. finely ground filberts

Beat butter with sugar, egg yolk, water and peels until very light and fluffy. At low speed of mixer, beat in flour and salt just until mixed. Refrigerate until easy to handle. Form dough into 1-inch balls. Roll in unbeaten egg white and then in ground nuts. Place on a greased cookie sheet and bake in a 350° oven 15 minutes or until done. Store in a tightly covered container. Makes 2 dozen.

GLAZED PFEFFERNUESSE

1¼ c. butter
1¼ c. brown sugar, packed
¾ c. molasses
½ c. warm water
½ t. baking soda
Dash pepper
½ t. cloves
½ t. allspice
¼ t. nutmeg
¼ t. mace
1½ t. cinnamon
⅛ t. crushed cardamom
6 c. sifted cake flour
½ t. salt
Few drops anise oil or 1 t. anise extract
2 c. chopped nuts
Confectioners' sugar

Cream butter; add sugar and cream well. Blend in molasses and half the water. Dissolve soda in remaining water. Sift together dry ingredients. Add to creamed mixture with soda, water, anise and nuts. Mix well and chill. Shape dough into 1-inch balls. Place on greased cookie sheets and bake in a preheated 375° oven for 10 to 12 minutes. Dip top of hot cookie into glaze; coat with confectioners' sugar. Makes 12 dozen cookies.

GLAZE

1 c. confectioners' sugar
3 T. hot milk
¼ t. vanilla

Blend together confectioners' sugar, milk and vanilla.

RUSSIAN TEACAKES

1 c. butter or margarine, softened
½ c. confectioners' sugar
1 t. vanilla
2¼ c. all-purpose flour
¼ t. salt
¾ c. finely chopped nuts
Confectioners' sugar

Cream butter, sugar and vanilla. Work in flour, salt and nuts until dough holds together. Shape dough into 1-inch balls. Place on ungreased cookie sheets. Bake in a preheated 400° oven 10 to 12 minutes, until set but not brown. While warm, roll in confectioners' sugar. Cool; roll again in sugar. Makes 5 dozen.

EASY ROLLED SUGAR COOKIES

1 c. butter
1 c. sugar
2 egg yolks
1 t. vanilla
½ t. salt
3 c. sifted flour
1 t. baking powder
⅓ c. milk

Cream butter; add sugar gradually. Mix in egg yolks and vanilla. Blend in sifted dry ingredients and milk. Chill. Roll ⅛ inch thick on a well-floured surface. Cut with cookie cutters and place on greased cookie sheets. Decorate before baking with colored sugar or wait until baked and cooled, then frost. Bake in a preheated 350° oven 8 to 10 minutes. Makes 5 dozen.

SPRITZ

1 c. butter
½ c. plus 1 T. sugar
1 egg
¾ t. salt
1 t. vanilla
½ t. almond extract
2½ c. sifted flour

Cream butter and sugar. Blend egg, salt, extracts and flour. Knead dough in hands until soft and pliable. Force dough through a cookie press onto ungreased cookie sheets. Decorate and place in a 400° oven for 8 minutes. Makes 5 dozen.

MONDCHEN

1 c. butter
1 c. sugar
1¼ c. unblanched almonds, grated
1 c. sifted all-purpose flour
¼ t. salt
1 t. grated lemon rind
1½ c. confectioners' sugar
1 t. vanilla
2 T. hot water

Cream butter; add sugar gradually. Blend in almonds, flour, salt and lemon rind. Roll dough ¼ inch thick onto floured canvas or board. Cut with a crescent cutter and place on greased cookie sheets. Bake in a preheated 350° oven for 10 to 12 minutes. Blend confectioners' sugar, vanilla and water; spread on hot cookies. Makes 7 dozen.

CANDY CANES

1 c. shortening or ½ c. butter, softened
1 c. sifted confectioners' sugar
1 egg
1½ t. almond flavoring
2½ c. sifted flour
1 t. salt
½ t. red food coloring

Combine shortening, sugar, egg and flavoring, mixing well. Sift flour and salt together; stir into shortening mixture. Divide dough in half and blend red food coloring into one half. Take one teaspoon of each color dough. Roll each into a 4-inch long strip on a floured board. Place strips side by side, pressing together lightly. Twist into a rope. Place on ungreased cookie sheets and curve top of each piece to form a crook. Place in a preheated 375° oven for 9 minutes or until lightly browned. Remove while still warm. Makes 4 dozen.

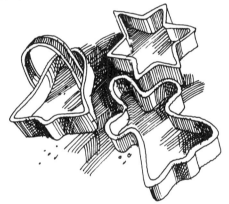

SWEDISH GINGER COOKIES

½ c. dark corn syrup
½ c. sugar
½ c. melted butter
6 T. light cream
½ t. ginger
½ t. cloves
½ t. cinnamon
½ t. baking soda
2 T. light cream
3 c. sifted all-purpose flour

Boil syrup 1 minute; cool slightly. Add sugar, butter, 6 tablespoons cream and spices. Dissolve soda in remaining cream and add to syrup mixture. Blend in flour. Refrigerate. Roll ⅛ inch thick on floured canvas and cut into desired shapes. Place on greased cookie sheets; decorate before baking. Bake in a 350° oven for 10 to 15 minutes, depending upon the size and thickness of cookies. Makes 4½ dozen.

BROWNIES

Old favorites; always good.

2 1-oz. squares unsweetened chocolate
⅓ c. butter or margarine
1 c. sugar
2 eggs
½ t. vanilla
½ c. flour
½ c. chopped nuts (optional)

Melt chocolate and butter in a saucepan over low heat. Remove and let cool. Beat in sugar, eggs and vanilla. Stir in flour and nuts. Spread in a greased 8 x 8 x 2-inch pan and bake in a preheated 350° oven for 25 minutes. Cool slightly and cut into squares or bars.

PEANUT BUTTER BROWNIES

⅓ c. melted butter or margarine
1⅓ c. brown sugar, firmly packed
½ c. peanut butter, smooth or chunky
3 eggs
1 t. vanilla
1 c. flour
¾ t. baking powder
¼ t. baking soda
½ t. salt
½ c. chopped peanuts

Melt butter in saucepan. Beat in brown sugar, peanut butter, vanilla and eggs until well blended. Add flour, baking powder, soda, salt and peanuts and blend well. Pour into an oiled 9 x 12-inch pan. Bake in a preheated 350° oven for 20 to 30 minutes until toothpick inserted in center comes out clean. If desired, frost with Broiled Frosting.

BROILED FROSTING

4 T. butter or margarine
1 3-oz. pkg. cream cheese
1½ c. brown sugar, firmly packed
½ c. chopped salted peanuts

Melt butter and cream cheese over low heat. Remove from heat and stir in brown sugar and peanuts. Spread over hot brownies when they come from the oven. Broil 3 inches from heat for a few seconds until frosting is bubbly. Watch carefully so as not to scorch. Cool and cut into bars. Makes 2 to 2½ dozen bars.

CHOCOLATE CREAMS

Delicious, creamy and chocolate. Make ahead and store in refrigerator (hide them or they won't last long). They also make an elegant gift.

1 6-oz. pkg. semisweet chocolate chips
¼ c. milk
1 t. rum extract
4 c. confectioners' sugar
½ c. chocolate jimmies

In a saucepan, combine chocolate and milk. Blend and heat slowly, stirring constantly. Add rum extract. Remove from heat and beat in sugar. When cool enough to handle, make into about forty-eight ½ to 1-inch balls. Roll in chocolate jimmies. Store in the refrigerator. Makes about 48.

SPEEDY CHOCOLATE FUDGE

1½ 12-oz. pkgs. semisweet chocolate chips
1 15-oz. can sweetened condensed milk
⅛ t. salt
1 t. vanilla
½ c. chopped nuts (optional)

Melt chocolate over low heat, stirring. Remove from heat and stir in sweetened condensed milk, salt, vanilla and nuts. Pour into a waxed paper lined 8-inch square pan; spread evenly, smoothing surface. Refrigerate until firm, about 2 hours. Turn candy out on board and peel off paper. With a sharp knife, cut fudge into desired size pieces and store in an airtight container.

MINT PATTIES

Tint these a pale pink for peppermint, pale green for wintergreen.

3 c. confectioners' sugar
1 c. boiling water
10 drops oil of peppermint or oil of wintergreen
Food coloring

Boil sugar and water to a soft-ball stage (234° on a candy thermometer). Add flavoring. Remove from heat and beat until mixture begins to thicken. Beat in coloring. Drop from spoon onto waxed paper to form small thin patties. Keep mixture over hot water while dropping patties. Cool. Makes about 48 patties.

Pictured opposite:
Mint Patties

MARZIPAN BARS

½ c. butter or margarine
½ c. brown sugar, packed
1 egg yolk
1 t. vanilla
2 c. flour
½ t. baking soda
¼ t. salt
¼ c. milk
1 c. raspberry jelly

Cream butter and brown sugar; beat in egg yolk and vanilla. Combine flour, soda and salt. Blend in alternately with milk. Spread in bottom of a greased 15 x 10 x 1-inch pan and cover with jelly. Pour Filling over jelly layer. Bake in a preheated 350° oven for 35 minutes. Cool on rack. Spread with Icing and cut into small bars.

FILLING

8 oz. almond paste, cut in small pieces
1 egg white
½ c. sugar
1 t. vanilla
3 T. butter or margarine, softened
3 eggs
Drop green food coloring

Combine almond paste with egg white, sugar, vanilla and butter. Beat until smooth. Add eggs, one at a time, beating after each addition. Add food coloring to desired tint.

ICING

2 1-oz. squares unsweetened chocolate, melted
1 T. butter, softened
1 t. vanilla
2 c. confectioners' sugar
¼ c. hot milk

Combine all ingredients; beat until smooth.

MOUND BARS

2 c. graham cracker crumbs
¼ c. confectioners' sugar
½ c. melted butter or margarine
1 15-oz. can sweetened condensed milk
2⅓ c. flaked coconut
1 4-oz. bar semisweet or German sweet chocolate
2 T. butter

Mix together crumbs, sugar and butter. Firmly press into bottom of ungreased 13 x 9 x 2-inch pan. Bake in a preheated 350° oven for 10 minutes. Combine milk and coconut and spread over baked layer. Return to oven and bake an additional 15 minutes. Cool. Melt chocolate with butter over low heat. Spread evenly over coconut filling. Cool; cut into 2 x 1-inch bars. Refrigerate or freeze until served. Makes 4½ dozen bars.

DUTCH CHOCOLATE BARS

1 c. sifted flour
1½ c. sugar
½ t. salt
½ t. baking powder
½ c. butter, softened
1 egg, slightly beaten
2 1-oz. squares unsweetened chocolate, melted
1 t. vanilla
1 c. rolled oats

Sift together flour, sugar, salt and baking powder into mixing bowl. Add butter, egg, cooled chocolate and vanilla. Mix until smooth. Stir in oats. Spread into greased 13 x 9 x 2-inch pan. Bake in a preheated 350° oven for 25 minutes. Frost with Peppermint Frosting. Cut into small bars. Makes about 32 bars.

PEPPERMINT FROSTING

¼ c. butter, softened
2 c. confectioners' sugar
1 t. peppermint extract
Few drops green food coloring
3 T. light cream (about)

Blend butter, sugar, extract and food coloring. Add enough cream to make frosting of spreading consistency, beating well.

CHOCO-NUT BARS

½ c. peanut butter
6 T. butter or margarine, softened
1 c. sugar
2 eggs
1 t. vanilla
1 c. whole wheat flour
1 t. baking powder
½ c. salted peanuts
½ c. chocolate chips

Cream together the peanut butter, butter and sugar. Beat in eggs and vanilla. Combine flour and baking powder and stir in. Add nuts and chocolate chips. Pour into an 11 x 7½ x 1½-inch pan and bake in a preheated 350° oven 25 to 30 minutes. Cool and cut into bars. Makes 24 bars.

INDEX

OTHER COOKBOOKS AVAILABLE
All Holidays Cookbook
American Cookbook
Barbecue Cookbook
Christmas Cookbook
Christmas Gifts from the Kitchen
Cookie Cookbook
Country Bread Cookbook
Country Kitchen Cookbook
Family Cookbook
Farmhouse Cookbook
Festive Party Cookbook
Fish and Seafood Cookbook
From Mama's Honey Jar
From Mama's Kitchen
Gourmet Appetizer
Gourmet on the Go
Gourmet Touch
Guide to Microwave Cooking
Have a Gourmet Christmas
Junior Chef Cookbook
Meatless Meals Cookbook
Menus from Around the World
Naturally Nutritious
Nice and Easy Desserts
Simply Delicious
Soups for All Seasons
Tempting Treasures
Whole Grain Cookbook

Editorial Director, James Kuse

Managing Editor, Ralph Luedtke

Production Editor/Manager, Richard Lawson

Photographic Editor, Gerald Koser

Copy Editor, Sharon Style

compiled by   photo stylist
Pamela Wilke   Marybeth Owens

artwork by
Jim McGath